THE OF
TAROT & YOU

THE ORIGINAL TAROT & YOU

RICHARD ROBERTS

Ibis Press
An Imprint of Nicolas-Hays, Inc.
Berwick, Maine

Published in 2005 by
Ibis Press, an imprint of
Nicolas-Hays, Inc.
P. O. Box 1126
Berwick, ME 03901-1126
www.nicolashays.com

Distributed to the trade by
Red Wheel/Weiser, LLC
P. O. Box 612
York Beach, ME 03910-0612
www.redwheelweiser.com

VG

Printed in the United States of America

11	10	09	08	07	06	05
7	6	5	4	3	2	1

The paper used in this publication meets the minimum requirements of
the American National Standard for Information Sciences—Permanence
of Paper for Printed Library Materials Z39.48–1992 (R1997).

Contents

The reader will find this book rather different from other Tarot materials now available, which deal primarily with the history and occult meanings of the cards. Just as a volume on astrology would have less applicatory value if it presented only theory without any actual horoscopes, so it seems that previous books on the Tarot have been lacking in this respect. I believe that this volume may initiate a new trend in the field of Tarot, presenting as it does numerous authentic readings.

There is a further respect in which other Tarot books often prove a hindrance rather than a help to those who would give readings themselves, and for what other reason does the deck exist? Imagine the neophyte reader, armed with book and deck, commencing a reading. First card: now what does so-and-so say that means? Just a moment while I look it up. Or, I remember so-and-so says such-and-such, but how does that meaning fit in here?!

Let us consider another hypothetical situation. The would-be reader has at his disposal a computer programed with interpretations on every one of the Major and Minor Arcana constituting the 78 cards of the deck, gleaned from all the books written, let us say, in the past 100 years. Now the cards are dealt, the computer activated, and the reader awaits the results. Obviously fuses would begin blowing; chaos would be the result. No matter that writers have expressed vastly divergent opinions on the meanings of the cards, the important thing to remember is that another's value, or another's way of seeing can only become one's own when discovered for one's self.

Introduction

Just as a "dreambook" of rigid symbolic interpretations is fallacious because symbols have various meanings, and really only *come to mean* in the *context* of the dream, so, too, I do not intend that the reader of this volume follow my interpretations when giving his own readings. As another's shoe, another's symbol is not usually a good fit. Indeed, I remark many times during the readings that a similar card had occurred in another's reading, and that it meant one thing then—in the context of his reading—whereas now—given a different person—it seems to mean something very dissimiliar. Naturally also the *position* of the card in the reading will have considerable bearing on its value interpretation.

How then will this book be of use to a reader of the Tarot? Primarily as it presents the how of an actual reading, it will encourage him or her in the free-association method, which is the "way" of a reading, the cards serving as activators of the unconscious. This, then, is the "magic" of Tarot—their evocative ability. Thus the deck is a kind of Rorschach test of the reader's level of consciousness at the moment of the reading. He regards the cards and allows his mind to drift over them, almost as in conscious fantasy, free-associating, holding back nothing that may seem relevant. Anticipating the objection that one is therefore "reading into the cards", the answer is of course. What else?!

Why is it then that divinatory methods often are successful? And also what happens when they seem to be inaccurate? A few months ago in a sermon at a San Francisco church I said that the divinatory form was not really the most important part of divination. After all in past ages, casting the bones, reading clouds, or divining by entrails had been—along with astrology—the accepted methods; yet today no one that I know goes around telling cotton futures by the color or lie of a gizzard, or choosing a wife by the form of a passing cumulus.

I believe the success or failure of the method is determined by the level of consciousness of the person using the particular divinatory method—and not the method itself.

Yet one can pick up a book on the Tarot and read "the magic is in the cards". Ah, how wonderful, we don't have to do anything! Everything is in the hands of Fate. Man always loves whatever enables him to relinquish willful choice and responsibility. Probably each society has heaved a collective sigh of relief as progressively it forsook direct, personal communication with God, shamanistic religion, for an interceding priestcraft that advised individuals on their moral conduct and the steps to be taken in insuring salvation. For, after all, if one tries on one's own to communicate with God, and there is no answer, may not the conclusion be that God is dead?

Today Tarot, astrology, palmistry, and *I Ching* are given the same fervent devotion by the young which their parents showed for orthodox religion. However, granted disenchantment with orthodoxy, I see no reason to endow the cards with supernatural numinosity. Why then all this great interest in the occult? Are we really in the Aquarian Age and experiencing a true spiritual revitalization? I am not as convinced as some of my colleagues. Very often it seems that we are merely supplanting one priestcraft with another, the new chanting in Hindu or Encounterese rather than Latin. Again Fate is the old bugaboo. If one has bad stars, bad karma, or bad Tarot, then there is fatalistic self-reassurance whenever life turns hag. The flies in the soup are not one's own doing but Fate's unhappy hand. Conversely, those with good stars, good karma, good Tarot need only wait for Fate to fulfill its promise to them. Yet this is a most serious misconstruction of all occult philosophy and ultimately spiritually debilitating to the one who holds to it. Willful change, conscious evolution, spiritual growth, all discovered inwardly, are the grand cornerstones of prophetic divination.

Hence, in this short introduction, I wish to de-emphasize tools

4

of divination and instead place the accent upon the reader, and also upon the one given the reading, whom we may call readee. Because Tarot cards are archetypal, therefore allowing the psychic, unconscious, and imaginative functions of both reader and readee a wide field of play, they lend themselves to perceptive, in-depth readings.

Another factor in a good reading is rapport of reader and readee. Resistance never yields profound results. Thus, at least the pragmatic reason for "unbelivers" to be routed out of the temples of the occult. But the same axiom applies equally well to the delicate relation between analyst and analysand on the psychiatrist's couch, and also to salesman and salesmanager.

In this text I give readings using each of the standard spreads, and have added a new form which evolved out of a series of readings and letter exchanges with the eminent scholar of mythology Dr. Joseph Campbell. I have been particularly gratified by the responses to the new form from those persons given readings, and hence, gladly pass it along to the reader, with again the reminder that what works for one may not for another. However, for a reader readily in touch with his intuitive self, one spread will probably prove as valuable as another. However, my new form, which I call the Jungian spread, enables one to comment (if he is able) on the inner psychological life, specifically the Jungian archetypes, of the individual given the reading. No other spreads of which I am now aware have actual archetypal stations (card points).

Just what is Tarot? Fifty-six cards of four suits equivalent in number to present-day playing cards, except that an extra face card—the Knight—has been added for each suit. Jacks are called Pages, however. These fifty-six cards are the Minor Arcana. In addition, there are twenty-two Major Arcana, or Key cards, ranging from Key zero (The Fool) to Key twenty-one (The World).

The roots of Tarot are variously attributed to the Egyptian Book of Thoth (no relation to Crowley's volume of the same title), the Hebrew *Kabbalah,* and to China, India, and Tibet, as well as to many other countries.

The first known appearance of Tarot cards is placed in Europe during the late 14th Century. The name Tarot appears to be an anagram of ROTA, Latin for wheel, thus the Wheel of Life. Tar is said to be Greek for Thoth, an Egyptian god equivalent to Greek Hermes. The Book of Thoth, one of the ancient Egyptian hiero-glyphic papyri, is said by many occultists to be the prototype for the medieval Tarot packs. Usually this information is offered without the slightest bit of scholarly evidence, other than to say that two Frenchmen, Court de Gébelin (1728-1784) and P. Christian, attributed the origins of Tarot to the Book of Thoth. Since my own backgrounds are of the university, I felt that these assertions could not be accepted at face value without checking further. Occultists are woefully inclined to cite legendary sources without ever resorting to the hard work of scholarship.

I discovered that only fragments of the Book of Thoth are in existence. What is available has been translated mainly by 19th Century European archeologists of the post-Rosetta stone era (1799). In West Coast libraries I could not find a single translation of any of the fragments of the Book of Thoth. I found the book I wanted in an East Coast library. In the German material I read there was nothing to tie the Book of Thoth to Tarot.

History of the Tarot

Ouspensky, among other occultists, asserts that Egypt is the source of Tarot because of an initiation discussed by P. Christian in his *History and Practice of Magic* (1870). In this the initiate is led past twenty-two leaves or paintings on which appear the supposed source figures for the twenty-two Major Arcana. Naturally, whether or not one accepts this depends upon the closeness of correlation between the Egyptian and Tarot figures, *as well as upon the authenticity of P. Christian's sources.* Checking this I found a definite parallel, and also the uncredited source of A. E. Waite's subsequent Rider pack. Unfortunately the trail of the Tarot tends to dwindle with P. Christian's sources. This is what I found. Iamblicus, 4th Century A.D., is the author Christian cites as having written a treatise on the aforementioned initiation rite occurring within the structure of the Sphinx of Giseh near the Great Pyramid. This source may or may not be extant today; it is recorded as an Oxford folio: *Iamblichi de mysteriis Aegyptiorum* (folio Oxonii, 1678).

However, in Tarot there are parallels to all of the world's great religious systems, as well as to the esoteric truths hidden beneath exoteric doctrine.

Therefore, I have arrived at the opinion that all speculation about Tarot origins is equally meaningless, not only for the reason that it is purely speculation and must remain so until the unlikely time when a very, very lucky archeological find will *prove* its ties to a particular country and religious system, but also because the ultimate importance of Tarot is that it is a symbolic system of *cosmic, moral,* and *natural* laws, each of which has the same underlying principle *operating in all areas relevant to human endeavor,* and which ties together all three systems.

Thus there is no religion that does not have some parallel to Tarot, because reduced to its essence each system displays a certain sameness. In certain ways, therefore, Tarot is a symbolization of any and *all* religions. Certainly this is not immediately apparent to the average reader the first time he uses the cards or studies them. But the more one probes their depths, the more rewarding the richness of their symbolism. Each of the Major Arcana is in effect an entire world. Taken together they constitute a galaxy of universal principles, truths to live and die for, revelations about the divine Self, as well as the personal workaday

7

self. Yes, they also have a practicality when applied to business or love, family or friends. They are only limited by those using them—the consciousness of reader and readee.

TAROT & YOU

By now it must appear obvious to the reader that Tarot interpretations available today are not of an original spiritual fountainhead, but reflections of the psyche of the author offering the interpretation. The figures of Minor and Major Arcana have undergone transition and have been colored by the persuasion of each author writing on Tarot; hence my line in the introduction about computers blowing if all the conflicting interpretations were to be programmed into them.

Whether or not the reader is aware of it, he will find that Tarot also fits into his own way of looking at the realms of earth, mind, and spirit, diverse as his way of seeing may seem to be from that of traditional occultists. Indeed, his own approach is the more reliable, simply because it is his own.

Why is Tarot so universal, why can it "work" for anyone? The images depicted, particularly in the realm of the Major Arcana, are primordial and archetypal.

In his preface to *The Secret of the Golden Flower* by R. Wilhelm, C. G. Jung may as well have been writing about the symbols in Tarot. "The spontaneous fantasy products . . . concentrate themselves gradually around abstract structures which apparently represent 'principles,' true gnostic *archai.* When the fantasies are chiefly expressed in thoughts, the results are intuitive formulations of dimly felt laws or principles, which at first tend to be dramatized or personified."

Activated by the evocative imagery of the Tarot, verbalization of the "thought/fantasies" is the free-association approach to Tarot reading. One says what he feels. Do not allow the original impression to be restricted or modified by dictates of what one thinks he should say about the card—what he has read or heard others say. Let the pure intuition shine forth unfettered by logic.

Tarot is above all a symbolic system of self-knowledge, self-integration, and self-transformation. Vital to integration is the union of opposites within, a process which Jung says "on a higher level of consciousness is not a rational thing, nor is it a matter of will; it is a psychic process of development which expresses itself in symbols." (*The Secret of the Golden Flower.*)

J. E. Cirlot (*A Dictionary of Symbols*) confirms the relationship of Tarot to Jungian concepts of integration: "Present-day psychology has confirmed . . . that the Tarot cards comprise an image (comparable to that encountered in dreams) of the path of initiation. At the same time Jung's view, coinciding with the secular, intuitive approach to the Tarot enigmas, recognized the portrayal of two different, but complementary struggles in the life of man: (a) the struggle against others (the solar way) which he pursues through his social position and calling; and (b) against himself (the lunar way), involving the process of individuation. These two ways correspond to reflexion and intuition—to practical reason and pure reason."

Thus it is in the following readings that the reader of this volume will hear me speak frequently of Selfhood, the goal of the individuation process. Selfhood represents a totality of being. Jung says the Self is "a God-image, or at least cannot be distinguished from one. Of this the early Christian spirit was not ignorant, otherwise Clement of Alexandria could never have said that he who knows himself knows God." (*Aion: Contributions to the Symbolism of the Self.*) Jung also has said, "Christ exemplifies the archetype of self." (*Aion*)

There will also be references to the four functions, sensation, intellect, feeling (in the sense of value judgments), and intuition, because development of the least of these in anyone is vital to integration of the mature adult. And I shall speak of the Law of Attraction, which implies that restrictions within (the lunar level) may block attainment on the mundane plane (the solar level), or even attract misfortune to the individual.

Since the Tarot cards are divided into four suits, a possible relation is suggested to the four functions of Jungian psychology. Pentacles is the suit I assign to the sensation (sense perception) function. This function tells one that a thing exists; he perceives it through his five senses.

I relate the thinking function to the Swords suit, although some may associate it with Rods or Wands. The phrase, "the sword of intellect" comes to my mind and is probably the reason I make this association.

Rods I link to the intuition function. Whereas thinking tells one what the thing is that is perceived, intuition may tell one the history of it and even its future. The feeling function is not to be confused with the emotions. It is the rational process of making a value judgment, a weighing of factors. This function I associate with the Cups suit.

When one discusses the main function an individual uses in relating to his world, he is describing that person's *superior* function. The quality or approach the individual uses least is his *inferior* function. This function is repressed or largely unconscious. The fully integrated man is able to utilize all four functions. I often refer to this symbolically as the square of consciousness. As a quaternary, or quaternity, the square is a symbol of psychic wholeness, and of order and stability within the life.

Further, I make a correlation between the four elements, Fire, Earth, Air, and Water, and respectively the four suits, Swords, Pentacles, Rods, and Cups. This has led to astrological speculations that have proved rewarding in my readings. Again I reiterate that if the reader is at home with a different set of correspondences, he should use them instead.

The Jungian Spread

In the summer of 1969, I was visited in California by Dr. Joseph Campbell and his wife, Jean, who is known as Jean Erdman in the world of modern dance. Dr. Campbell is the author of *The Masks of God,* a four-volume series encompassing the entire range of mythology from primitive to creative. He also has written *The Hero With a Thousand Faces,* a book which I read again each year, and about which I have difficulty restraining my enthusiasm. It literally changed my life, and will do the same for anyone ready to commence his own "heroic journey." The rest of Dr. Campbell's works are too numerous to mention; however this year (1971) he has edited *The Viking Portable Jung,* which will be of special interest to readers of *Tarot and You.* As a most elementary introduction to the psychology of C. G. Jung, I recommend the text/picture volume *Man and His Symbols,* available in paperback and also in two hardbound volumes.

On this particular afternoon in 1969 we had nothing to do, and the fog being in, we decided to experiment with a Tarot reading. (His reading of that day is not the one reproduced in this book.) The results kindled our interests, and subsequently we exchanged many letters regarding the meaning of the twenty-two Key cards of the Major Arcana. I quote from Dr. Campbell's letter of October 7, 1969. Key cards one through four "reveal Jung's basic collective archetypes: Animus and Anima (I and II), World Mother (III), World Father (IV) . . ." These words were the inspiration for my Jungian Spread.

In clarifying what he means by archetypes, Jung has this to say: "My views about the 'archaic remnants,' which I call 'archetypes' or 'primordial images,' have been constantly criticized by people who lack a sufficient knowledge of the psychology of dreams and of mythology. The term 'archetype' is often misunderstood as meaning certain definite mythological images or motifs. But these are nothing more than conscious representations; it would be absurd to assume that such variable representations could be inherited. The archetype is a tendency to form such representations of a motif—representations that can vary a great deal in detail without losing their basic pattern." (Jung, *Man and His Symbols.*)

I do not recall now whether it was Jung or someone else who likened the archetype to the axial pattern in crystals. That is to say, even while in solution, while there is still no trace of a solid crystal, the solution itself possesses the potential for the crystalline pattern. So too the mind before consciousness possesses the archetype.

In Dr. Campbell's linear scheme, the Zero Key, The Fool, was placed either at the beginning or end of the other twenty-one Keys. Thus it was Alpha *and* Omega. It occurred to me that since Key I and II represented pre-birth, pre-conscious factors in the individual, they then required an origin card. Further, The Fool as Alpha and Omega suggested the snake with tail in mouth, that is, beginning and end, the uroboros, the Orphic egg out of which all life comes, and to which it returns at death. The number Zero also had suggestions of an egg, and of a "no-thing" center out of which matter differentiated. This meant that The Fool could be placed only at the center, while outside the Wheel of Life revolved. Additional insights into what The Fool symbolized soon came. He was also the World Navel, "the still point of the turning world . . . there the dance is," as T. S. Eliot has so beautifully put it in *Four Quartets*.

No human can represent this concept, and the creators of Tarot were wise to have such a foolish figure here. On another level we may say divine wisdom seems folly to men. Thus I place face down the first card drawn in a reading of the Jungian Spread—out of deference to the fact that nothing (Zero) can represent it. It is Nature's veil that man will never lift, the Unmanifest, the divine Mystery of the Cosmos that man will never penetrate to its depths, since the very universe that he seeks to know is receding before him at nearly the speed of light!

This flying-out from the center is the impression that the other cards present in the Jungian Spread. The Unmoved Mover, the No-thing, is the stationary hub of the cosmic wheel. Are we now perhaps defining God? The human mind cannot concept- ualize this idea. We are more at home with Biblical depictions of an all-powerful, bearded gentleman on a throne. Since kings were the most exalted beings humans have had for models throughout the world's cultural history, it is not surprising that our Biblical authors depicted the loftiest concept as a king/judge on a throne.

On an interior, or psychological level, the Zero card also repre- sents what Jung called the collective unconscious. ". . . Just as the human body shows a common anatomy over and above all racial differences, so too, the psyche possesses a common substratum transcending all differences in culture and consciousness. I have called this substratum the collective unconscious. This uncon- scious psyche, common to all mankind, does not consist merely of contents capable of becoming conscious, but of latent disposi- tions toward identical reactions." (*Alchemical Studies.*)

Thus the collective unconscious preserves and transmits a common psychological inheritance for all mankind. Naturally one

12

cannot conceive of entering his own (and all men's) collective unconscious; yet the fantastic and psychedelic trip near the end of the film *2001* is a depiction of a world in which ordinary physics does not apply. Then "inside" may become "outside"!

The position of Key Zero required a face-down card in my arrangement of the Major Arcana. Next came the placement of Keys I through IV. Of these four cards I made a square around the face-down card (four diagrams are presented in the section of Jungian Spread readings.) Here I allow the reader ample leeway in arranging these cards. For example, card one, occupying the position of Key I, may be followed by Key II directly below it, or to the right of it. Most important is that one understands that these four cards symbolize the Mother and Father of the person given the reading as well as one's own inner masculine principle (if a man), and his *anima*. If the reading is given for a woman, two of the cards will represent her inner feminine principle, as well as her *animus*. Now we have come to the two terms that are probably unfamiliar to the reader. They are not difficult concepts, and I shall explain them as simply as possible. Very generally they may be thought of as the ideal woman and the ideal man within the unconscious of a man and woman respectively. Remember, however, that they are archetypes, and pre-conscious, pre-birth in origin. Thus the archetype is a determinant of what the subsequent conscious ideal will be like. In some, this figure is negatively constituted as an archetype *before the person is born.* Thus the life quest for a mate will always be full of problems for such a person because that person selects only negative persons in seeking the fulfillment of his or her anima or animus. He or she never finds anyone who is good for him, unless he becomes more conscious of the anima and consciously sets out to transform it.

When the anima or animus is positively constituted *before birth,* that person then has excellent relatedness to his own opposite side, be it masculine or feminine. For example, a man with a positive anima has excellent potential as a creative artist. His harmony with his feminine inner self constitutes a state of dynamic equilibrium. Such a man should not be confused with a homosexual, who is in a state of imbalance, the unconscious feminine elements dominating the masculine consciousness.

Through astrology I am able to determine the preconscious

13

constitution of animus and anima in women and men, and how it will affect them in their later adult lives. I tested this theory with a prominent Jungian analyst and writer whose horoscope I cast and interpreted. Although with some persons archetypes are not as great a factor in their lives as with others, I have found that this approach functions remarkably well in all the charts I have cast, so it was natural for me to adapt it to the Jungian Spread. From the remarks of the readees given the Jungian Spread, you will read that my analysis of these unconscious formative factors matched these archetypes as the readees had come to know them consciously. Persons interested in horoscope charts cast with a view to unconscious as well as conscious factors may address inquiries to me at P. O. Box 581, San Anselmo, California 94960.

Jung has this to say in defining the nature of the anima: "Every man carries within himself an eternal image of woman, not the image of this or that definite woman but rather a definite feminine image. This image is fundamentally an unconscious hereditary factor of primordial origin and is engraved on the living system of man." (*Contributions to Analytical Psychology.*)

There are four stages in the development of the anima. This does not imply that every man's anima is ultimately raised to the highest level. In men who see women primarily as sex objects, the level involved is obviously the first, or lowest. "The first stage is best symbolized by the figure of Eve, which represents purely instinctual and biological relations. The second can be seen in Faust's Helen: she personifies a romantic and aesthetic level that is, however, still characterized by sexual elements. The third is represented, for instance, by the Virgin Mary—a figure who raises love (eros) to the heights of spiritual devotion. The fourth type is symbolized by Sapientia, wisdom transcending even the most holy and the most pure." (von Franz, *Man and His Symbols.*)

Since the anima is unconscious, she is very probably behind those encounters of "love-at-first-sight" that many of us have experienced. As long as one's awareness of her remains unconscious, the power of her image may be projected out of a man's unconscious and onto a quite ordinary flesh-and-blood woman, who suddenly acquires extraordinary mana for him, inspiring his friends to wonder at "what he sees in her."

Likewise womankind bears within itself an archetypal image

14

of man known as the animus. Being opposites, animus and anima function in quite different ways within the psyche of woman or man, and a discussion of this occupied much of Jung's own works; hence it is beyond the scope of this short history.

However, the animus also has four stages of development within the woman's psyche. At the level of purely physical attraction to man, Tarzan was once the embodiment of this figure. Today a Joe Namath or a Paul Newman may find that his mass attractiveness to women is the result of his fulfillment of this animus level. The second stage is marked by the romantic minstrel/poet. In his day Dylan Thomas had immense appeal for women even though he was not especially handsome physically. Following in his footsteps on this level were figures such as the Beatles' Paul McCartney, and Bobby Dylan. At the third stage, the man is the "bearer of the word for his nation and culture." John Kennedy was such an animus figure for many women. At the highest level, the spiritual, a girl's own personal guru becomes her initiator into the higher mysteries of self and spirit. (In the foregoing examples, I have updated the persons at the levels given by von Franz in *Man and His Symbols.*)

Remember, a man has an *anima,* a woman an *animus.* Generally, it is quite an easy matter to spot the card among the first four upturned which stands for the animus or anima. Usually a figure of the opposite sex is depicted, and very often an idealized figure. Study the examples connected with the four persons given readings by the Jungian Spread.

Now the other archetype involved in the first four cards is of the same sex as the readee, and I call it the masculine principle within (for a man), or the feminine principle (for a woman). In cases in which it functions in a negative or repressed way, I call it the shadow. Jung meant by this term the unconscious side of the ego, personified in dreams by someone of the same sex as the dreamer. Thus, with two cards at the beginning of the reading representing figures of the *inner life,* it is at least potentially possible to discern the nature of these archetypes within the psyche of the one read.

The next two cards, World Father and World Mother, (may) refer to the mundane parents in the life of the individual. In cases in which the psychic life of the readee is not yet at peace or in harmony with the parents, these cards may stand as representatives of father and mother *imagos,* images yet residing in the unconscious. Or they may stand as *exalted* images, Rex and Regina, or still further, as the fructifying World Parents of the mythological realm. Most often, however, the cards describe our apple-pie Mom and Dad as we know them.

The fifth upturned card is placed below and between the two cards for the World Parents. It falls naturally in the position of the fifth Key card, that is, The Hierophant. Just as the forces of the higher spiritual world are channeled through him to the mundane plane (in the role of medium of the message), so too the forces of the person's inherent world (cards one to four) are directed outwardly to the mundane plane. The fifth card is thus the *gestalt* of his life, or the way in which he relates to the world, and the world experience, which is described by cards six through twenty-one. Card five often symbolizes, by the suit of the card, his superior function, or the orientation he uses in dealing with life. For this relation of the four suits to the four functions, see my words at the beginning of this section.

Generally, the first card stands for the inner masculine or feminine principle. The second represents the animus or anima. Cards three and four are Father and Mother. Lay out these four cards and arrange them in an order to fit your own associations.

The Wheel of Life is represented by the outer circle of cards. They proceed in a clockwise manner, and the reader is free to begin at the six o'clock point (directly below card five) or at one o'clock. Generally I begin at one o'clock with persons over fifty because the cards then proceed down to what Dr. Campbell has called the "belly of the whale," or the dark night of the soul— life's most difficult time. With younger persons this experience may still be in the future, and as is the sun their cards are marching upward to the zenith of life.

I have now given you the Jungian Spread. With all the other simple spreads of cards available to you, there is absolutely no reason for you to utilize it when attempting a reading. However, if you find—as I do—that matters of inner space are as exciting as outer space, then you may wish to know more of Jung, how your own archetypes affect you in your life, and whether or not you can discern these effects in the lives of others—through Tarot.

16

I have already heard from people who have used the free-association technique in their readings with excellent results. None of them has studied any of the interpretation books. Remember, a symbol or image can be interpreted from an infinite number of points of view. You, the reader, must find the spread of cards with which you feel most confident, most at home. Whatever you "see" in the cards will be your meaning, the cards' meaning. Perhaps one day Tarot will be recognized as a truly helpful tool for developing intuition. Do not approach a reading with a sense of inferiority; "give" as much as you can to it. Your accuracy will surprise you. One way to begin is by reading for yourself. If you have a question which may be answered by a negative or positive response by the cards, then use the "Yes-No Spread." Or try a one-card reading by simply cutting at random to a single card. Then you may tell the readee, "This is you at present. I see such-and-such in the card. The feeling it gives me is . . .," etc. Gaze at a cloud, and see what it resembles. Allow the unconscious freer rein, and it will take you far. With most of us, the everyday consciousness, the logical, rational mind sits too heavily upon the unconscious. Give the unconscious its due.

Shuffling the cards can be the process whereby the readee implants his vibrations into cards, or unconsciously orders them so that they can be read by you, the reader. I prefer a method of three shuffles, then a cutting into three piles with one of the piles reversed (if the spread calls for reversals). This entire shuffle/cut process should be repeated three times, a total of nine shuffles.

As a last note I want to say something that is still thrilling for me. I believe I have cracked the Tarot "code." There is supposed to be a way by which the cards are arranged that will reveal the esoteric meaning of each card and its relation to all others. The great occultist A. E. Waite evidently knew this but would not reveal it. He switched Keys eight and eleven from older Tarot decks which had Justice following The Chariot. He has never given a reason for this, other than to say, "As the variation carries nothing with it which will signify to the reader, there is no cause for explanation."

Perhaps at some future date I shall publish this thrilling scheme. For now it is decidedly outside the limits of this book.

Happy readings.

17

All right, this reading will illustrate the so-called "Ancient Celtic Method." I say so-called because to my knowledge there is no historical basis for relating the Tarot to the Celts. Certainly the Tarot is known to gypsies in all countries—the deck is more commonly known as gypsy fortune telling cards—and there are gypsies in Ireland, usually called tinkers, but the gypsy strain is foreign and not Celtic. I think perhaps the reason for the name of the spread comes from the appearance of the form—resembling an ancient Celtic cross.

The person given the reading, or the readee, as I like to call him, has been brought to the reading without knowing anything about Tarot. Is that correct?

W: I didn't even know they were cards until you brought them out.

R: O.K. Also, we have never met before. I asked my friends to bring you here without telling me anything about you before so that you will serve as a control in the reading. I will ask you to verify or deny what I say, but don't volunteer any information until after I have finished speaking.

W: That's fine with me.

R: First, this method involves picking a card that stands for your-

The Ancient Celtic Method

self in the reading. Persons of blond hair and blue eyes are represented by the suit Rods, or Wands, as it is sometimes called. Cups are for persons with light brown hair and eyes; Swords for dark brown hair and eyes; and Pentacles, or Coins, for persons of black hair and dark eyes. It's curious that red heads are never mentioned, but I guess the color of the eyes would determine their category. Now your hair is kind of in between dark brown and light brown, so would you rather be a King of Swords or a King of Cups?

W: A King of Swords! Definitely.

R: O.K. Then the SIGNIFICATOR card for you is the KING OF SWORDS . . . Oh, yes, I should say at this point that a mature man would be represented by a King of the suit that applies, and a woman by a Queen, a young man—oh, say age 15 to 30—by a Knight, and a young girl or boy would be represented by a Page.

W: (Laughing) Couldn't I have a Knight then?

R: You're decidedly over thirty, and therefore, we can't trust what you say, or so the saying goes. (Laughing)

W: Then I'm stuck with a King. I wish I was playing poker.

R: All right, now shuffle the cards once, cut them into three piles, reversing the direction of at least one pile. Repeat this

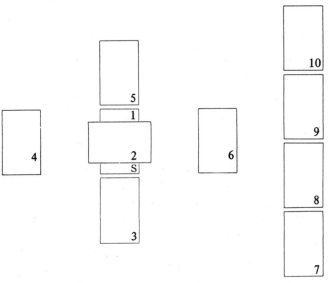

Significator, King of Swords
1. Three of Rods
2. The Hermit
3. Eight of Pentacles
4. Five of Cups (Reversed)
5. Four of Cups
6. Three of Swords (Reversed)
7. Six of Swords
8. Four of Pentacles
9. Two of Cups
10. Knight of Cups

19

shuffle/cut process two more times—three altogether . . .

W: (Cutting and reversing one pile) Like this?

R: Right . . . O.K. Now I'll lay out all eleven cards at once, and then deal with them individually . . .

I'm supposed to say here "this covers him," in respect to the first card, which I have placed on top of the SIGNIFICATOR. However, anyone who knows my theories on why Tarot works, knows that I don't believe it makes a bit of difference what one says.

W: No magic words?

R: No magic words. But for the sake of pointing out what each position represents, we may say that the first card, having been placed on top of the card that represents you, engulfs you, cloaks you, or *covers* you. In other words, it is the psychic situation surrounding you, enveloping you. I am assuming that you were hoping to receive some kind of insight into yourself, or into a particular situation, and if that is true then your unconscious knew the order of all the cards—and this is important—*even though you had not seen the cards before in your life and did not see the order with your eyes even now.* My theory is simply that through a kind of psycho-kinesis—if you know what that means? . . .

W: Uh, the mind can cause things, objects to move around. It was mentioned on "Startrek" on TV one time.

R: Right, mind over matter. So your unconscious directed the cards to a meaningful order that would outline your question or problem, and possibly enable me to throw some light on it for you.

W: Was I supposed to have been thinking of a question?

R: Yes and no. This form supposedly answers a question for you, but again according to my theory, if there is a question or problem on your mind, then your unconscious will psycho-kinetically direct the cards and the order.

W: Great. There has been something on my mind for several months.

R: Then it should come out in the reading. The card that covers you is the THREE OF RODS, and as I said before, it is what is psychically enveloping you. Perhaps we could say the atmosphere, or the life-situation. Maybe also, your feelings.

20

This is a man with his back to me. The three rods suggest a portal or gateway of some kind. The garb of the man is rather regal, so it is easy to associate him with the King SIGNIFI-CATOR. Maybe he has a new threshold to cross in life. He hasn't gone through these portals yet. He is hesitant . . . Oh, the thing that stands out about this card is the completely blank sky. It reminds me of a poem I wrote entitled "Camus' Death", and there was a line, "Just before you were to die/You looked again in the eye/That blank sky . . . " It's as if the man in the card is facing a blank wall. There is also the term the "existential vacuum;" it stands for a lack of value, a sense of meaninglessness. This man seems to be in a vacuum, but whether or not it is existential I don't know.

Let me look at the next card and I'll try to see what it is that is causing these feelings in him. The next card is THE HERMIT. This card "crosses you," so let's call it the opposing forces. You know the expression, "Don't cross me"? I think this card is inter-esting because it points out the fallacy of attempting to attribute a rigid meaning to each card without considering it in the context of the reading. In other words, for me symbols come to mean in the context of a given situation. Usually THE HERMIT is a symbol of wisdom, or the Jungian archetype of the wise old man, who so often appears in dreams as a symbol of the Self, but I don't get that feeling here at all. In other words, if I were to try to make that standard interpretation fit this reading, my approach would be like a Procrustean bed. Procrustes was an ancient highwayman who forced travellers to come to his castle and lie in his bed. If they were too short, he stretched them on the rack until they fitted his bed. If they were too long, he chopped off whatever hung over.

So let me free associate with the card . . . Again, the figure's face is averted from the viewer, as in the previous card. To me he seems to be going back into the monastery, rather than leaving it in order to re-enter the world. That is not encouraging. The word hermit suggests to me isolation and seclusion, hiding. Maybe he is hiding something. Now we must remember that this card is in the position of the forces opposing you. But since studying psychol-ogy and the occult, I have been made aware of a very great truth; what is known in hermetic circles as the Law of Attraction. It

21

means one receives what he gives. The principle is that we give off psychic vibrations that permeate the ether and attract to ourselves others, or situations, that are of a similar vibration. If we are of a low vibration, then destructive situations and people are the unvaried pattern of our lives. So that in summing up one might say that the outer world life situations are a concrete manifestation of the inner world psychic condition. The thing about the man depicted in THE HERMIT is that he doesn't seem to be giving off—or giving out—anything. But it's not the peace of atonement. Cloistered and secluded is the way I feel about him— emotionally that is. He isn't giving out with his emotions, his feelings; he has secluded, hidden them. Does hermit have a verb form—to hermit, to hide? I don't know, but the figure depicted is the kind of person I would like to see thrown into an encounter group ... O.K., then if this is the force that crosses or opposes you, then I would have to say it is of your own doing, coming right out of yourself and thence manifested in the world where you see others seemingly allied against you.

Well, let's come back to this card later, because I'm sure it's very important and will shed light on the other cards. (Laughing) I wasn't consciously making a pun, but now I am aware that the figure carries a lantern ... Now can you associate yourself with this card?

W: Not at all, because I'm very sociable. I live in the world and have never had any inclinations to seclude myself.

R: That wasn't necessarily what I meant. You may not seclude yourself physically, but you may seclude your emotions or feelings, that is hide them away inside yourself. People can make an hermitage of themselves to the extent that others in their lives who need their love—or whatever—find the emotions sequestered—yes, that is a good word for it—and unavailable to them.

W: Could I change the ground rules here just a little. Would it be all right if I didn't say anymore 'til I've heard some more from you—maybe after a couple of more cards?

R: Absolutely. This reading is like a puzzle, and I would like to find a few more pieces myself ... O.K., the next card is the EIGHT OF PENTACLES. Completely different from the previous card! Maybe I had you all wrong. (Laughing) ... I'm supposed to say here, "This card is beneath you", which means that this is the past, or that which went before and contributed to the present situation. When I look at this card, I think of the expression, "Be happy in your work." Here is a man who *is* happy in his work. He is obviously a craftsman—Lord knows there are few enough of them left in this world—let's call him a businessman, highly successful, and he holds the hammer he uses to "hammer out" his deals. Hard-driving also comes to mind with "hammer out." He is hard-driving because he is happy working. He really feels "at home" while working, so he doesn't mind doing a lot of it. Perhaps he has trouble understanding why others do not share this feeling with him . . . Ah, on his head he wears a cap that looks like the old-time beanies kids—tough kids—used to wear in the old days. The beanie was covered with buttons that had on them what were then regarded as inflammatory slogans, like "So's your old man." They would be very mild today. I never wanted to meet up with a kid wearing a hat like that because with all the slogans challenging you he was an open invitation to fight. You had to put up or shut up when you met a kid wearing a cap like that.

Well, the man on the card has a cap covered with what appears to be coins. So it's as if the Pentacles on the wall had continued right into his head. It's a preoccupation, then, almost an obsession, that he has with working and making money. He sees only the mallet or hammer, not the beautiful sky outside his window. Maybe that's why the sky had become blank in the first card.

All right, the next card is the FIVE OF CUPS . . . This card is reversed, and again we have a figure with the face averted or hidden. I really feel a sense of loss in connection with this card. Since the suit is Cups, I think the loss is on the side of emotions, rather than monetary matters as it might be if the suit were Pentacles. Oddly enough, this is a case in which the card seems to me to have the same value or meaning that it did in another reading. Oh, here I am supposed to say "this is behind you." It represents a situation that has just passed, or let us say took place within the past year. The last card was a kind of long term foundation or basis for the disruption of cups—or emotions—which we see represented in this card. Yes, overturned cups definitely mean to me an outpouring of emotions. I am reminded of the film made from D. H. Lawrence's "The Virgin and the Gypsy." The

23

pent-up energies were symbolized by the dam which held in the waters. When the dam burst it flooded the rectory, symbol of the repressive, puritanical Christianity, and then the rector's daughter, the virgin, bedded down with the gypsy, symbol of the elemental forces.

In this picture there are three overturned cups, and I get the feeling of a disruptive emotional outpouring involving not just yourself, but your entire family—since there are three cups. You are married and have children?

W: Yes.

R: O.K. I have a hunch now as to how all the cards so far fit together—what the story is. But I'd like to look at the next card and then go back to the beginning. The next card is particularly important because it represents your hopes in respect to the situation. It is sometimes also called what *may* come to pass.

The next card "crowns you." It is the FOUR OF CUPS. We see a gloved hand coming down out of a cloud. Obviously this cup is a gift for the man under the tree, and the interesting thing is that added to the other three cups it constitutes a quaternity, which always reminds me of the Jungian four functions—sensation, intellect, feeling, and intuition . . . Now I think I'm ready to go out on the limb in the picture. The fourth cup represents your inferior function, which I take to be the feeling function. This may have got you into trouble with your family.

W: Why?

R: Well, women expect feeling to be demonstrated as a sign of love. When it isn't, they infer that they are unloved and begin looking elsewhere.

Now let's go back and look at the first card that "covered you," the one representing the atmosphere relevant to the problem. No, I think perhaps I'd rather speak about the second card first. O.K., this card was THE HERMIT, and my feelings about it were that he was not giving out with his emotions, that they were cloistered, sequestered within. If your inferior function is feeling, that would fit . . . As I said before, the opposing forces seem to lie without in the world but in reality they lie within, perhaps the result of not giving out the expected emotions in life situations.

Remember we said the next card was completely different— this was the EIGHT OF PENTACLES, the businessman hard at

24

work. Well, for persons who find feeling relationships difficult, work—rather than a monastery—is the sanctuary for them. They take refuge in their work because impersonal—rather then intrapersonal—relations are the order of the day. The other three functions can all be valuable in the business world—intellect and intuition particularly, and possibly sensation. But if one has to be ruthless and gain his own ascendancy at the expense of others, the less feelings one has for his fellow man the better. I'm speaking pragmatically now, from the business point of view and not from my own. After all, business is dog eat dog, survival of the fittest—or slickest.

So here we have a man who feels at home not at home but in the competitive world of business. But this gets him into trouble because—feeling more at home away from home—he devotes more and more time to his work. He becomes very successful— look at all the Pentacles! In effect he heaps these at his lady's feet in what he believes to be a demonstration of love, but she is not fooled, or shall I say fulfilled, by material wealth. She is operating on another plane and needs merely a few simple signs of affection. Not just sex, but a certain empathetic relationship which he is bewildered as to how to give. So we came to the inevitable next card, the card I have just discussed having been the foundation of the matter—over devotion to work.

And in the next card, the FIVE OF CUPS, there is emotional disruption and chaos in the family. Looking at it now, it looks like blood spilling out of the cups, and these family quarrels are always like cutting an artery. You see what happens is this. The wife's resentment finally spills out in violent accusations of "you don't love me." You do however love her, you just don't have any idea of how to go about expressing it, or saying it. So your emotions spill out uncontrollably too. You get angry, and say something like, "Why the hell do you think I work six days a week, then, ten hours a day?! Do you think I enjoy it?!" Of course, we know now why you do work so often. You feel more comfortable at work since you have trouble expressing feelings. Some persons come from families where the emotions are easily demonstrable in the family, so as children they are outward going with their feelings. Probably it was your luck to have come from a family—those of the "best breeding" are like this—in which

25

show of affection was reserved for birthdays, Christmas, anniversaries, *et cetera*. In such families the parents look upon emotional displays as bad taste, as taboo as incest might be. *The Forsythe Saga* comes to mind. So you learned from your parents—unfortunately.

W: But my wife comes from a family where her father and mother are either kissing and hugging all the time or fighting. So she can cry in a movie, or at something on the TV, or anything.

R: It seems to have been a case of opposites attracting with you two. Of course, between her home life and your home life there is probably a middle-ground that is better suited for growing up stable yet expressive.

O.K. Now the third spilled cup in the picture represents the child or children's emotional disruption caused by the situation. There is an absolutely fantastic book by Frances Wickes called *The Inner World of Childhood*. All the other child psychology books can be thrown away. She points out that the child usually picks up on the unconscious level of the parents, so it's not what's up front that counts, but the undercurrents. As a matter of fact, where there was a disturbed child in the family, she began by treating the parents, clearing up the unconscious conflicts which the child had intuited.

Let's go back to the first card again, the atmosphere around the problem. Remember I said the man in the THREE OF RODS seemed to be on a threshold which he was hesitant to cross, and ahead of him was that blank sky that suggested meaninglessness. Ohhh, I see something that really ties him to that businessman in the third card who was working too hard. Look at his head-gear—he has the same cap of coins that the businessman has. It's really easy now to associate the two figures. So let's say that the atmosphere around him has left him doubting himself. All he believed in is about to be left behind, and ahead is only a blank void. So I would say he should not cross that threshold, but should go back to his wife. The atmosphere seems to be one of impending divorce. Now I've gone out on the limb so you talk for a while.

W: This is really amazing . . . My wife and I are separated now. She has been asking for a divorce, but, as you say, I am hesitant to take that step. I don't look forward to starting a new life.

R: Uh, huh, I can sympathize with that.

W: What about the last card, where you said I'd get the cup as a gift?

R: Oh, that shows some promise for you. It may come into being that the fourth function—feeling—will be added to you. Don't ask me how to go about it, that's a difficult problem at best and probably a job for an analyst. However, the anima, the feminine side of yourself—in Jungian terms—is the archetypal figure that can lead you inwardly, put you in better touch with your feelings, and perhaps effect relatedness. Because of the appearance of this card in this position, I would say the prospects of this happening are rather good in your life. However, I would see a good Jungian analyst, and then perhaps have him see your wife and try to explain that you have problems expressing your love for her, although the love for her is there and trying to find a means of expression nevertheless.

Well, now we've reached the point where the rest of the reading is in the realm of speculation.

W: How do you mean?

R: Well, for the next card I say "This is before you." In other words, you won't be able to verify or deny what I say, but the card should somehow fit into the pattern I have described.

W: I see.

R: O.K., this card is—ouch!—the THREE OF SWORDS!

W: Wow!

R: Here we have a picture of a heart pierced by three swords. The card is reversed, which suggests to me an inversion of pain—a psychic pain—rather than external physical pain . . . This is a good card for you at this point. If you are going to strengthen your inferior function—feeling—you of course have to begin to feel more deeply, and because of the separation from your wife, feeling will be painful for you initially. Even heart-rending, one might say. Yes, there will be great emotional suffering ahead for you, but if you can see that it is the result of your earlier desires to avoid the experience of human relatedness, your desire to live at the surface of life rather than in its deeper aspects, then you may be able to see this suffering as purposeful, and in the long run rewarding. In other words, no cross, no crown.

W: I think I see it.

R: All right, let's try the next card. Including it, there are four more cards to be turned over, and in connection with them there are no magic words to be said.

W: Are they supposed to indicate how things will turn out?

R: The very last card indicates that, unless it is ambiguous, in which case we would use the last card as the SIGNIFICATOR, and begin the reading again.

W: I'm going to have to leave in about thirty minutes to an hour, so we couldn't do that all over again tonight.

R: O.K., then I'll hurry along with the last four cards. Next card—SIX OF SWORDS. I have heard various interpretations assigned to this position. Some say it represents the person himself, probably at some point in the future. Others say this card personifies or symbolizes the fears of the individual. Let's just look at it as a continuation of your journey towards acquiring greater feeling consciousness. There is a solitary figure *poling* himself along in a boat pierced by six swords, double the number of the previous card. The pole is immersed in water, which to me suggests that you *will* be making contact with the emotion/feeling side of yourself. However, as opposed to sailing, poling is hard work, so this will not be accomplished without great effort on your part . . . The pole seems to be more than a pole. It has a pair of wings at the top, which suggests that it may be a sceptre of mastery of some kind. So again I think you will be successful in developing the feeling function. The odd thing about the swords is that they are piercing the bottom of the boat, and seemingly are also touching water at the tips. O.K., something comes to mind here. The boat equals the vehicle. The vehicle equals the consciousness of the individual. By piercing or probing down to the very bottom of consciousness, one reaches the waters of the unconscious. In other words, your feelings lie buried deep within your unconscious, and must be brought up into consciousness where they can function in your interpersonal relationships.

Now if we look upon this card as symbolic of your fears, we might say that it appears to be a lonely journey—and he is indeed solitary—so perhaps you fear the loneliness of this journey. But—again—it is a journey to wholeness—psychic wholeness, and must be undertaken if you are to heal the rift between yourself and your wife. My associations are with the heroic task, the slaying of the dragon. The hero is separated from his beloved and must

28

enter the dragon's realm—the waters of the unconscious—but when the dragon of unfeeling is slain, he may then return—whole—to his lady. But, if he had attempted to remain at home (or at work) and avoided undertaking the perilous journey all would be lost.

No, I think this bodes well for your future. There *will* be more suffering—SIX swords—but the challenge is being met, and ahead there is a truly glorious sky just over the mountains.

W: Great.

R: The next card has to do with the environment surrounding the problem and particularly the influences of family and friends. This card is the FOUR OF PENTACLES . . . Huh, this is a tough one—I have been empathizing so much with you that I'm drawing a blank on the influence and point of view of family and friends—Well, this figure is almost a caricature of materialistic concern. On the breast, where the heart might be, is a giant pentacle. Above the head—or mind—is another. And to the right and left are two more. So, let me take a guess at this. Are the concerns of your so-called friends and in-laws, in regard to the separation of you and your wife, mainly materialistic in nature? That is, are they dwelling excessively on property settlements to the exclusion of the feelings and emotional suffering of the two people involved?

W: Definitely . . . Definitely. My wife's brother is an attorney and he has been after her for a year to divorce me. Her mother and father don't even want her to talk to me anymore. After all this is California, and if we split our community property she would come out very well off . . . My so-called friends, as you called them, seem to worry most about how much the divorce would wind-up costing me. None of these friends, and none of the family—even my own parents—seem to want to see us get back together again.

R: O.K., this atmosphere is a kind of trap for you, therefore. Because in times of feeling lonely and sorry for yourself—as when you're alone in that boat of the previous card—you may want to play off these feelings of being misunderstood against those of your own friends, who would be a welcome sounding board for such ideas. You must resist this temptation. Don't get me wrong, I'm not saying you're totally to blame as the cause of the separation, but going on this journey, strengthening your feeling function, can only result in your being a better person ultimately. Ahh, this is important. Even if you don't accomplish your goal, which is reconciliation with your wife, your chances of achieving a stable relationship with the next woman you love will be tremendously enhanced by what you accomplish now.

W: I understand. Great! This is better than going to a shrink.

R: (Laughter) . . . O.K. Let's look at the next card, and that is the TWO OF CUPS. Oh, this card is in the position of your hopes and ideals regarding the matter. Here the knight has returned from his journey and is reunited with his lady. Here we have a pledge of cups or feelings. I wonder about the origins of toasting another person as a show of affection and feeling. Or an exchange of cups as symbolical of an exchange of feeling. And this is important! This is the first time a figure in the cards of your reading is shown facing another human. Always before there was only a solitary figure, and very often that figure faced away from the reader or seemingly averted his face, so in the openness of *facing* the lady, as in the open exchange of feeling symbolized by the exchange of cups, your hopes for a solution seem to be reconciliation based upon a newfound ability for openness and display of emotion. The inferior function has been brought to consciousness and is in this card working to effect relatedness. What do you think?

W: When I saw the face of the lady, it reminded me of my wife. She has those same kind of intense eyes.

R: Good . . . Also, it is the *two* of cups, and the number two in occultism numerologically signifies receptivity and relatedness. Now undoubtedly you did not know that; yet this card represents your unconscious hopes for the resolution of the problem, so your unconsious selected this card as symbolical of the ideal solution—an excellent example of the way the unconscious works its psycho-kinetic powers.

Another thing that seems important is that there is a golden border around the top of the card. Also, the two cups are golden. Gold in color symbology signifies harmony, spiritual atonement, and life fulfillment. Gold is also symbolical of the "treasure hard to attain"—the Self, with a capital "S."

W: The last card tells me how things will turn out.

R: Right . . . I'm really afraid to turn it over. I've taken you this far, and given you reason to believe that there will be a happy ending, and if there isn't I'd almost want to blame myself.

W: We're right back to the first card—where you said the man was unwilling to take the step.

R: Very good! Yes, this is like crossing a threshold for the reader as well as for the life being read . . . O.K., here we go. The KNIGHT OF CUPS. All right, the problem that came to the fore during the reading had as its root cause the inferior function of feeling. Raising this into consciousness so that it could work for relatedness in life was the heroic task posed. In the service of this task, the knight has his heart pierced thrice in the depths of his suffering, yet is reunited with his lady, and stands finally as a knight of feeling—a knight of cups. I don't know if it is possible in Jungian terms for the inferior function to become the superior function at a later stage in life, but I would certainly say that as a knight of cups you would acquire sufficient sensitivity in your personal relationship with your wife to work out a happy reunion. I think the chances are excellent—at least according to the Tarot—and I shall be anxious to know how things work out.

W: This is the first good news I've heard about it . . . Amazing is all I can say. Looking at all the cards now, I see the whole problem laid out just as you said. But I don't think I could have seen the same things by myself. And I don't know if I'm convinced they will come true.

R: Maybe not, but you did shuffle the cards in an order necessary to make the reading meaningful.

W: My unconscious did the shuffling. (Laughter)

R: (Laughter) Right! Whether or not they come true I can't speak about. I don't pretend to be a prophet.

W: Well, thanks very much for the reading. If it doesn't work out the way you say, I'll be back to work you over. (Laughter)

R: I just thought of something that may help. After I have this tape typed up, suppose I give it to you, and you can play it for your wife. I think it might go a long way towards convincing her you are willing to work on your problem.

W: That would be great! She was always trying to interest me in stuff like this—astrology and palm-reading, but I never was interested before.

he person given this reading is well known to me; hence I decided that she should not conceal from me the matter of the reading, as guessing could be a factor in my reading her cards. Furthermore, she herself felt that the reading might be enhanced if we were both able to contribute to each card with a full knowledge of the matter under consideration. We decided, therefore, to attempt two readings to see if the second substantiated the first, which should be the case if Tarot is a valid form of divination. The matter under consideration for both readings is phrased by her as the question, "Will I survive?"

R: The date is December 13, 1970, and this is a reading for Erin Walsh by the Ancient Celtic Method. We have selected as the SIGNIFICATOR, the QUEEN OF RODS. Covering this card is the PAGE OF CUPS. Ordinarily I associate the Cups suit with the individual's unconscious, because it is often depicted in myth and fairytale by bodies of water, or containers of water—such as wells, or jars containing genies. The fish emerging from the cup represents an unconscious content that has come to the surface and been manifested in the conscious life. It may be positive, leading to self-reflection within the individual, or it may be a

The Ancient Celtic Method

negative manifestation, in which case it may unwittingly dominate the life. At all events, this "covering" card represents the influences on you, and because of this I would definitely say that the shaping forces exerted upon you now are from within the psyche, manifesting themselves in material form on the mundane plane. They *appear* to come from without, but in reality they are the inner forces made manifest without.

Since your experience has been reading ordinary playing cards, perhaps your interpretation is not the same as mine, but I am sure the readers are interested in hearing from you the meaning given them.

E: My interpretations from playing cards? First of all, my experience with the PAGE OF CUPS has been good. Usually he brings news or a message. However, he's called Jack of Hearts. The TEN OF PENTACLES crossed is isolation. For me it means "have to", as business, duty, things I have to do which, however, isolate me from myself and from social enjoyment.

R: Yes, the third card represents the opposing forces in your life, and at this time they are mainly economic. With so many pentacles in the card, if it appeared in a more favorable place in the reading, it might betoken financial security, materialistic

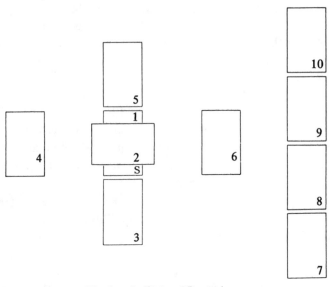

Significis, Queen of Rods 6. Eight of Pentacles
1. Page of Cups 7. Queen of Pentacles (Reversed)
2. Ten of Pentacles 8. Four of Cups (Reversed)
3. Nine of Pentacles 9. Knight of Pentacles (Reversed)
4. King of Swords 10. Seven of Rods
5. Five of Cups

well-being, but in this case it is in the position of forces opposing you, so we have to interpret it as economic expediencies—and a great many of them.

The next card, the foundation of the matter, seems to be a continuance of the money matters theme.

E: The NINE OF PENTACLES, or Nine of Diamonds, in ordinary cards is the devil's wish card. It's like the monkey's paw; it means be very careful in your wish, because you might get it. The Nine of Hearts is the good wish card.

R: The fourth card represents an influence upon you that is in the process of passing away. This is the KING OF SWORDS. This is a man of great intellect with many grandiose schemes and plans. I see this in the elegant cloud forms behind him, suggesting to me air castles. Since you've had only one man in your life, and since I would call your husband an intellectual, I think this card represents him, but his influence seems to be on the wane in your life.

The fifth card, which I shall turn up now, represents an event that may come about. When I see the FIVE OF CUPS I feel sorrow and a sense of loss.

E: In my experience, it's the end of the love affair. It's not supposed to be felt too deeply. It's not so bad as some of the other cards, but it is the end-of-a-love-affair type card.

R: Well, I think that kind of substantiates what I said about the previous card.

E: Yes, it does.

R: The next card is in the place of representing a future influence. This prospect is before you, and here we have the EIGHT OF PENTACLES, suggesting to me hard work, getting down to business. Also, the number eight is composed of four and four, in other words, two full quaternities, or two worlds of four quarters each. Summing it up, completedness.

E: (Laughter). EIGHT OF PENTACLES in my reading is the same thing. It represents a sort of equilibrium between spiritual and financial matters.

R: Two different worlds.

E: Yes.

R: The seventh card represents you in the sense that it is your attitude personified. That's interesting!

E: She haunts me!

R: When we were considering which card to represent you as the SIGNIFICATOR, I chose the QUEEN OF RODS, because you are a Gemini, but you said you would have chosen the Queen of Cups. Now this card is the QUEEN OF PENTACLES, reversed.

E: I have a fight between the Queen of Cups and the QUEEN OF PENTACLES.

R: In what sense.

E: The QUEEN OF PENTACLES. She's energetic, she's ambitious, but she's self-interested and difficult. She does manage to keep going, but not with understanding—through prevailing over others. I don't like her. And she keeps cropping up. I get her again and again.

R: Yes, I don't think her consciousness is as high as the other queens. She is perhaps preoccupied with material matters—note the way she gazes so intently at the pentacle. However, we have been told that is what opposes you, and the foundation of the matter is pentacles, or concern with money problems, so it makes sense that she does appear at this point.

E: Yes, it makes perfect sense.

R: Next we go to the environment surrounding you. Looks like a gift is coming your way, not so much from the material plane as from the astral plane. The hand proffering the cup, in the FOUR OF CUPS, comes out of a cloud. To me this card suggests the Buddha in meditation under the Bo tree, so inward turning and contemplation are suggested. I think this is a trend I saw in you about a year ago. I think you will return to that more equable state of mind. This will be a gift coming from within yourself that will give you a new direction in life. Perhaps the PAGE OF CUPS and the EIGHT OF PENTACLES, and what we said about them, foreshadow this. Now you're pointing to the TEN OF PENTACLES.

E: Isolation. The TEN OF PENTACLES can be a card of choice. It's the "hermit's cell." You are stuck and you stay there, or else you leap out and make a journey. You can take risks and try something else.

R: This is of course the card for the environment, and since it is reversed I think we have to say that it represents dissatisfaction with the environment. If this were a Pentacle suit card, it would be representative of the environment as established by that suit in our reading. However, the connotations of this card suggest a turning away from that particular direction and concern, so I must infer acute discontent with material preoccupation.

E: Yes, the whole money thing is exhausting.

R: The next card stands for your wishes and longings . . .

E: And fears.

R: And fears. So we turn over this one.

E: "Jack of Diamonds is a hard card to play." It's the KNIGHT OF PENTACLES, and it's also upside down. It's sometimes related to the Hanging Man. In my mind, the Jack in ordinary playing cards is a combination of Knight and Page. Probably my association is with the folk song also. You do everything wrong, even though your intentions are the best. The most generous way I can describe it is as a sense-making card. But reversed like this, it becomes a "harder card to play." To me it suggests infidelity, unreliability, existential dirty tricks—if there is such a thing. The energy is all misdirected. He does try to make sense out of things, but he is upside down.

R: All right, the outcome of the matter is the SEVEN OF RODS. Why don't you talk about that because I see you are doing a flash on it.

E: This is the Seven of Clubs in ordinary cards, and it means trusting too much, thinking all is well when it is not.

R: Because this man is in a defensive pose, if the card were upside down I think I would say it represents paranoia. It certainly means strife, and there is a great deal of opposition against you, symbolized by the six rods confronting the man holding the one rod. He stands alone, and his back is to the wall, so to speak, so he is not without courage.

E: Having been the main source of support for my son and my-self for fifteen years, I can identify with that! At least there were not any Major Arcana in my reading. Thank God for that!

R: If you can amplify on the circumstances of the past year, and show how this reading reveals those circumstances, it will make this reading clearer to those reading the book who are not familiar with your life.

E: Well, mostly it's been a year of disastrous economic situations. Last week was the topper. I lost my job. My rent was raised. I was turned down for a graduate study program at State College, and as a symbolic manifestation of all this, I walked into the bathroom and the ceiling fell on me. The sky fell on me! I don't have any money to pay the higher rent, and there isn't anything available for less rent. I haven't had much of a chance to think about anything *but* the mundane level. I don't like the TEN OF PENTACLES crossing because it means that I will continue to be isolated and in bondage to this necessity. The only thing that can keep me going is my FOUR OF CUPS, which is my faith card.

R: Ah, now I know what it means! You've been preoccupied with what you call your loss of grace in your life. It seems to me that the hand out of the cloud offering the cup is the return to you of the state of grace at some future time. Again, for the sake of the reader, can you amplify on this concept of loss of grace for those who are not versed in it.

E: (Laughter). I guess my philosophical cliché has become that I feel that God has been unnecessarily cruel. There have been too many accidents, too many bad things, and I'm losing my resilience. A large part of it is that while I'm losing all the human things, I still have economic responsibilities. So my life has become largely one of just trying to survive, and I really don't have time for any kind of thought, any interior feeling, and all that is left is just making money, and just barely doing that. Somehow, the QUEEN OF PENTACLES is capable of doing it if she were right side up, getting into it, surviving, prevailing. But I don't like that QUEEN OF PENTACLES. It's a role I don't want to play.

In my own readings, I've had the cards make an absolute fool of me. They lie, they cheat, they make jokes. I've thrown them so many times that they know me too well. For example, I've known what I needed, what I hoped for, and they'll come up and say ha, ha, ha, here we are. Like that time I was absolutely suicidal, and they came up all black, all spades, no clubs except bad clubs. Or else they've got to be just jolly happy. "The world is yours!" One time I walked about three miles in my house—up one side and down the other before I finally stopped crying and turned over my card. It was the Nine of Hearts, which is the gypsy wish card, and I looked at that and I laughed like a loon. I said, "Yes, O.K. kids, what else do you have to say?" They turned up Ace of Hearts, you know anything nice, goodies. It was *sarcasm* on the part of the cards! (Laughter). You get to that point where it's not just truth but *sarcasm!*

The Ancient Celtic Method

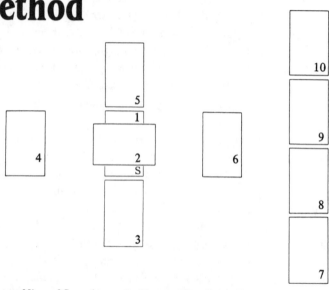

Significator, Nine of Swords
1. The Hierophant (Reversed)
2. Seven of Rods
3. King of Swords
4. Page of Swords
5. Ten of Rods (Reversed)
6. Three of Pentacles (Reversed)
7. Wheel of Fortune (Reversed)
8. Judgement
9. Four of Swords
10. Three of Swords (Reversed)

ll right, we went through this first reading rather rapidly so that we could do a second to test the cards. Only this time you said you did not want to pick a SIGNIFICATOR, but whatever card that came up first would stand for you, not so much for your physical person as for your total being, including your mental and emotional state at this difficult time in your life.

E: Correct. Turn it over!

R: (Whistle).

E: I am a dead woman. I am a dead woman.

R: The NINE OF SWORDS.

E: Bad, bad news.

R: O.K., then the atmosphere covering you ... THE HIERO-PHANT reversed.

E: A guy called himself that who did my spread about two years ago. He died lousy!

R: How did he die?

E: Well, I don't want this on tape—this is private.

R: I'll edit it out. (*This material was not included, therefore*) ... I've got to get this reading back to you now. We've been talking about him but we're not reading his cards, and we're not reading my cards, it's your cards. The question is how does THE HIEROPHANT relate to *you* here? And the association that I see is someone who goes between two worlds, in this case not the world of drugs but maybe the world of alcohol. Is this the atmosphere around you now, what do you think?

E: What you said about two worlds is really good. It is two worlds but alcohol is a symptom. It's my need—The Hierophant need—to be alone. It's my need to be by myself to *find* myself. I could be a crazy old lady if I were left by myself—but I have the pressure of the pentacles. In other words, I'm split between two things. I have no *time* anymore for my own quietness, for my own knowing. And I get angrier and angrier at God. There was a book that I read that said primitive man treated the universe as a partner—the universe, God, whatever you want to call *the other*—and would rather die than have that universe be unfaithful to him. ... Well, I've said it. The relationship is so meaningful, so strong, and so powerful that it is superhuman, almost. And if the disappointments in this relationship—the meta-relationship—*(Laughter)* the meta-disappointments—are so hurtful, then one would rather die than maintain a situation he does not believe in, one that he cannot tolerate.

R: All right, then this is the atmosphere around you now. How do you associate that with THE HIEROPHANT?

E: O.K. Let's make him a male saint. He's living in two worlds so he's a dual personality.

R: How do you associate this with yourself?

E: I want to be a saint. A perfect person.

R: Really?

E: Yes.

R: So it's your drive for perfection, which you can't possibly fulfill, that makes you fail—do all the pratfalls perhaps.

E: Yeh, I do everything badly because I can't do anything perfectly.

R: Uh-huh.

E: Yes, it does follow this way. I have been thinking about that problem.

R: O.K. I think we're getting a little deeper in this reading.

E: But why in the name of God do you want to have me on tape?! (Softly) I'm a useless human being.

R: Huh?

E: I'm a useless human being.

R: To me you are a very special human being, but why the tape? Because the amazing thing is the way the problems come to light through Tarot. I think we're starting to get into the causes that are making so many negative cards appear. You know that yourself. You've been reading for yourself for years with an ordinary deck of cards. And you know how true that's been? So let's just push on for a moment.

The next card—what?—crosses you, representing the opposing forces. Correct? This was our outcome card before, the SEVEN OF RODS. We said before it suggested strife.

E: Yes, and in the center of the spread like that it means I am perhaps unconsciously causing it. Like I'm not handling it right, or not doing something I'm supposed to be doing.

R: I think this is interesting because it comes right next to the Hierophant, and there are unconscious forces, which we haven't fully laid bare, which are bringing the adversity into your life on the surface level. But the magnetic attraction force is operating within the unconscious.

E: That's what you've told me before, and that's why I keep bringing up the notion of bad luck. Because I'm *not* thoroughly convinced of . . .

R: The Law of Attraction.

E: . . . That. Or the fantastic intelligence of the Superego. I'm really not. But that shows in my horoscope also. I am a Gemini skeptic, and the opposition between Saturn in Pisces and Neptune in Virgo makes me even more of a skeptic.

R: Your attitude then is basically anti-holistic, anti-spiritual in

40

approach, wouldn't you say? In other words, you don't see, for example, how bad fortune may have a transformative effect upon an individual. You see it more as a stultifying, totally negative force oppressing the individual?

E: Not the individual—the people! I'm an emotional democrat. I was also kind of precociously religious.

R: And you lost your state of grace.

E: I lost my state of grace and my only concern now is to survive. No, to prevail.

R: But doesn't an individual desire to survive or prevail *in order to* fulfill some goal or purpose?

E: I'm not going to go any place to which I can't take my friends. (Laughter) That includes Heaven or Hell!

R: What about that question? Isn't the purpose of surviving to individuate as a completely unique human in some way?

E: Yes, and I have the feeling that my purpose is somehow to make peace.

R: Now we come to a new interpretation for the Hierophant— that of mediator. That fits then?

E: Yep, yep.

R: What kind of mediation do you see yourself effecting in life?

E: Well, it's really hard because I don't manage to succeed. I can make peace locally, but then people go off and do what they want to anyway, and there's so much ugliness and misunderstanding between people. I don't like it, and sometimes I can change it—put people at ease. I am a psychological servant, serving this world. At the same time I resent it. I want to be king too, my lap full of apples. But I don't maneuver in that way. Instead I am the king's fool. And not a holy fool either, a mundane fool, up to my nostrils in human offal.

R: All right, then let's see what the foundation is that has caused this. . . . Guess who came up?

E: (Looking) Oh, you brought up (name of husband deleted). The KING OF SWORDS again.

R: In the other reading he was ahead one position—meaning an influence that was passing. Now he occupies the foundation of the matter. You did shuffle these cards a second time?

E: Very, very carefully. You think I wanted the same bad news again?! Before, you related this card to my husband, so since this

41

stands for the foundation of the matter, maybe it's not all my fault.

R: Well, let's see what comes up in the position he occupied before. . . . This is quite remarkable. Again a male face card of the Swords suit, only this time he's been demoted in rank from King to PAGE OF SWORDS, but that figures because we had said that he was a waning influence in your life. You may be right when you say it is not the Law of Attraction operating, as this card's position tends to place some of the blame with your husband. But the Law of Attraction was in operation when you selected him and he selected you. What are your associations with this card?

E: He's the bad lover. He's the guy who will let you down. And they all have, one way or another. They may come back later, but when the chips are really down—they all cut out. And it's the Queen of Swords who lets that happen.

R: Then men have treated you in what you call the Jack of Diamonds tradition, which is rather offhand and cavalier?

E: No, they've been very gallant, and secretly demanding. But a guy can be very gallant and he'll rip you off for everything.

R: Well, then, you feel the men in your life have ripped you off, and you include God in the same sense because we talked about the primitive's participation mystique with the *other* . . .

E: Yep, yep, yep! The primitive who regards the *all* as a partner. And I have the feeling that I have been taken advantage of.

R: On the cosmic plane as well as the mundane plane?

E: Yes, because I've tried to be nice, and as good as I could, but when things go wrong . . . then it turns bad . . .

R: The next card represents what may come into being. TEN OF RODS. Reversed.

E: Reversed. It means bad times, of course.

R: To me it looks like a terrific burden, almost like carrying a cross. It's in the same spirit of—what was it—the Five of Cups we had before in the previous reading.

E: Yes, where the cups were all overturned. But a burden is different from a disappointment. A burden you can continue with, but an empty cup is a fact.

R: I think the fact that this card is reversed indicates that the burden may be doubled because the individual is misusing her

42

powers—the force of the card is not straight up and down.

All right, what's before you is the reversed THREE OF PENTACLES. I see this as a kind of recouping of some of the losses you have sustained. Starting to get things together in a material way. Probably it represents hard work, as did the Nine of Pentacles in the previous reading. Its power is backwards again, so you're not realizing anything from the hard work.

E: How true, how true.

R: The seventh card represents your attitude, the WHEEL OF FORTUNE reversed.

E: (Laughter). Do you want me to die right here?!

R: Zee cards never lie. If you cannot take the cards, you should not come to the gypsy.

E: I didn't come to the gypsy, the gypsy came to me! O.K., WHEEL OF FORTUNE upside down.

R: I think this relates to your connections with the HIERO-PHANT and the PAGE OF SWORDS. Your being misused by fortune is the way you summed up your attitude towards life.

E: That was really good. You are clever. That took a super intuition right there.

R: I'm starting to wake up.

E: What's my family and friends influence? I'm afraid to touch it because it may come up reversed.

R: This is good because it's straight up and down. However, since the card is JUDGEMENT, there will be some kind of assessment or valuation made upon you. This card on the surface is often associated with resurrection, but the judgement may be negative. (Whimsically). At Judgement God may decide to use you in the same way He may feel you have used Him during your lifetime.

E: I didn't do anything bad to Him. I was loyal and faithful for years, after years, after years.

R: (Again whimsically). Uncomplaining?

E: Uncomplaining. I had faith. And it went on and on and on until finally it broke. It broke about six years ago.

R: I wonder if God reserves His greatest attention for those faithful few whom He thinks He can try the most.

E: I keep trying to give up—like I'll put my hands in the air—but then something else will happen—something nasty will come down—not necessarily to me but to somebody else! It's not serf

E: I've heard that before and, listen, all I want to say is "uncle"!

R: (Laughter). That's very good. Did You hear that up there? This is on tape—she is capitulating.

E: (Laughter). "Did You hear that up there?" For some reason I have the feeling that I pick the hardest way to do everything. I'm ready to cop out and say, "O.K., I bit off more than I can chew." Like I can't do what I thought I could do. Perhaps before this life I said, "Hey, God give me a really hard incarnation this time." And He did! I haven't given up yet, but I have the feeling I'm doing everything the hardest way possible. . . . I guess to make it the most important.

R: That makes sense. . . . One thing you are assured about is a feeling of God's attention. There are many in this world who have a feeling that God is deaf to them, does not see them, and for that reason they conclude He does not exist. You have a feeling of God as the arch antagonist in your life, and this description is usually reserved for the Devil. Someone once said, "The Devil is God, as He is misunderstood by the unenlightened."

E: I'll put it this way. I have a *sense* of God, and we had a longstanding love affair. Things got worse and worse and I got mad at Him. And you don't get mad at God. Because He's got all those things on His side. I liked the separateness between us, the fact that He was unavailable and gone all the time, but then I lost faith. No! I didn't lose faith; I just got mad!

R: It sounds to me like the Absent Parent syndrome projected onto the divine level. Absent Daddy, absent Holy Father.

in heaven, ruler in hell so much. Really I guess I'm going to be wretched on principle.

R: Well then, you seem to know what you're doing.

E: I do and I persist in it.

R: It reminds me of the classic study of antagonism to God of Prometheus, who was punished by God by having his liver gnawed out daily by a vulture. Of course, God also arranged that it would grow back in each day. And finally Prometheus is told that if he will apologize to God and utterly capitualte . . .

E: He can't!

R: . . . he will be forgiven and freed. What does he say, do you remember? He says, "Tell God I utterly despise Him."

E: At this point I'm crying.

44

R: It's all right. We only have two cards to go in the Passion of Erin.

E: (Laughter). I'll be dead by then.

R: Umm . . . well, your hopes.

E: My hopes!

R: Your fears.

E: My fears!

R: Oh, oh. Your fear is of what looks like a funeral scene. This card is the FOUR OF SWORDS. Do you have a preoccupation with death?

E: Developing. . . . Yeh, I'd just as soon be dead except I have no guarantee that when I'm dead God won't be there. I'd hate like hell to find myself again in some meta-school, meta-otherworld, you know, where I'm going to have to learn again, go through the same old scene again, and Big Boss will be there!

R: (Laughter). I've really never known anyone before who has as personal and endearing a relationship with God as you do!

However, let's get back to the FOUR OF SWORDS. It is not necessarily a card of death; it may mean for you a kind of psychic recuperation after great striving and anxiety. So on the positive, or hope side, it may be parallel to the nature of your interpretation of the Hierophant, in that he represented a quiescent state—almost like meditation—in which you could get back to yourself.

E: In ordinary playing cards, the Four of Spades is the recuperation after illness. I like that card. It means surcease, a kind of ending, and I'm not so hip on beginnings as are other people. I've begun too many times, so I'm mostly interested in resting.

R: All right, now we'll do the outcome. The outcome that we had before was Seven of Rods, which in this reading became the opposition card. I think this represents a philosophical insight, perhaps into your whole life. Certainly it represents an insight into the reading. The fact that the outcome of the first reading became the inner opposing forces of the second reading suggests that the inner and outer world are not as far apart or as separate as you like to think. The outer opposition is also within yourself, in other words.

E: You mean I'm doing it.

R: I've been saying before in readings for people that the Law of Attraction is the greatest wisdom one can understand, and I think

45

you disagree with me completely.

E: Well, I resent it. I have to. Because if I'm as miserable as I am, and at the same time *doing* it, calling it down upon me . . . but I already said I was doing it, didn't I? Because I said I had picked out the hardest row to hoe, the hardest way to do things in this life. Well, I can't handle that in an evening.

R: I think that the Tarot pattern and the life pattern—the one reflecting the other—will not change until the inner attitude changes. And I don't like to put the last card out because I just feel that it will be extremely negative. I don't see how it can be avoided if your inner thinking does not change.

E: I want to see the card anyway!

R: Right. It's the reversed THREE OF SWORDS.

E: That's the card I hate most.

R: Of all the cards?

E: Of all the cards. Like the Five of Cups it's the end of a love affair, but the pain here is felt more deeply. A heart is pierced by three swords, and in the Waite deck the skies were crying also . . .

R: Wait! There's an important point! I was just trying to establish the parallel between outer and inner world, so if the skies are *crying* it is the inner world projected onto the outer world. Well, this is a card of great sorrow and unhappiness, and that's all we can say about it. The outcome is thus more severe than the previous reading, but the outer world *outcome* became the inner world *opposition.* If that is true then the reverse must be true. The inner world oppositions also may become the outer world outcomes.

Let's wind this up. We are now signing off up there, and if any of the angelic hosts are listening . . .

E: Hey, God. Will you listen to me for a moment. Be my friend, just for a while. I've tried very hard. Would you be my friend? I'll prove myself, I'll be a really good girl. You hear me?!

(To the reader) Do you think God will hear?

R: The loss of grace when projected onto the outer world becomes a *modus operandi* in the life.

E: I've given you much evidence for your argument.

R: O.K., signing off. Back to our sponsor.

This way of laying out the cards takes the form of two inter-penetrating triangles with the outcome of the matter at the center. The first triangle is simply composed of past, present and the near future. Cards 4, 5, and 6, comprising the second triangle, require some amplification.

Card 4 may represent a person or persons who are exercising a favorable influence on the matter in question. Or, it may operate on an altogether different level—psychological and emotional rather than external. In which case, it may represent the inner vibration which can effect a beneficial outcome in the 7th card.

Card 5 stands for the surroundings of the readee—his world in a nutshell. This also may be interpreted on an inner rather than merely an outer level. In such an instance the card will give one a picture of the state of mind of the querent, or of those he has attracted to his world.

Card 6 represents what stands in the way of realization. If these forces of antagonism and opposition are stronger than the beneficent factors, the outcome will probably be unfavorable. However, if the contrary is true, a happy realization will be respresented by this card.

In this reading, Mr. Carter is denoted by the abbreviation M.C., and his wife by A.C.

The Magic Seven Spread

1. Seven of Swords
2. Ace of Pentacles
3. Six of Swords
4. Queen of Cups
5. Eight of Rods (Reversed)
6. Eight of Swords (Reversed)
7. The Sun

R: The date is December 14, 1970, and this is a reading for Mr. and Mrs. Carter. Incidentally, I think I should say that we have not met before today, and we did meet in a store when I heard you inquiring about the figures in the Tarot posters. From there it was an easy matter to get you to my house for a reading on the promise of a drink. (Laughter from Mr. and Mrs. Carter)

A.C.: Some of the stores in San Francisco give free cocktails while you're shopping, but not in this hick town.

M.C.: Well, it's good business. You get so stinko you don't know what you've been charged until the next month and then it's too late! Say what is this ale, where can I get it?

R: MacEwan's Edinburgh ale. It comes from Scotland.

M.C.: Now I know you don't go to Scotland every time you need a case.

R: Some of the liquor stores will order it for you, and some say they don't know where to get it. Just ask around.

A.C.: This is really strong! I don't mean in taste, but it *must* be over 3.2 percent.

R: It's over ten.

A.C.: How can they get away with it?!

R: It comes in under the wine license since it's an ale. Beers are what have to be cut in alcohol . . .

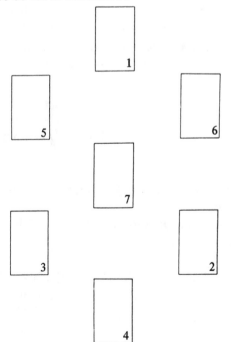

All right, I'll start by laying out the three cards of past, present and near future. They are SEVEN OF SWORDS, ACE OF PENTACLES, and SIX OF SWORDS.

A.C.: And away we go!

R: First of all, an immediate pattern is apparent—one of material success for the present. But the past was not so rosy. The figure in the SEVEN OF SWORDS sends me a vibration of unrealized effort. He is trying, but more often than not things do not work out for him. He does manage to achieve some gain, and this keeps him going, until somewhere in the past—between cards one and two chronologically—a big break came and the reward for all the effort was attained. Does that pretty much describe what happened in your life?

M.C.: Exactly.

A.C.: Uh-huh.

R: Well, it's right there in the cards. The ACE OF PENTACLES denotes material well-being, among other things, but this was the impression I had from these cards.

Now the near future is depicted by the SIX OF SWORDS, and this is a little more difficult for me. In some way, I get the feeling of an attempt to break away from an old pattern, the old business pattern, but at the same time I don't feel that this means that you want to start a new business, or go into a new line of work. Let me see if I can phrase this correctly. Your question does have to do with breaking away from your old business routine, but it does *not* involve a new business? Is that correct?

A.C.: That's right.

M.C.: Very, very true.

R: Hmm. At the same time, I'm getting a vibration of strife or conflict. Do you and Mrs. Carter disagree over what you should do in this matter?

M.C.: Yes we do.

R: She's smiling, however, so I don't think it's a very serious conflict between you.

O.K., card 4 is the QUEEN OF CUPS, and I think this represents Mrs. Carter.

M.C.: Why?

R: Because the card is in the position of the favorable influence. She *is* in favor of the matter, and you are not. Right?

A.C.: Right!

R: Very often I associate the Cups suit with the water signs of the Zodiac, and I'm getting a flash now that Mrs. Carter is a Scorpio.

M.C.: (Laughter). Now what tells you that in this card?!

R: She nodded yes, so she is a Scorpio. It was just a hunch. Actually in physical appearance she does look like a Scorpio.

A.C.: I didn't know I was supposed to look like any particular type!

R: Scorpio women have a lot of power. It's not necessarily all out front though. They can control a group or a situation from below the surface, and the impression I was getting was vibrations rising out of the cup. The cup equals the unconscious and the power is in the cup and coming from it. I think she really has her mind set on this, and she's probably going to get her way, and since—again—this card is in the position of a positive influence, then why shouldn't she have her way? (Laughter).

A.C.: That's what I've been telling him for two months. (Laughter)

M.C.: Looks like the cards are against me too.

R: They may be *for* you in the long run if they enable you to capitulate to her—gracefully, that is. It's definitely going to be easier to live with her if you give in on this.

A.C. and M.C.: (Laughter together).

R: Now the next card, because it is reversed, presents the first adversity in the matter. Although she opposes you in this matter, hers is a positive influence. However, this card, the EIGHT OF RODS, stands for the surroundings, and topsy turvy is the word that comes to mind. Also, the phrase "at the sixes and sevens" comes into my mind.

A.C.: Are those supposed to be flowers?

R: Rods. A flight of Rods through the air. Activity is the usual association with this card, and my feeling is one of a hectic pace. And you are not thriving in this atmosphere—the effect on you is negative.

M.C.: I'm not sure I agree with you there.

A.C.: *I* agree with him.

R: Well, if you are a businessman, and you must be with the ACE OF PENTACLES in your spread, it's not difficult to imagine that

51

there is a lot of frenzied activity connected with it. Are you your own boss?

M.C.: Yes.

R: Usually when this is the case a man drives himself harder than he would for anyone else. And you may tend to take the job home with you. I think this is what this card is telling us. Somewhere the rods have to come to rest again, and you will have to learn how to unwind.

This leads us right into the EIGHT OF SWORDS, which symbolizes the forces antagonistic to a successful realization of this matter. And this card has a doubly negative influence because it is reversed. The bondage of the figure suggests to me a psychological bondage on your part.

A.C.: What do the swords stand for?

R: Usually I go one of two ways with them. They may suggest intellect, and the world of the mind to me, or all the associations that go with warfare, such as strife, conflict, aggression. In this case, I feel that the strife is internalized in Mr. Carter. He is literally agonizing over what the outcome should be, perhaps unnecessarily so because the ACE OF PENTACLES already indicated that he "has it made." That is to say, he may be worrying without just cause. I feel anxiety connected with this card. I feel unrest. I feel uncertainty. You just can't make up your mind can you?

M.C.: Well, it's easy enough to make up my mind, but another thing to be sure I'm doing the right thing.

R: I understand. But this card indicates that you yourself may be your own worst enemy in this matter. Mrs. Carter is nodding her head. What I mean is a decision, one way or the other, may not be as bad as the anxiety you are experiencing over the problem. Am I right?

M.C.: Possibly, but you don't know all the factors involved.

R: I think the outcome involves a change for you, and you are reluctant to undergo that change, but I believe it will be good for you.

A.C.: No question about it.

R: It's a change on the side of a break from the frantic activity shown by the EIGHT OF RODS in the environment card, so generally speaking, the matter in question simply must be getting

52

away from the job for a while.

Now the outcome or realization of the matter is shown by card seven, and it is THE SUN. . . . Most of these cards may be interpreted of different levels, or they wouldn't work so well. THE SUN functions on at least three levels, and I'll kind of run through them for you. As a general symbol of light, it may stand for illumination—spiritual illumination, "seeing the light" so to speak. On a psychological level, it may represent a centering within the individual, in the same way that the sun is the center of our solar system. This is called individuation, or Selfhood, in Jungian psychology. It represents an at-one-ment of being. I'm not trying to put you down, but I don't see your interests or energies directed along these lines. There are a lot of couples nowadays who are going off for weekends at Esalen institute in search of something like this, but I don't think this is the case here.

On the mundane level, sun is . . . sun. I don't know what else to say. I'm drawing a blank. There should be some abstraction coming into my head, but all I get is "sun is sun." Fulfillment, realization? Well, the position here is the realization or outcome place, and THE SUN *does* stand for that on one level, so whatever the matter is, it *is* going to come about.

A.C.: How does this last card differ from the card that was supposed to stand for the near future.

R: Uh, that was the SIX OF SWORDS. I said that represented an attempt to break away from the old pattern. The man is commencing a new journey by boat, and he winds up . . . at THE SUN, the outcome card. Is this a cruise?! Like a vacation to the South Seas, or Acapulco, or something like that?!

M.C.: (Laughing together) Yes!

A.C.: It seemed so obvious, I wanted to tell you.

R: "The sun is the sun"—that's all I could think of, but it didn't make any sense to me!

A.C.: Can we go back through the cards? Everything you said was right! I have been trying to get him to take a vacation every year for the last five years! Except when he got the flu, he hasn't been out of that office more than two days in a row.

M.C.: We went to Las Vegas for three days last year.

A.C.: I forgot that! Mr. Roberts, if your cards convince him to take some time off now it will be more than doctors could do.

53

R: Is there a health problem?

M.C.: None whatsoever. A cold or two is all I've ever had for as long as I can remember.

R: But the EIGHT OF SWORDS and the EIGHT OF RODS suggest that even though you are *physically* healthy, a great deal of mental stress is going on, and in the long run this can be just as negative in its effect on you—if not more so.

A.C.: (To Mr. Carter) What have I been saying?

R: Just what is the reason why you hesitate about taking this vacation? Most people would jump at the chance to take a cruise if they had the money—and if they were their own boss.

M.C.: But you see it's not that easy. Situations can come up about which only I can make the decision.

R: Well, perhaps you should delegate more authority in your business.

M.C.: It's not that large a business where I can afford hiring executive types that can make such decisions. Thousands of dollars could be lost if I was not there. Probably nothing like that would come up, but it might.

R: But does the chance of losing a few thousand dollars make it worth never having any time off? I mean, it seems like a vicious circle.

A.C.: My very words.

M.C.: Well, you know I'd pretty much decided to take a chance this time, although most of the time I'd rather be home anyway than in a motel or traveling. But I'm really a sucker for a cruise. (To Mrs. Carter) You didn't know that did you? It was her idea, and as soon as she mentioned it my sales resistance was lower than usual.

A.C.: You never told me that!

M.C.: You're damn right I didn't. But I think we'll probably wind up taking this cruise.

A.C.: What do you know, I finally made a believer out of him. (General laughter). Now if I get a deck of cards like this will I be able to do what you did?

R: You'll probably do better.

The date is November 6, 1970, and this is a reading for Larry Collins, owner of the Abraxas Bookstore in San Anselmo, California. To begin, I shall read the three cards connected with past, present, and future. They are KNIGHT OF SWORDS, KING OF PENTACLES, and FOUR OF PENTACLES.

The figure of the knight suggests someone setting out on a journey by himself. Did you make an early break with your parents, or are you still in touch with them?

L: Still in touch.

R: And on good terms?

L: Yeh . . . I can suggest what the break may have been. More of a splitting from my immediate group of people—setting out on my own.

R: I see. Very often the parents establish the standards of the peer group for an adolescent, and he revolts against the parents rather than the peer group. Anyway the journey of the knight is lonely and solitary. I can see here a similarity between your past and my own, particularly in respect to a mutual interest in the occult. For one not hung up on the concerns of the peers for baseball, football, and the countryclub ball, marching to a different drummer can prove to be a lonely way . . . The sky behind the knight is kind of a strange color. A certain visionary, inspira-

The
Magic Seven
Spread

1. Knight of Swords
2. King of Pentacles
3. Four of Pentacles
4. Nine of Pentacles
5. Four of Cups
6. Judgement
7. Five of Rods

56

tional sense on your part is suggested to me by the clouds, where-in I see figures forming. Swords I normally associate with the Jungian function of intellect, so can we say that this has been your main way of relating to the world in the past?

L: Right.

R: Now the second card, the KING OF PENTACLES, represents the present. That bull almost seems to be leaning over the shoulder of the king, seemingly trying to get more to the fore with the king. I take you to be the king, but do you have a girl who wants more attention from you now who is a Taurus?

L: (Laughter). Taurus moon.

R: Well, interpreting the suit Pentacles in a psychological way, I relate it to the sensation function, which leads me to speculate that at present your approach to life is now less intellectual and more down to earth. There is more of a body consciousness and a heeding of the message of the five senses than in the past when your approach was intellectual.

L: Definitely.

R: Now the mundane interpretation of Pentacles associates that suit with money matters, and material things generally. Of course, as a storekeeper you cannot ever overlook this, but at present is there some financial concern that is particularly pressing?

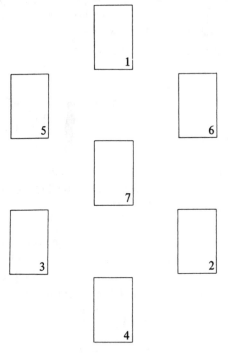

L: I would like to take out a loan and increase my stock of books.

R: I see, then let's look at the card that stands in the place of the future, and that card is the FOUR OF PENTACLES. Here is a person wearing a rather strange bonnet or cap, topped off by a giant pentacle; therefore, I would think that there will be a favorable financial resolution for you in this matter. This card suggests affluence to me, so there should be a happy outcome. If you can withhold your comments for a time, we can come back to these cards later.

L: O.K.

R: The fourth card is the NINE OF PENTACLES, the fifth card the FOUR OF CUPS, the sixth card JUDGEMENT, and the seventh, FIVE OF RODS. Cards four, five, and six are the points of the spiritual triangle which penetrates the mundane triangle with its points of past, present, and future. The midpoint where the two overlap is the outcome and the position of the seventh card.

O.K., this fourth card depicts a very regal woman gazing at what I take to be a peacock. A feeling of peace and atonement is the vibration I receive from the card. Also, I associate this with the feminine side of yourself, the anima, in the archetypal world of your personal unconscious. We have both talked about what planet in the horoscope we believe represents this archetypal figure, and my intuition tells me it may be the planet you were "born under."

L: (Laughter). That is correct.

R: All right, conscious control of your life is dependent upon how well you utilize the highly charged yin vibration that she transmits from your unconscious.

L: Right, right.

R: Now the spiritual environment in which you are operating is represented by the fifth card, and that is the FOUR OF CUPS. Are you meditating at present?

L: Twice a day.

R: This card reminds me of the Buddha in meditation beneath the Bo tree, whereas the hand coming out of the cloud presents a kind of gift of divine inspiration from above. Linking this scene to the last, perhaps we can say that the peaceful, muse-like vibration and offering to you—from the archetypal world—will lead to fulfillment of your desired goal.

L: Very true.

R: And then we come to the sixth card, representing the bad vibes, or the forces that would hinder the attainment of the goal. This card is JUDGEMENT. I feel that the antagonistic forces are those of *ordinary* society which will judge you. The figure blowing the horn holds the banner of St. George, which is associated in my mind with the forces of arch-tradition and orthodoxy, so I think the main antagonism in this endeavor will come from the quarter of what is already entrenched and established.

L: I can certainly believe that.

R: The outcome of this is a little more difficult for me to determine. The card here is the FIVE OF RODS. The outcome seems to be on the side of sociability, or social activity. Whatever the endeavor, it is definitely not a solitary one because there are four persons depicted. It seems to involve exchange between persons in the group.

I get a flash of Socrates, Plato, and the kind of democratic Athenian school they held on the street in ancient Greece. So I see the desire for an exchange of knowledge, and free and easy communication between people as an outcome of this fulfilled goal.

Would this be a kind of school or group activity involving studies of the occult, particularly astrology, which you would like to start yourself?

L: One part of it. A school somewhat fashioned after that of Alexandria.

R: Also, this is the first time that there has been more than one person to a card in the spread, so a coming together with others is the dominant theme. With the rods, the figures are making almost a kind of mandala pattern. One could connect the tips by drawing in straight lines. The angles might then resemble the aspects in your own horoscope, although I have never seen your chart.

L: (Laughter). It does! It really does!

R: All right, then for the sake of the tape give your overall impression of the reading.

L: Pretty good, pretty good! What I wanted to see realized was the coming together of the world.

59

R: The world?

L: In a brotherhood of human beings.

R: Oh, I see, universal brotherhood.

L: Yes.

R: So I was more or less reading a question for the world than for you personally.

L: But I would like to have something to do with it.

R: Uh, huh.

L: That's why that last card really hit home. It is the only card with more than one person. But the school thing that you mentioned has also been something that I've been interested in for a long time. In the larger sense of my own personal concept of a school where ideas are freely exchanged, I would like to see . . .

R: Universal brotherhood.

L: Yeh!

R: I can see now in retrospect how that pattern does work. If we go back to the first card, the knight must then be associated with the warrior caste. This then is the *past* of humanity generally— warlike! The present is less concerned with warfare as a noble endeavor as it was in more chivalrous times and in the crusades. Now we go to war out of financial expediency—the king wearing that great material pentacle. And over the shoulder of humanity peers that arch symbol of power and aggression—the bull! Also, the animal could represent the essential animal nature of man, man as killer, that Robert Ardrey writes of in *African Genesis.* Ardrey also is concerned with world peace and brotherhood, but fears a reversion to our lower nature.

Then the figure in the FOUR OF PENTACLES suggests a possible coming together from the four quarters. Four is the number of completedness and unity.

The following card was the NINE OF PENTACLES. This is interesting viewed in our present light. A similar card, with woman and bird, turned up in another reading. I remember at that time my associations were with Leda and the swan. You recall the myth?

L: Yes I do.

R: For the sake of those who do not know the story, Zeus often assumed forms öther than his divine self in order to impregnate mortal women. The poet Yeats wrote a magnificent poem in

60

which he asked, "Did she put on his knowledge with his power . . . ?"

This card then may serve as a depiction of the divine (Zeus means "bright sky") coming down from the heavenly plane, the sphere of the bird, to the human level, the mundane. Furthermore, the woman represented has that peace-instilling visage of the Virgin Mary, so the scene almost suggests the Annunciation. Thus if we are to have universal brotherhood, one way to effect it is through a kind of Second Coming, another assumption of human form by a divine being, as in the case of God in Christ.

I just flashed on what is really meant by the Second Coming. I do not think there will ever be an actual physical appearance of Christ on earth again. The Second Coming really means the incarnation of the Christ spirit in man. When we have that, there can be no strife, but only universal brotherhood.

L: I'd agree with that.

R: So looked at in this light, the hand coming out of the cloud in the FOUR OF CUPS symbolizes divine inspiration, or revelation of the principle of love offered as the true meaning of the concept of the Second Coming.

L: Uh-huh!

R: So JUDGEMENT, the next card, would not represent the judgement of antagonistic forces, but transformation, resurrection of all of mankind. The figure then is the angel Gabriel blowing his trumpet.

L: And the sunrise!

R: Yes, the sunrise in the background. The dawning of a new era, measured not as a historical period, but as a spiritual quality.

Then, finally, the coming together from the four quarters of the world, as shown in the FIVE OF RODS. North, East, South, and West uniting as one, as foreshadowed perhaps in the FOUR OF PENTACLES.

So the spread does seem to work on both levels.

L: It does. Very much so.

R: Do you see any further things in the cards?

L: I'd really agree with all that. Your interpretation fits both my personal and universal wishes. If I can achieve peace on the personal level, the others can also. And what works on an individual level, works on the world level.

R: Ah! This is what I said in my last sermon. There is no politics that can solve the world's problems.

L: Definitely.

R: What is needed is transformation on the individual level all through humanity. And then, when that has been effected, the political situation will be naturally resolved. In other words, we try to put the cart before the horse in the world arena. We look to politicians to solve the problems, when in reality *we* have to do it on the individual level.

L: Right! Very much so.

(As a footnote to this reading, a month later Larry Collins informed me that a beneficial Taurean woman had come into his life, fulfilling the prediction of the KING OF PENTACLES).

The date is January 3, 1971, and this is a reading for Mary Curtice. Also present are her husband, Robley Curtice, and Miss Coco Cutler. The readee has not asked for the answer to a specific question, but desires a general reading about herself at present.

The first three cards are in the position of past, present, and future, and they are THREE OF PENTACLES, THE HERMIT, reversed, and KNIGHT OF SWORDS. My association with Pentacles here are money matters, material concerns. The implications are "getting the house in order." The figure is nailing up a wall, or perhaps buttressing it, shoring-up a shelter of some kind. This is therefore a constructive card. In the past, you have done a lot of hard work is what this card says. In connection with this, can you comment?

M: I was the only one of us working most of the time, particularly when Robley went back to school for his teaching credential.

R: What kind of work were you doing?

M: Clerical.

R: Your husband was interested in becoming a writer and you were willing to work without begrudging him the time to develop his talent?

M: Oh, there were times I begrudged him this.

The Magic Seven Spread

1. Three of Pentacles
2. The Hermit (Reversed)
3. Knight of Swords
4. Page of Swords
5. Two of Swords
6. Ace of Rods (Reversed)
7. The Sun

R: Mainly at six-thirty in the morning.

M: (Laughter). Sure. But I felt that he had to find himself.

R: O.K., the card that deals with the present is reversed, and it is THE HERMIT. Well, you've had two children, the economic problems have been resolved—are behind you in card one—and now you're beginning to wonder what the next phase in your life may be. In connection with this, there is a retirement from the world. You're not interested in working anymore. Correct?

M: Right.

R: Also, since the card is reversed, introspection, an inward turning is also involved. The hermit is holding a light, which implies a quest for value or meaning. The figure retires from the world in order to find the inner light. Does my description of this card also describe the kind of change in orientation you are undergoing now?

M: Yes, this is the first time in my life I've thought about these things for any length of time. Maybe it's because I don't have to work anymore and *can* think about them. I think the hermit is really me at present.

R: Good. Now regarding the future, the card is THE KNIGHT OF SWORDS. Often this suit seems to fit that part of the individ-

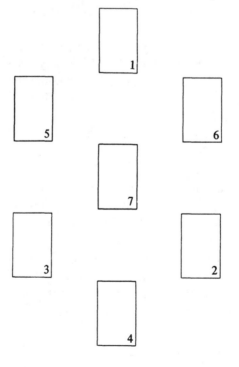

ual's mode of expression which Jung calls the intellecual function. For fuller development of this in you, a helpful guide is the inner archetype called the animus, or the masculine principle within. The capacity for self-reflection on deeper levels is something that can be the result of rapport with this archetype. During this time in your life, you may be asking yourself questions such as, "Who am I?" Development of your masculine principle may help to provide the answer through a greater capacity for logical, ordered, sequential thought. So I see you reading a lot in the future, concentrating on books that themselves have protagonists who are questioning the meaning of life. I just noticed something. A knight is usually associated with a quest or pilgrimage of some kind, and the spirit of the previous card, THE HERMIT, is also one of spiritual quest—the lantern with the star-shaped light within—so I would say this is what's on your mind at this time.

M: My goal right now is definitely spiritual—to achieve a kind of selflessness.

R: I had no idea these kinds of changes were taking place in you. Always before whenever I got onto spiritual topics with you and Robley, I had the feeling that you were amused at what I said, and were pooh-poohing the whole subject.

M: I think that was true before. But now I am more interested in these things.

R: All right, the next card represents a helper for you in fulfilling your goal, and it is the PAGE OF SWORDS. Maybe I got ahead of myself with the description of the animus because this card could serve for it as well as THE KNIGHT OF SWORDS. Or, this may stand for a flesh-and-blood person. Well, why not Robley, because with all his interest in books and writing, he is in effect a servant or page of the intellect?

M: I think it is Robley.

R: O.K., so he will be encouraging you along lines of suggesting what books you may read that fit your present interests, and also he will be a sounding board for you to discuss your discoveries with him.

M: I think that's true. Intellectually I haven't developed at all, and Robley certainly tries to help me in that respect. I think now I am open to accepting this new development, whereas before I was not. I feel more complete now than ever.

R: Good. Now we come to the TWO OF SWORDS, representing the surroundings as affecting what you hope to attain. Sometimes this card conveys the idea of balanced forces. Let's say spiritual and intellectual forces are functioning harmoniously together for you. Or, the two forces may be the feminine principle and the masculine principle. Heretofore, only the feminine side of yourself was fully operative, but now the animus is aiding the intellectual development so there is more of a balance to your personality. At this point you are concerned with that side of your consciousness that will lead away from a strictly feminine orientation to the world towards a self-reflective attitude—in some ways meditative—that will ultimately lead to a total realization of the inner reality of self.

M: I think if I do develop my intellectual side I will be better balanced and more complete. That will make Robley happy too.

Robley: Maybe she doesn't want to develop intellectually.

R: Well, each of us has a masculine and a feminine side, and it would be her animus fulfillment. It's development of a side of herself, the same way that a man should want to fulfill his feminine side also. That's what I have been doing with the intuition thing through reading Tarot. Intuition is naturally easier for women. Perhaps that's why it has always been called "women's intuition." In other words, we have to be in harmony with ourselves, and we are a yin and yang—each of us.

Coco: The whole life suffers if either the masculine or the feminine side is neglected or not brought into some kind of balance. It's not a balance that reaches a status quo, but an interplay when both sides are released.

R: They do a cosmic dance together in joyous celebration.

Robley: (To Mary) What do you see in that card?

M: I noticed the blindfold right away, and this meant to me that I had been blind to some aspect of myself—that I was leaving out something.

R: That's a good interpretation. The next card is the ACE OF RODS reversed, and I think this indicates again an inward turning, particularly since I ordinarily relate the Rods suit to the intuitive function. In this case we have an ace, so a great deal of power is indicated and I don't really feel that the power is attenuated by the reversal. What it signifies to me is inner orientation.

Furthermore, the ACE OF RODS in this position opens up a whole new interpretation for the TWO OF SWORDS. We can say that the eyes are blind to the outer world so that the inner sight can be developed. And, of course, inner sight is intuition, which follows immediately in the ACE OF RODS.

In the same sense, the hermit turns his back on the outer world and goes into his hermitage. So the successful outcome of this matter depends on your going into your own inner world, your own unconscious. These three cards, THE HERMIT, TWO OF SWORDS, and ACE OF RODS, seem to be variations on this same theme.

Now let's turn over the outcome card. Well, this is quite beautiful!

M: What does it mean?

R: To my mind you couldn't have a more explicit card come up at this point. THE SUN is a card that perhaps stands for many things, but the first thought in my mind when I see it is "Self-hood." This is a Jungian concept for the fully individuated person. In modern jargon we might say that it is someone who "has it all together." Its appearance here in the outcome position means that you will get it all together—both the intellect and the intuition, joined to the sensations and feeling functions, which I am sure have already been fully operative in you.

There is another card, called THE STAR, which also conveys the same value to me. The star-shaped light within the lantern of the hermit is transformed from "out-there" to "in-here," to within the individual. Or better yet, the light never was "out-there," but was waiting to be fanned into fullness within. So think of it in the sense almost of becoming a light unto yourself.

M: Then the spiritual quest, or my drive to develop will be realized?

R: Absolutely! You see there really is no opposition to your attainment.

Let's sum up. You don't want any power in the business world, and you are not greedy, you don't want to keep working—as you are in the THREE OF PENTACLES—so you retire from the world—THE HERMIT. Together you develop your mind and your masculine principle—KNIGHT OF SWORDS, aided by your intellectual husband, PAGE OF SWORDS. Going into your unconscious you attain better balance and free your intuition, TWO OF SWORDS and ACE OF RODS. The long-term result will be Selfhood, THE SUN.

So where would the opposition to this come in? The ACE OF RODS is in the *position* of the opposition card, but I don't see it functioning that way. Except, of course, if we consider the prohibition in your Japanese background against a woman developing intellectually and functioning as an equal with man. I suppose in the sense of authority that could be one meaning of the word *rod*. Well, in connection with that, would you talk about your father?

M: I didn't really know him. We never really talked, and he was never close to any of the children. He read most of the time. He was from the old country.

R: By "old country" you mean . . .?

M: Japan.

R: Well, I can see how this experience of the man who reads by himself was a causal factor in the development of your animus. This is why now you want to find out what kept him away from you during those times. There must have been something of great value in the books because you recognized your own value and what you had to offer to your father. So now there is something in these books which you would like to investigate yourself. This is one way of getting closer to the father again.

M: I think it was just the kind of culture.

R: But he's a little bit unusual for that old country culture.

Robley: (To Mary) Yeh, that's what you said about him once before.

M: Yes, he *was* different because he used to read. None of the others used to read.

Coco: Did you admire your father?

M: To a degree. But I felt . . .

R: A little left out?

M: Yes. There was no communication. I never approached him because that was never done.

R: This is what I'm driving at here in connection with these two figures, one representing the husband, and the other your own male principle, the animus, both represented by what I take to be symbols of intellectuality—the Swords suit. Around the house

69

Robley is always recapturing the nostalgia of the Lost Generation, Left Bank days, in which conversation about the arts is witty and urbane. And you have a feeling or have had a feeling of being left out. This is a re-creation of the father thing, and now you want to mend the fences and see to it that you are given your due. It's admirable, and I think this will have a successful outcome.

M: I can see the relation now.

Coco: When you talk of intellectual development in a woman there can be an implication of *competition* with men, whereas here I think in regard to Mary's situation it represents fuller development of her entire personality through an *innate* part of herself, not just in connection with her father or her husband. All intellectual delights do not come from having read all the books and knowing all the knowledge. It could represent . . .

R: It's discovery.

Coco: . . . Discovery of a higher level of consciousness.

R: I think that's a very valid comment, and the unfolding sun there suggests . . .

Coco: . . . The unfolding of Mary's whole personality. Certainly the animus, as that masculine portion of all women, can work negatively or positively, but it sounds to me as if it is stirring in a very positive way in you. As the Logos, or the representation of higher levels of consciousness, it has a larger connotation than is usually put on the word intellectual. It's a very positive thing going on for you, along with the very feminine spiritual stirrings—more than stirrings, needs, which you pursue quite consciously as well.

R: I think that sums it up much better than anything I have said tonight. . . . Let's have a comment from the husband. Have you been cognizant of these stirrings in Mary?

Robley: No.

R: I think it's interesting that I have known you and Mary for about ten years; yet I haven't been aware of these inner desires for change and growth within her either.

(To Mary) But they have been there for the last year or six months?

M: Yes, but something stopped me from developing. It was as if something innate was prohibiting me. A lot of times I wanted to

70

read, but something stopped me—like a block.

R: Isn't it culturally true that Japanese women are supposed to be very feminine and not partake of intellectual activities? So this might be construed as kind of stepping out of line.

Robley: I think that's true. Also you have a problem because you were part of a cross-culture.

M: Yes, that's a problem in Hawaii. I was mixed in school with the American culture, and then at home with the Japanese.

Robley: So your role was obscured.

M: Yes.

R: In other words, when you were interested in these intellectual pursuits and you said something always stopped you, it was probably an innate pressure from your Japanese heritage that prevented you.

M: It could be. I don't really know why.

Robley: Well, it could be a sum of factors.

R: Well, as I have said, the father, the inner archetype, and you—where does one leave off and the other begin? I can't tell where her father leaves off and you begin except by these California cowboy boots. (Laughter)

These are the kind of witticisms I have to listen to . . .

Robley: . . . that are good in October.

R: . . . that are good in October but begin to sour in January.

Coco: Do you cringe over some of them that you have to spend hours listening to?

R: Sometimes I have to go back over the same part of the tape four or five times to hear what someone said who was mumbling, then I have to hear my same joke over and over.

Robley: That is your Purgatory.

R: I do believe it's curing me of making jokes.

Robley: Thank God for that. (Laughter)

his layout of cards is often utilized when giving a reading for a person who has a wish or goal which he would like to see fulfilled.

In selecting a Significator, a card representing the querent, follow the procedure set forth in the Ancient Celtic Spread.

The querent shuffles the deck, then the reader fans the cards face down on the table. Usually the querent then draws fifteen cards at random while concentrating on his wish. He may then re-shuffle those fifteen cards, whereupon they are spread out in the pattern shown. In this case, the reader decided to see if he could attune his unconscious to the conscious wish of the querent by selecting the Significator and the first twelve cards of the reading. The last three cards, representing the realization of the wish, were selected by the querent; however, the reader decided if these three cards did not fit the pattern of his reading, he would then draw three more himself. The author/reader is denoted by the letter R. C. denotes a mutual friend. The querent is denoted by the letter B. The tape opens with her friend Frank speaking.

Frank: (to Reader) Can she tell me what her wish is—without telling you?

The Wish Spread

Significator Two of Rods
1. The Magician
2. King of Rods (Reversed)
3. Page of Rods (Reversed)
4. Eight of Rods
5. Three of Cups
6. Five of Rods (Reversed)
7. Three of Swords
8. Queen of Rods (Reversed)
9. Knight of Rods
10. Emperor
11. Four of Rods (Reversed)
12. Queen of Pentacles
13. Ten of Cups
14. The Lovers
15. Five of Cups
16. Five of Swords
17. Ace of Cups (Reversed)
18. Ten of Swords

R: Umm, she could whisper it.

B: (to Frank) I'm not going to tell you!

R: This will be a demonstration of the Wish Spread. The Significator card was selected by the reader from the face-down fanned deck laid out across the table. In this case, the card was the TWO OF RODS . . . This is a squire or knightly man, and he carries in his hand a globe, which suggests to me the earth or the mundane plane. Does your wish concern in part material remuneration of some kind?

B: Yes, that's right.

R: Free-associating with this figure, I notice that while the right hand carries the mundane globe, the left hand carries the rod, and the second rod is somewhat ahead of the figure. His eyes seem to be fixed upon it, not on the globe. However, we already established that this is a symbol of something material, so let me ask you this. Would the fulfillment of the wish be not an end in itself but the furtherance of a distant goal that you wish to attain and have your eyes on?

B: Yes, uh-huh.

R: The other interesting thing about this card is that on the figure's left sleeve he has a kind of insignia that I take to be a rose

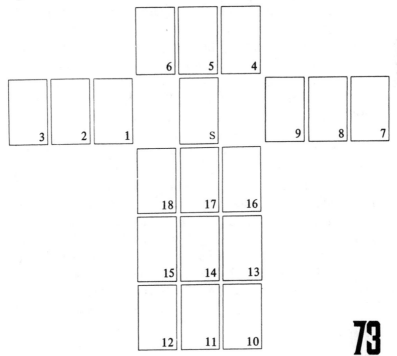

and a lily. Both are associated with Christian mysticism and the left-hand path to God. That is to say, traditionally the right-hand path is through reason and sensation, the left-hand way is by means of feeling and intuition. So can I speculate further that the long term goal in connection with your wish has psychic or spiritual integration or fulfillment as its quest?

B: Yes, for me it does, but not necessarily for others.

R: Well, it does in this specific case?

B: Uh, huh.

R: All right, we'll turn up these cards now. The first three cards—dealt from right to left—concern what surrounds you. The three cards above represent the factors describing your wish. The three cards to the right stand for what opposes you; on the bottom, what comes to your home—again represented by three cards, and immediately below the Significator card the three cards you selected telling us what you will realize.

You're looking at the entire spread, let's first have your reaction generally to what you see.

B: Well, in the center it looks like hearts and flowers, but surrounding it there seem to be thistles—a whole thicket of them. Maybe they represent problems.

R: What you're calling thistles are actually rods, but I can see the similarity. There is a preponderance of rods, but my interpretation is not that of yours. The interesting thing about the three that you selected is that they don't seem to fit into the pattern, so I'll try to interpret from your three cards when we get there, and if that doesn't work I'll pick three others as the resolution cards to go with the other twelve I selected.

O.K., the three cards representing what surrounds you are THE MAGICIAN. KING OF RODS (Inverse), PAGE OF RODS (Inverse). Now I usually associate the suit Rods, or Wands, as they are sometimes called, with the intuitive function of the Jungian four functions. The interesting thing about the first card, THE MAGICIAN, is that he carries in his hand a rod. This is the only Key card that I know of in which this occurs. So there is a definite pattern here of a theme of rods going through the first three cards. This is kind of a legacy, and the interesting thing about this first card, THE MAGICIAN, is that he looks very much like Frank. Do you see the similarities, particularly in the

74

moustache?

B: Yes.

R: Are you looking to Frank for help in fulfillment of this wish?

B: No.

R: Then I'd say this figure is not representational, and we'll go into your unconscious. To me this is a natural figure for the animus, because, if you're familiar with my Jungian Spread, this is the One Key card and it falls into the natural position of the animus. On the table in front of the figure you see the four suits—cup, sword, pentacles, rod—which are symbolic to me of the four functions—feeling, intellect, sensation, and intuition. He carries an extra wand. So I would say, very largely surrounding you in connection with this wish it would depend on the intuition function within you.

B: Yes, it would.

R: And naturally the use of intuition involves a turning back into the unconscious. The second and third cards are inverted, and you might find help in the unconscious in fulfillment of the wish, using the powers of the unconscious, the untapped resources there through the intuitive functions for fulfillment of the wish. O.K., just generally speaking, you don't have to tell me what the wish is about or anything, tell me what you think of my interpretation so far.

B: Absolute concurrence.

R: Good, then I'll quit right now and go leave the next twelve cards for someone else. (Laughter) The next three cards are called factors describing your wish. Again we have a whole bunch of rods—the fourth card is the EIGHT OF RODS, the fifth card is the THREE OF CUPS, and the sixth card is the FIVE OF RODS, inverted. The EIGHT OF RODS is a card usually of activity, some see it as flight of arrows, but it does suggest action and activity or movement toward a goal. So you're not just wishing now about this goal, you're doing something actively to fulfill it?

B: Yes.

R: O.K. The next card is the THREE OF CUPS. Here we have cups, and we have a kind of triune here, three very lovely, muse-like figures. I don't think this is true, but I'm going to ask you the question because the line of thought that I'm following doesn't include this interpretation, but I would think in an ordinary reading, according to the Hoyle of Tarot reading, this question would be asked. Although I don't think this is a possibility, but since there are three women here, the ordinary question would be are you involved with two other women in seeking this goal? An activity involving them?

B: No, but I live with two other women.

R: Well, we could say this, that on the mundane plane that maybe something connected with the living condition would have an influence on the job outcome, or not?

B: No.

R: All right, I'm going to get off this mundane plane, because my feelings upon seeing this card were to continue on with the Jungian interpretation strictly. You have what looks like a giant lotus flower in the background, and a flower suggests unfolding, lotus-like with the Self or Selfhood. My feelings would be that the fulfillment of this wish involves a working with people on an exchange of feeling level, particularly where they express their feelings to you, and you, by using the intuition of the four cards containing rods earlier, help to resolve situations that they are involved in, and this further leads to an opening of the feminine principle within you, the flower unfolding and blooming. And the toast of cups—an exchange of feeling is part of the activity involved!

All right, now we go to the FIVE OF RODS, and this is a card of very great activity, about as much as the EIGHT OF RODS. And I would say that here we don't have the solitary figure that is associated with all the rods before, but we have four figures, five rods, so I would say you are using intuition. If you got your wish, you would be using intuition in inter-personal relationships, because of all the people and all the activity of the rods. You see, they are crossing all directions, but it doesn't mean a thwarting of purpose necessarily, but it means a use of the intuition on your part in inter-personal relations.

B: Are you talking about intuition versus feeling?

R: Evidently both functions are going to be operating here, because in the previous card I talked about feeling, and exchange of cups is exchange of feeling, so I would say two levels will dominate—those of feeling and intuition. O.K.?

B: Yes, I think that accurate in describing my approach to life

76

generally.

R: All right, looking again at the FIVE OF RODS, I notice that it is also inverted, as were the KING OF RODS and PAGE OF RODS. Nineteenth century Tarot interpretation inclined to label cards appearing inverted as signs of setbacks or adversity. However, since Jung postulated in 1930 the theory of the unconscious mind, I like to regard inverse cards as possibly representing an inward orientation to the unconscious, particularly here in this case, since I have associated the suit Rods with the intuitive function. Keeping with the spirit of flexibility which I suggest for any reader, let him experiment to see which approach is best suited to his own readings.

So to sum up the factors describing your wish, you desire an endeavor involving inter-personal relationships in which you can utilize your own feeling and intuition.

B: Yes, that's quite true.

R: O.K., now we go over to the right of our spread to see what opposes you. The cards involved are in the position of seven through nine, and they are THREE OF SWORDS, QUEEN OF RODS, inverted, and KNIGHT OF RODS. In terms of what this last inversion may mean in the unconscious, the ready association is with the shadow, the woman within you. If the archetype is negative, impatience, temper, and general lack of self-control could lead to trouble. Unlike my own Jungian Spread, this particular form does not enable us to go into the nature of your shadow; however, if positive, then the QUEEN OF RODS, leading back again into the unconscious is going to help you immensely here with the activities that you desire which involve your intuition. And the KNIGHT OF RODS again—we've had KNIGHT, PAGE, and KING OF RODS, and we've had the QUEEN OF RODS; you have all the court cards. All of the court cards are here. Having a full court with the cards that I associated with intuition, I'd say that your prospects are overwhelmingly good, because if you're going to use intuition in this particular pursuit, you will have more than what you need. Again we have a flower here with the QUEEN OF RODS, which again suggests the flowering of the feminine principle that we saw earlier. Now the joker in the deck is the THREE OF SWORDS, and the heart there is being pierced by three swords. This came up in my reading last week, and I think the person's problem there was one of feeling function, and he had to suffer to find fulfillment and be able to fulfill others with whom he was involved. In this relationship that you are wishing for, is your association with that, that you need to feel more? Will that help you to realize your wish? I wouldn't interpret it that way.

B: No, I think it's just the opposite.

R: O.K., good. See, the swords represent the intellect function, and maybe what has to happen here is that you have to have a marriage of the heart and feeling function and intuition with the intellectual function. You would agree with that then?

B: Yes.

R: The swords are coming down out of the clouds, which suggests a sort of Logos Principle being brought down to the mundane plane. This came up in a man's reading last week, and I told him he would have to suffer more and feel more. And in this case, we have a fulfillment of all the things on the feminine side, and now we're trying to search out and find what function has to be added for the fulfillment of the activity, and the sword again is associated with the intellectual function. It comes down and is married to the heart, adding the animus side of reflection, differentiated thinking, as logical, ordered, sequential thinking. There is a nice trine. You have a sword of logic, order, and sequence going right into the heart and making for a marriage.

This last set was what was opposing you. This next set is what comes into your home. So we can sum up by saying that the only thing that opposes you in this desired activity is the inferior function of intellect.

B: Yes, I think that is right.

R: Now what comes into your home. This card is beautiful. Every time I see it I think of the quaternity of the four functions. FOUR OF RODS. We have the sought-after delectable mountains, the wish-fulfillment lying right there at the center of the spread. To me it means that the four functions will come together in the individual. For the sake of the reader, the three cards that come to your home are THE EMPEROR, FOUR OF RODS, and QUEEN OF PENTACLES. The FOUR OF RODS is reversed; all of our rods have been reversed, except the EIGHT OF RODS, and they are perpendicular really. Now in the tenth card we notice

78

that the figure of THE EMPEROR holds a ball similar to that held by the man I picked as your Significator, the TWO OF RODS man. This suggests that the figure either represents you and fulfillment on that plane in reaching your desired wish, or it suggests to me someone with whom you must deal in order to be able to effect the use of your intuition and feeling in the interpersonal relationships. In other words, he looks like the head of a department or a head of state. Could he be the head of a medical department?

B: It doesn't really fit. I would say he's some kind of administrator.

R: Yes, that's a good word. He's on a throne of some kind, so he has dominion over the mundane plane. Now we come to the FOUR OF RODS, which suggests the four functions hinted at in the first card, THE MAGICIAN, where symbols of the four suits were lying on the table. Now in this card we have a symbol of the quaternity of the four functions, the square of consciousness. Then the QUEEN OF PENTACLES wears an ermine robe and holds a large ball, symbol of coins or material reward, fulfillment on the mundane plane, which we saw earlier in the ball held by the man in the Significator card. Cards number thirteen, fourteen, and fifteen are in the position of what you will realize. They are TEN OF CUPS, THE LOVERS, and the FIVE OF CUPS. These are the only three cards that you selected. If I were to follow along with the same pattern of interpretation, I can see how the first two cards may fit into the pattern, but the last one doesn't hold true. The TEN OF CUPS represents an ultimate fulfillment on the side of feeling. The feeling shown by the THREE OF CUPS has been more than tripled, and I would say that there would be a definite fulfillment of the wish. THE LOVERS suggest that the operative abstraction in the activity will be a compassionate love such as that shown by the Buddha in his regard for long-suffering humanity. But when I come to the FIVE OF CUPS the suggestions are of a break-up in the family, and my intuition tells me that interpretation does not fit here. There is a bleakness about the scene depicted, an emotional disruption suggested, but I cannot see that coming through for you. I don't think it's true, but I will ask you anyway. Would pursuing this activity result in disruption in your family in some way? There would be no strife there? No, I didn't think so. Well, what I want to do then is to pick three cards myself for your realization cards . . .

This first one that comes up is the FIVE OF SWORDS, and I think this fits in very nicely with the other Swords suit card which we had earlier—the THREE OF SWORDS. We said that there had to be a marriage between the heart and the intellect, or the intuition function, the feeling function, and the thinking function. I like this card. It shows a warrior collecting fallen swords on a battlefield, and this simply means to me that through study and research you will be able to utilize the intellectual ideas of others in what will be for you a meaningful way, because they will be reinterpreted by your feelings and intuition. In other words, it may be a rusty concept that has long lain on the academic battlefield and no one has put it to good use, but you will come along and use it in a meaningful way in your particular endeavor.

B: Uh, huh.

R: Now the next card to me means that you will attain this, and it signifies complete fulfillment on the side of feeling. This card is the ACE OF CUPS. Something comes to mind here. Can you see the symbolic pattern between the THREE OF CUPS above and the ACE OF CUPS here? Over the three women exchanging their cups we have this gigantic flower, which I said looked like a lotus, bursting into bloom. It dominates the entire top of the card. The inverse ACE OF CUPS is turning back into the waters of the unconscious again, and the base of the cup is resting on the waters, and we have three flowers—obviously lotuses—that are very similar to the large flower in the THREE OF CUPS. And, then out of the cup bursts the sun! If we know what the lotus symbolizes in mythology—spiritual unfoldment, and if we know what the sun symbolizes in Jungian psychology or alchemical occultism, we have here the sun of Selfhood, the individuated One in the Many and the Many in the One.

I want to say now what I think your wish is—what I think you'll be doing. In my terms it's a spiritual activity—service in the highest sense—a working through of the two seemingly separated planes of spiritual and mundane in an exchange with people. Now I'll go out on the limb, because the whole pattern points to only one thing on your part—inter-personal relationships utilizing your intuition, feeling, and intellect. Therapeutic counselling of people—this is your wish. I would say that it will be fulfilled.

B: Yes, uh-huh.

R: Now this next card is a very heavy trip, the TEN OF SWORDS. It suggests to me that you may be injured in the line of duty, so to speak. You might be murdered, raped, or severely beaten. But you know when you go out into the world and are open with the world, this is always a possibility.

Frank: Why couldn't it be the death of the self on the mundane plane?

R: Well . . .

Frank: Inwardly, not outwardly?

R: Since this involves the future and I don't pretend to be a prophet, I will leave it that way. We don't know what it is, but since you are so open with people you must be careful . . .

C: Why are these swords menacing and not those of the THREE OF SWORDS?

R: I saw those dealing with the heart and animus relatedness, whereas these seemingly kill the person.

C: But you're taking one literally and not the other!

R: Fine, but all we're doing here is free-associating with the cards, and I have to give what I get from it.

B: I was given a reading in February with fortune telling cards, and the person said there was the possibility of injury at the hands of another person. I'm aware when I leave my job late at night that it is a dangerous area. I am constantly aware of the possibility of something happening. Usually someone will walk out with me. It's not just my own paranoia, but I am always aware of the possibility.

R: Well, then is your wish really being fulfilled now?

B: Not on a material level, and not on a full-time level, which is what I want.

R: I see, you would like to become a full-time therapist?

B: Um, hmm.

R: And reap the benefits that would accrue—as shown in the QUEEN OF PENTACLES, wearing ermine and holding the pentacle . . . (Laughter) I'm being facetious, but this card does suggest you will make your living at it. Another thing I notice in this queen, in the headgear we have a symbol associated with what figure?

B: Zeus?

C: Athena . . . what's in your mind, Richard?

R: Well, I'm thinking of Mercury.

B: That's what I was thinking of—winged feet.

R: Mercury represents the intellectual function in astrology—stands for the mind—so this means that the five swords that you collect, and the marriage of the sword to the feeling function will be effected and this will result in the mundane fulfillment which you sought in the Significator card as the man who was holding the globe of the earth. I said you wanted mundane remuneration but it was a means to a more distant goal, which evidently involved intuition—the rod he was holding—and its use in inter-personal relationships. But I would say be careful in these relationships so that in some way your compassion is not misinterpreted to be something else which would cause others to be angered if you denied them yourself . . . I think we could say that there are three possible interpretations for the TEN OF SWORDS. In one of my theories, everything exists simultaneously on three levels and is subject to interpretation according to those three levels, which are the mundane, the psychological, and the spiritual. And in a reversal of my usual form, I gave the mundane interpretation here. The psychological interpretation fits with our other two swords cards—that you have added intellect so that you are functioning with greater conscious rationality—to work with the legacy of intuition and feeling which you already possessed. And, finally, Frank gave the spiritual interpretation—death on the mundane plane for further fulfillment on the individuated side. This would fit certainly with the previous card, which was the cup of Selfhood.

But again, since this represents a future possibility, let's keep all three potentials in mind. The first you want to avoid, the second you would like to add—greater intellectual development, and the third—apotheosis. Don't forget though, after you have died on the mundane plane, you have to do what the Buddha did and return to life again and the inter-personal relationships, shown in the FIVE OF RODS and the THREE OF CUPS. So all in all, my feelings are that it is a very beautiful spread, and with so much going for you, I can't see how you can miss.

82

Now I'd like you to give your overall impression, and whether or not you can see what l have delineated from the cards. In other words, you can see the associations I've made?

B: Yes, I can see them, not only job-wise, but also through relationships of various kinds the development of feeling and intellectual relatedness. I'm conscious of the need for both. It seems like it's pretty well spelled out. I think it's a very clear-cut reading.

R: May I use this reading in my book?

B: Yes, I don't see why not.

R: Will you give us your name then. I know your first name is Barbara, but I don't know the last name.

B: Skaggs.

R: Scandanavian?

B: German

R: And the place where you are now doing some therapy is . . . ?

B: The Haight-Ashbury Clinic.

(The recorder was turned off at this point, and then turned on again for additional commentary)

R: We were given a fourth interpretation of the TEN OF SWORDS after the recorder was inoperative, and since I think it is quite brilliant, we're now recording again. In her own humble way, Mrs. Coco Cutler waited until after the recorder stopped before presenting it to our group, but now we shall have her theory. She pointed out that the first time a sword appeared in the reading it represented the intellectual function. Then in the FIVE OF SWORDS, the gathering of swords represented concepts, theories, and approaches to therapy, external intelligences, in other words. But the danger from this is a kind of animus possession in which the individual no longer realizes that the ideas she has appropriated belong to others. The dominant, feminine functions of feeling and intuition are then lost to her.

C: She is then in danger of being *used* by the intellectual concepts rather than using *them*. This card indicates a warning against being possessed by the ideas.

R: (to Barbara) You can see that interpretation in relation to yourself?

B: Definitely. I know when I have listened to someone else and then used an idea in a situation against what I felt to be another

83

answer, I later on found that my own feeling had been more important and valid. I think my feelings are really important, and I need to rely on them, and at least not lose sight of them.

R: The figure in the card is dominated by the swords, so we could say that he has lost sight of the other functions. So there is the danger implicit. However, I don't feel that this will be the results in your own work. I get another flash on physical danger, so I'd say buy a forty-five and put it in your purse. (Laughter)

B: There's something else I'd like to say about the spread in general, particularly all the rods. I got the impression of being in the center of the layout surrounded by thorns and thistles. I related that to the story of "Sleeping Beauty" when she was asleep or enchanted. Her Prince Charming had to break through the thorns and the thistles and get to her, and when he kissed her she awakened to consciousness.

R: I see what you're saying. The Significator seems to be in a thicket because there are rods all around—thirteen on top, three to the left, two to the right, and there are four below.

B: And also the swords add to the barrier.

R: Well, when you said that, I had an immediate flash because you said the prince would come to awaken her to consciousness. And the association of intuition and feeling are with the unconscious, the feminine side of the individual, whereas the intellectual function is associated with the consciousness and the masculine side of the psyche. So the task of awakening Sleeping Beauty from immobility, stasis, and the sleep of unconsciousness belongs to the animus, the masculine side of her own nature. It seems to me all fairy tales are extremely interesting when interpreted in the light of psychology, particularly Jungian psychology. So I see the story of Sleeping Beauty as a symbolization of woman's anticipation of relatedness to consciousness through animus fulfillment.

The date is February 3, 1971, and this is a reading for George Hernandez. The form is the Wish Spread. We should probably have a "figure" to represent you, George, and I'm just going to select the KING OF RODS. This is what we call the SIGNIFICATOR, and it stands for you at the middle of the spread.

The initial three cards in this reading are the FOUR OF SWORDS, FIVE OF SWORDS, and QUEEN OF SWORDS; these cards are in the area of the forces surrounding you, or it is called "what surrounds you." The force surrounding you, the element around you at present, is the FOUR OF SWORDS, a card that is associated with death, but it obviously is not here, because it is an impetus card for you, because it is at the beginning of the reading. What my eye is immediately attracted to here is that the swords are hanging over the body, but not in the way that they were in the last reading I gave, which was the Sword of Damocles and where they were threatening swords. But here to me they are inspirational swords. The astral plane comes to mind, and they are kind of infusing the body of this knight with their power. He is in a state of absolute receptivity to them. The sword under him suggests to me his own sustaining principle, the logos principle, in his life. Some may call it the God principle. Even though he is

The Wish Spread

Significator King of Rods
1. Four of Swords
2. Five of Swords
3. Queen of Swords
4. Page of Cups
5. Ace of Cups
6. The Star
7. The Tower
8. The Devil
9. Temperance
10. Page of Swords
11. The World
12. Four of Rods
13. Three of Rods
14. Two of Rods
15. Ace of Swords

depicted wearing armor in this card, I really don't get a defensive motif at all; I feel a sense of openness to what may come down to him from the astral plane.

The FIVE OF SWORDS suggests possibly two "paths" in the foreground, and there is a lot of hard work going on in the intellectual realm, where you are gathering all the philosophies. In effect you have become a kind of synthesizing intelligence for the philosophies of the rest of the world. You are examining them with great care for whatever value they may offer, because you recognize that these swords will stand you in good stead in your most violent hour, in your moments when there is only God and yourself in life.

G: It is true that different philosophies at one time or another have seemed to have a special helping quality for me.

R: This next card is the QUEEN OF SWORDS. I am associating this card with an inner state of mind, what Jung calls the anima figure. Are you aware of what he means by that?

G: Anima means "soul" in Latin . . .

R: It is one of the archetypes, as Jung defines them; this one is the archetype of the feminine principle that is within all men.

G: Right.

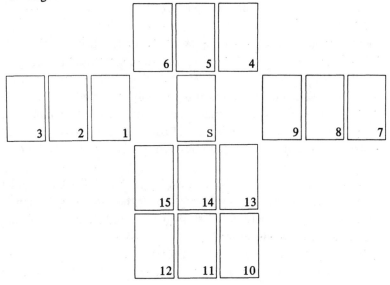

R: This relatedness to this figure gives one sensitivity and opens up one's own psychic side. So I have this feeling of receptivity and intellectual questing, but it is done in a spirit of relatedness to your own intuition and to your own psychic development. I don't see it as a figure in the outer world, a woman of an intellectual nature who is in your force field or who is surrounding you now; I could be wrong on that.

G: Well, I don't know of anyone.

R: All right . . .

Now the three cards on top represent the elements of your wish.

G: That's interesting, because my wish was threefold.

R: The PAGE OF CUPS to me is associated with something from the unconscious, and since I related the previous card, the QUEEN OF SWORDS, to the archetypal world of the unconscious and your feminine principle, this PAGE OF CUPS is viewing the fish rising from the cup as a kind of messenger from the unconscious. The messenger motif is also borne out by the winged adornment on the hat of the page on the card. I haven't had my eye attracted to the two buds in the card before, but I get a feeling here of a kind of a budding consciousness. I don't know if this could describe your particular wish . . .

G: Yes, yes.

R: . . . And my mind is jumping all around. I think in the way that you approached the reading in your own consciousness, you said it was a threefold wish. My mind is jumping around from level to level, and I'm seeing this not only as something from the unconscious, but the fish makes me think of the fact that on a spiritual level it is a symbol in Christianity for Christ. So your wish is a relatedness between your own unconscious and a kind of Christ consciousness.

We come now to the second card, the ACE OF CUPS, which we discussed briefly in our laying out of the cards to get them in the proper order before the shuffling. I think that this was the only card that we discussed.

G: Yes, or at least one of the very few.

R: As is so often the case with this kind of situation, it turns up as the very center card in your wish here. We had mentioned the fact that it had turned up as the outcome card in the reading of a man for whom the Grail myth meant a great deal in his life. He happened to live in the same small town that you do.

G: The image conveyed by the ACE OF CUPS does bear a relation to my wish. The picture of the cup does, and the opening lotuses, and the sun falling into the cup.

R: Yeh. In our discussion of this earlier, I pointed out that the ACE OF CUPS was associated in a legend with the Silver Chalice of the Holy Grail. The word grail wasn't familiar to you, but the word chalice was. I pointed out how this card seemingly unites the spiritual persuasion of East and West because the figure of the Grail is sitting on the water on which the lotus floats. The lotus is always the symbol for the unfoldment; the phrase is "the jewel is in the lotus" in Buddhist philosophy. The jewel of Selfhood, in Jungian terms, or the jewel of spiritual unfoldment, is in the center of the lotus.

Oddly enough, the very next card after this is THE STAR, which, when I encounter it in other readings, I often say is the symbol of Selfhood in Jungian terminology. I realize you haven't read Jung; maybe I'm being presumptuous, but . . .

G: Yes, just brief passages, but for that purpose we could say that I haven't read it.

R: Considering the vast amount that he did write, I probably can say that I haven't read him either. (Laughter).

In the dreams of patients who are in Jungian analysis, the star is a symbol of, again, unfoldment of the individual and the concept of Selfhood, which is really, in religious terminology, spiritual at-one-ment. It represents harmony of all phases of the life. The really exciting thing about these three cards is that there is no discrepancy; they all say the same thing on various levels. Since this is the first time you have ever seen the Tarot deck, you may not realize this; but I have read so many times that here is that inner world symbolized by the cup, the waters of the unconscious leading back ultimately to God, out of which the fish springs, the Christ principle, which has to be made the vivid force in the life of the page viewing this. The sun and chalice, again symbols of Western spiritual consciousness, unite with the Eastern symbol below, the lotus, and again the star in Jungian terminology is a symbol for Selfhood. Jung was acutely aware of the value of Eastern philosophies.

R: Now the next three cards are in the position of "what opposes you." These cards are KEYS 16, 15, and 14, a reversal of their normal order, which would be 14, 15, and 16, of course. My appraisal of THE TOWER in recent weeks has been a little bit different. I see now the elements of a new consciousness appearing here—the new consciousness is symbolized by the lightning bolts from above. They are inspirational; and the life of the individual as he knew it before, his accommodation to society, is totally shattered . . .

G: You mean when these bolts of inspiration come?

R: Yes. For your particular wish to be fulfilled, or your hope to be fulfilled, there will have to be a new you.

G: Yes, I believe that.

R: And the old you is symbolized by the tower, a symbol of an extension of the mundane plane, perhaps aspiring towards the celestial or divine above. But it is in great peril, and it must be for the wish to be realized. It is also being assaulted by the unconscious in part; it is being assaulted from below as well as from above, the waves breaking at the base of the structure.

I don't know if I should ask this—just give me a simple yes or no. I don't want you to give this away because we have more cards to come. Do you have a desire to know God within your own heart?

G: Yes.

R: I say that because THE TOWER took on a completely new meaning when I saw it this time; and do you realize what this would mean for an ordinary human being? It would resemble in symbology a tower on fire. In other words, it would almost be more than what the human being could hold in his consciousness.

G: That's true—yes. I have read the *Autobiography of a Yogi*, by Paramahansa Yogananda, and there is a part in which a student is seeking cosmic consciousness, and he wants the teacher to grant him this gift. The teacher tells him that his nervous system will not be able to take it. He likens it to an electrical circuit where the wire is not thick enough to handle all the current and burns out.

R: I can see this here if we look upon this tower as a wire that is just not solid enough. Nothing in material form is really solid enough to sustain God.

G: (Laughter). I was very impressed by that card when we were putting the cards in order in the deck. It sort of caught my attention and impressed me quite a bit.

R: Uh-huh, well, you may talk more freely about it now because as I see it your wish is pretty evident. I normally don't get to the answer until the last three, the realization cards. But I think with the three cards that were in the description of your wish, your goal was so clearly spelled out already that there was no hiding it really. It's kind of a shining light within your life, and if you want to talk about how that impressed you . . .

G: Well, at first it looked a little frightening, but then it seemed more like a divinely ordered destruction for some good, not just a careless destruction brought about by a random bolt striking a tower. A divinely ordered destruction of something that . . .

R: . . . has to fall.

G: Right, yes.

R: It's often associated with the biblical Tower of Babel. I would say that a person of ordinary consciousness looking upon that card would approach it with the same sense of peril and trepidation as they would the card called Death. I do look at you as a person of higher consciousness, and as soon as you saw it you saw through that first level. You saw through to the second, that if something more is to be born, then what was has to fall.

G: Right. It sort of looks like an edifice that has been built and has served its purpose, but it can be looked at as one that has been built on wrong assumptions. The old structure has to be demolished so that a better one can take its place. No piecework will do the job.

R: Well put. We've equated this, therefore, with yourself and with your new consciousness. We've equated it with you really on the three levels, the mundane, the psychological, and the spiritual.

G: Right.

R: You are a tower who is standing open to the sky and inviting reconstruction from God. I get that again referring back to the Four of Swords card, where I said these swords are coming down from the astral plane, and the individual is open to them, and that they weren't periling him or threatening him. He is open to their inspirations.

G: Yes. This picture in the Four of Swords card is interesting because it does show the exact position that I lie in when I first go to sleep—very rigid, very straight, with my back down. In this position I usually feel some astral influences. At times they even get a little bit disturbing, but then the sword underneath, the one that is horizontal, represents the underlying faith and comfort, the guiding principle of the divine consciousness that I feel will carry me through the different levels that I will have to ascend to reach my goal.

R: I know the goal is threefold, and the swords above are three-fold.

G: That's right; the goal is threefold—it was twofold before, but now it has become threefold.

R: Here are the three and the two in the second card, the FIVE OF SWORDS. The two have been discarded and the man now holds the three swords.

G: That's right; I just acquired the third one. And I have acquired this third one perhaps consciously just recently, but it has sort of gradually been incorporated into my universe in the past four or five years.

R: O.K. Now we get into a little difficulty here with the next card, THE DEVIL. Since your wish is pretty much out front as I said, I shall ask you to free associate with the cards from now on and maybe help me more on this.

G: The name The Devil sounds a little frightening, but here he looks like a tired dog, one who has lost his power.

R: Why would he turn up in one of the cards that opposes you?

G: Well, I guess perhaps the dark forces do oppose goals of a higher spiritual nature. But it seems that The Devil looks kind of tired and really not too powerful; it doesn't seem like he's going to have his way.

R: That's interesting. It just occurred to me when you mentioned dark forces, that probably when you were in the classes of Reverend Becker* you had to meditate during the week at the same time of day, each day.

---

* Until her death in 1970, pastor of the Golden Gate Spiritualist Church in San Francisco. Personally the author regards her as the most highly gifted psychic he has known. More that anyone else, I credit her with the development of my own psychic side, primarily through the influence of her "unfoldment" classes.

G: Right.

R: The purpose of this, as she so stated, was that she was putting her band of guides around us, and she was in communication with us at this time. So it may be that there are forces that are antagonistic to the realization of your goal, and that they are operative on the mundane plane of the world. We see in all aspects of our lives attempts to thwart any development of the individual out of the mass mold of people. On a psychological level there are always within our own unconscious elements that are waiting to overwhelm us. Witness the towering waves in the previous card, THE TOWER. There may perhaps be a spiritual plane in which dark forces do try to fly on bat wings, symbolically, and it may be that they are in contention there as they are here below. Of course the great truth is, "As above, so below," so we could say, "As below, so above."

G: Right, it could work both ways.

R: I feel that you are, of course, opening yourself up a great deal through your receptivity, as I described it in the Four of Swords, so one of the forces that is opposing you may be categorized by the grand old name of The Devil. Again you have from the fourth sword a feeling of an underlying, sustaining principle that will probably see you through. Thinking of that, I just noticed that this particular devil almost seems to be decapitated, as if the sword of truth had lopped off his head. He doesn't seem to be grounded anymore.

G: Right, he seems to have lost his power.

R: He's at least been halved from what he might have been; he looks like a head and wings only, now.

The next card is TEMPERANCE, which has an implication of an exchange perhaps between the mundane plane and the spiritual plane, tempering one with the other. Since it is in the position of one of the cards opposing you, I think that one of the things you will have to temper is an awareness of the fact that you are still in the body form on the mundane plane. Your wish, as exalted and angelic as it is portrayed by TEMPERANCE, should be tempered with the knowledge that it is probably the aspiration of the next plane of your evolution.

G: I see.

R: In other words you may have foreseen or you are already

preparing yourself for your next stage of consciousness.

G: Temperance would say that I am not yet there, so tread carefully.

R: Do homage also to the mundane plane and to the poor body.

Now the next cards are in the position of "what will come to you."

I saw an old movie on T.V. the other night, in which a woman was giving a reading by the Wish Spread. She described these three cards as "what you expect." In some ways I like this interpretation better, because the very last three cards of the reading are called the "outcome" of your wish. It's similar to "what will come to you." So let's look at these cards along both lines.

These seem to be extremely felicitous. The PAGE OF SWORDS suggests again the underlying principle; the one sword, whether it be truth or discrimination or light, accompanies you on your journey and enables you to slay all dragons and all devils.

THE WORLD is a card of completeness and realization. It is in the form of a mandala, representing fully integrated consciousness. Four fixed signs of the zodiac are shown at each one of the four corners—the fixed sign for earth, Taurus; for fire, Leo; for water, Scorpio; and for air, Aquarius.

G: It's interesting that it would come up; I am a Leo.

R: It's interesting also that these signs represent the four evangelists on the portal of the Chartres Cathedral, Matthew, Mark, Luke and John. The four quarters are also perhaps the boundaries of the cosmos. And then we have the symbol of individual integration, the circle, the same as our snake with his tail in his mouth.

G: This is also the symbol for infinity.

R: Exactly, and cosmic consciousness. Key 21 is often regarded as the card of cosmic consciousness along with the card it leads into, the Zero card, The Fool. So you can see how this is a mandala, and there is a cross in the middle where maybe the logos principle of Christ manifests through Mary on the mundane plane. This again in the form of a trinity suggests the way in which your wish is threefold.

G: That's right; I see.

R: And then this card, the FOUR OF RODS, is another beautiful card because to me it represents the quaternary. It is a life in which all of the four Jungian functions are integrated; they are intellect, feeling, sensation and intuition. This is the fully integrated person, the one who has not overlooked any aspect of his being. These four rods make a kind of square in the picture in the same way that there are four evangelists and four fixed signs of the zodiac. Looking at that as what you expect, it looks like a kind of integration of consciousness sought at all levels of being. I think probably that sensation is your inferior function, and that is why it appeared represented by one of the cards in what opposes you. So if you are to achieve full integration, you must celebrate the body *a la* Walt Whitman, as much as the mind and the spirit, because only restricted vision keeps us from seeing that each is divine.

Now we come to the outcome of your wish; the three cards are the THREE OF RODS, the TWO OF RODS, and the ACE OF SWORDS.

G: The ACE OF SWORDS is one of the cards that impressed me with its beauty when I was ordering the deck before our reading. The two white roses at the side of the sword and the sky symbolizing a sky at dawn are new birth.

R: Uh-huh. I am immediately attracted to the relation between the ACE OF SWORDS and the Queen of Swords, in that there is a floral motif combined with the swords, which suggests harmony of the yin and yang principles.

G: It's a very lovely sword, although swords in general have a war-like connotation. But this sword has a certain quality that makes it look more like a resurrecting sword rather than a death-inflicting sword.

R: Yeh. This again relates to what has been said about the Four of Swords, where they were not menacing at all. I think that this is the qualification that you have given to the reading here because very often swords in ordinary Tarot readings are interpreted as representing strife. This is not the case here at all; they are transformed swords, and they are perhaps agents and symbols of a higher Logos principle that descends and pierces the mundane plane, maybe a principle that has split this rose bush in twain, if man can make of his consciousness a receptive rose awaiting the sword of God—again the lightning striking the tower from above. In the same way the tower may be split directly down the middle. These swords have a highly charged value to them in a very positive nature.

Now we must deal with our rods. Whenever these two cards have come up in readings, they have suggested to me a new quest in life. I think that your wish on the mundane plane is going to bring to you a whole new life. Your whole life may change in the ordinary day-to-day material way. This is again another interpretation of The Tower. On the psychological plane, I see a great reliance on intuition because I associate the rods with the intuition function. I think that following your intuition will lead to the realization of your goal. These cards are all directed inwardly; as a matter of fact they are all pointing up in the direction of the elements of the wish. We said before that that is a direction of harmony between unconscious and conscious elements.

G: That's right; they are pointing that way.

R: Very often they say that when the cards are reversed in the outcome it means a reversal for you, a setback; but I have been reading Tarot in a completely unorthodox way, and I am not going to change my style now. (Laughter). So I see you with five rods here, and the sword of inspiration, perhaps the sword of intellect, balancing the five rods. I see great reliance on the intuition. The THREE OF RODS individually suggests turning your back on the whole previous orientation towards life. It may refer to what you said earlier about becoming a bigger wire or a better conductor for the God principle in your own life.

G: Right. To be able to handle the full flow.

R: And then this card, the TWO OF RODS, is very rich; the two rods form a gateway or threshold which the man is passing through, so it is a threshold crisis. He is looking at this globe, which to me suggests a crystal ball.

G: Yes; that is what I thought at first, but then realized. You will see when I tell you what the threefold goal is, that here this is when I had the twofold goal. And then here, I am looking at the world, and the looking at the world is what added one more goal to the two and made it threefold. Here, having found or established the threefold goal, I am now ready to bring the twofold goal to the world.

R: This globe motif or world motif is picked up in the figure of the same size embellishing the left arm. And the lefthand path to

God is the way of intuition and the way of receptivity. I see in the rose and the lily symbols of Christianity. So I think that in describing your goal broadly it was, as I spelled it out in The Tower, to have the God principle fully operative within you, which entails that it function not only on the spiritual level but also as the twofold part of your wish on the psychological level and in your workaday world.

G: That's right, exactly. Here I guess may be the two powers merging . . .

R: . . . East and West, perhaps.

G: Well, no, though maybe in part, maybe more. I see there the mankind, or more the mankind in creation, and God merging together in one.

R: Uh-huh. The two becoming a third.

G: Right—matter and spirit. I see it surrounded by a circle which is the completion that perhaps would be descriptive of it.

R: Right. Well, I think that you have a beautiful spread of cards here; they are all right to the matter.

G: They seem to be really very much in agreement with the threefold goal. Do you want to know the threefold goal?

R: Yes, let's have you talk about it.

G: In Reverend Becker's unfoldment class nine years ago, in which she asked us to write on a piece of paper what our goal was, at that time I put truth and freedom. We are told that we shall know the truth and the truth shall make us free. In a sense it is a twofold thing; they are inseparable. But then in the course of the years, as the Two of Rods shows, I began to experience cosmic consciousness in the sense of a feeling of universal love, even for my so-called enemies. I think this was the God principle operating in my life, which you very definitely described in the reading. I'd experience this feeling oftentimes in the early hours of the morning before getting out of bed when I was still not fully conscious, but yet I was conscious enough of what was happening within to know that it was not a dream state, not a part of the subconscious deposits. This feeling of universal love gradually made me realize that I not only wanted truth and freedom for myself, I wanted to bring about in an accelerated fashion sort of a quantum jump in the process, which I've been impressed is happening in life. This process is a transformation of matter

97

into spirit. The spirit is the union of the principle which is all love and completion, and I realize that the process as it is now is not exactly to my liking. I think one could rationalize and say this is the best of all possible worlds, but this doesn't seem quite right to me because I think most people would agree that there are many changes that could be brought about, not only on the social and political scene, but changes in the basic stuff that life is made of that would bring happiness to every living thing. This obviously is not the case, and what I really look forward to is achieving a quantum jump for all of us. I don't mean just us human beings, but all creation. Later as I went through this line of thinking I realized that it was very prevalent in the mind of Buddha when he said that even the blades of grass will one day be enlightened. This would confirm the theory of the transformation of matter into spirit through evolution. It would be nice if we could take a quantum jump. As I see it, one day maybe I won't want it, but now this is my goal. So the threefold goal is truth, freedom, and the attainment of truth and freedom for all that is. Even a rock, in a sense, has a certain form of consciousness, although very difficult for us to detect.

R: Well, this topic came up just Sunday night when I was giving a reading, because the *Wizard of Oz* became the topic.

G: Do you mean the movie or the book?

R: The movie *and* the books, which I was brought up on and so many American children were brought up on. When I finished the last Oz book as a child, I closed it and began to cry because I realized that the door to this miraculous realm was now closed to me. There were no other books I could read, and I could never go into it again.

Anyhow, we were all watching the movie on television that night, and I started seeing these things and jotting them down inside the flyleaf of a book. I think that there is a very high level of consciousness operating in the *Wizard of Oz,* in that through the four adventurers on the path of life, the yellow brick road, we have a symbolization of the four states of consciousness. The Tin Man represents mineral consciousness, and as such he desires to obtain a heart, or become sentient.

G: Right.

R: And the vegetable consciousness is represented by the Straw

Man; he desires to become reflective, to have a brain. The animal consciousness is the Lion, and he desires an abstraction, courage. Perhaps that abstraction would put him on a human level. And the human being has what goal?

G: No, I'm just familiar with the movie, and I only remember a little. What was the goal?

R: Well, the little girl wants to go home, which I take as a metaphor of the bosom of God, or back to spirit.

G: That's right; that is the feeling that I do have sometimes very strong in the mornings, and I don't just want to go by myself; I want to take the Straw man, the Lion, and the Tin Man with me. I am well aware now that the path leads there, and what I am interested in is finding a quick way or a catalyst to effect the transformation. I don't know if it is possible, but I think that people are not guided by possibility in their aspirations. When Columbus was looking for a path to the Indies, he may not have thought it possible; but the aspiration was so strong that he went on.

R: All the maps said he would just fall off the edge of the world.

G: Right. And here the maps might be saying that Nature makes no jumps, which can also be interpreted that you cannot make quantum jumps in evolution, meaning from matter to spirit. But how do we know unless we keep on trying? Now by trying I mean in the sense of the Baghavad Gita, where it says that the thought that is foremost, at the time of transition, in a mind is the one that determines to where the man gravitates. This perhaps cannot be interpreted literally because a person might die in his sleep and there would be no thought at that time, but I think it is the sum total of what his aspiration has been that determines what he accomplishes or to where he goes. If somebody has just been aiming at trivial things all his life, he probably won't go to a very exalted plane; he might not be able to do a lot in terms of helping others when he passes on because his aspiration was not yet there.

R: The interesting thing about the *Wizard of Oz* is that Dorothy, the little girl, does help her three friends to attain their wishes by performing three acts of compassion. With the Tin Man, she oils him because he is crying, which is a substantiation of the fact that he has a heart, that he is a sentient being now. He has made the quantum jump from mineral to a higher state. With the Straw Man, she helps him down from his cross. With the Lion, she slaps him at a crucial moment, and this enables him to become courageous when he is about to revert to his old cowardly ways again. Of course, the spiral of the golden road is a symbol of the spiritual path in life, leading outward and leading inward simultaneously.

G: That book was read by little children; it's the type of book that adults would not read unless they have become, not childish, but child-like. For instance, you can now appreciate this book. I am sure that somebody who doesn't have the spiritual awareness that you have, might have appreciated it as a child, perceiving the very superficial level of the book. Then of course when they become adults it looks like nonsense and they are not interested at all. So I guess it is one of those books that is read on . . .

R: . . . three levels. And I think I do appreciate it on three levels.

G: I think the insight you have given me on the *Wizard of Oz* is very beautiful and also very useful.

R: The four witches are the four directions, or the four quarters that we talked about before, and the four aspects of consciousness. The monkey people who have the wings are perhaps symbols of men who are, as Nietzsche said of man, "half ape, half angel." On a secondary level, the winged monkeys may be interpreted as unconscious contents, certainly destructive because their animal nature is not yet integrated into the conscious ethical world. They suggest our simian forebears, to which we all too easily often revert. When the travelers were being pursued by these monkey people, it was the dog that escaped and crossed a threshold. The dog's name was Toto, and if you remember your Latin, that means *whole, entire,* or *all.* He is a symbolization through his name of the oneness of the four travelers. He is fully integrated; he is the four into one, and that is why he escapes the monkey people and becomes the means of their downfall. And Dorothy's final act of compassion, throwing water on the burning witch, is equivalent to a baptism which effects the travelers' salvation, since it causes the witch to melt and disappear. Furthermore, the second time the travelers visit the Wizard to again ask that their requests be granted, they do not realize that in the course of their journeys they have already attained what they wanted. This is true of life. Nothing important on the spiritual path is given us; we attain it through our own questing efforts.

The poppy field, in which one goes to sleep while passing through, is representative of slipping into a lower state of consciousness, the sleep of the spiritually unawakened. Sleepers awake! They are all on the golden road, and they are all trying to get to a higher state of consciousness, but there's that poppy field to contend with.

G: It's amazing, the things he got into that book.

R: Yes. And here's another example of "As above, so below." Her companions of the trip all have their counterparts on the physical or mundane plane. That is to say, The Tin Man, the Straw Man, and the Lion are the three farmhands or workmen on her Aunt Em's farm. They are transformed with Dorothy in the Oz world; the same actors portray them. The Wizard of Oz himself has his parallel in the medicine man, Professor Marvel, who has his patent medicines and his little traveling medicine show. So we can find God on the mundane plane as well as the Wizard of the fantastic plane.

G: As Ramakrishna would say, God manifests himself everywhere, from the highest to the lowest.

R: This idea of a quantum jump in the consciousness of humanity generally is what Richard Bucke discusses in his book *Cosmic Consciousness.* He says that the beginning of a cosmic conscious race is now among us, and he cites many cases of this exalted state of mind. Larry Collins of the Abraxas Bookstore told me that he feels that there is a cosmic conscious race now because of mutants; that is, the atomic energy in the atmosphere has created this. It has been a negative force, but it may have effected a positive purpose.

G: Yes, but you see, to bring that about, it is not just a matter of changing humans. All of nature has to change. Few are those who can live without material food. It is true there have been cases of illumined beings or saints or gurus who have attained the state in which they don't need food. They seem to be able to gather the energy by splitting the atom. We all know that when the atom is split the amount of energy that is released can light a city. So I think that this is what these people are doing; they are cracking the atom and getting all the energy they need. Theresa Neumann

101

would never eat, and she lasted many years in perfect health. But I think many people are not there when they think they are.

R: Not where?

G: They are not at the state in which they can do it, but they think they are.

R: Particularly those on macrobiotic diets? (Laughter).

G: Right. I am more inclined to agree with Sri Krishna that the diet, as long as it doesn't produce in us a turmoil—there are certain foods that produce a turmoil or make the mind lose its tranquility or evenness . . .

R: Does he cite any of these foods?

G: I think it depends upon the individual. There are people who can eat chili and have the most peaceful frame of mind afterwards. I eat one onion and I'm going to be aware of my stomach for the next few days!

R: That's true. Richard Alpert tells a story of a guru he met who swallowed all his LSD without losing his tranquility. Then he followed this by chewing up a block of arsenic, which some Indians carry to combat dysentery. The guru ate the man's entire supply for a year. Again, he had no adverse reactions, which suggests that a higher level of consciousness can make the body totally do its bidding.

Well, George, we're running out of tape, and we just have time to put in some quick biographical material about you. You are in the field of physics and electrical engineering.

G: Yes, what I do is "logic design" for electronic calculators.

R: Thank you for letting me read for you.

G: It was my pleasure. As you know, when you first told me about it I was very skeptical, but I think the reading was most accurate.

102

T he following is a reading given by a method known as the Pyramid Spread. After the cards have been shuffled, twenty-one are dealt face down from right to left according to the pattern shown. The first card to be turned over is Key I (card 5 counting from left to right). This card represents the culmination of the past and the beginning of the present. Subsequently cards 1-4 are then turned up. Proceed in this manner by next upturning Key II (card 9) and then the three cards preceeding it (6-8). Reversing of cards not used in this spread. This is Katherine's reading.

R: All right, the first card in a Key position is the SEVEN OF CUPS. Chronologically this card represents a time that is perhaps last week or last year, but it is significant as the end of the past and the beginning of the present. It's rather odd that this card comes up first in the reading, because it is the strangest one in the deck—to me at least—and therefore most open to varied interpretations. Also, whenever an artist drawing the Tarot comes to this particular card, he always exercises the greatest poetic license, so often there are many differences in what is depicted coming out of the cups. Loosely we might say that these things appearing from the cups represent the saying, "As you sow, so shall you

The Pyramid Spread

1. Ten of Cups
2. Six of Cups
3. Four of Swords
4. Two of Swords
5. Seven of Cups (Key I)
6. The Moon
7. Seven of Rods
8. Queen of Swords
9. Eight of Rods (Key II)
10. Seven of Swords
11. Six of Pentacles
12. Four of Cups
13. Judgement (Key III)
14. Wheel of Fortune
15. Strength
16. The Chariot
17. Two of Pentacles (Key IV)
18. Three of Pentacles
19. Eight of Pentacles
20. King of Pentacles
21. Ten of Pentacles (Key V)

reap." In other words, what may come to a person in his own life. Personally I often associate water with the unconscious, and thus here the water is below the rim of the cup—or the level of consciousness. Hence, these things rising out of the bottomless abyss of the unconscious represent to me unconscious contents that are rising to the surface of consciousness. I get suggestions of the conscious mind being overwhelmed by these strange shapes and forms.

K: Well, each one is not particularly strange by itself—except for the diving helmet—is that what it is . . . ?

R: Yes, I think so.

K: . . . all together, though, they have a strange effect.

R: That's a good point. The objects are kind of everyday things. Ah! That head is not so ordinary! This Aquarian Tarot is rather unique because of the realistic depiction of faces, but the man's head coming out of the cup is quite different from other faces in other cards. The eyes and mouth are blurred, and it suggests to me someone who has been underwater a long time—a man drowned, in other words. Maybe we could say that he was the man inside the diver's helmet, but got separated from it and his air supply and drowned.

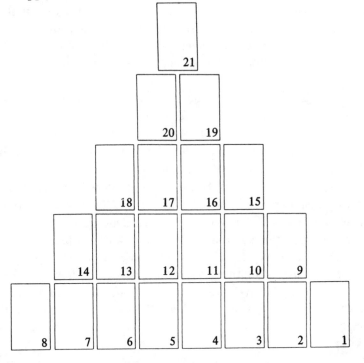

K: The hand at the top puts me in mind of the old adage a drowning man will grasp at straws.

R: Oh, yeh, one can imagine the drowning man's arm extending straight up over his head through the base of the cup above him. What the hand is holding is a rod, one of the four suits in the deck, and they are always drawn flowering in this deck . . . Wow, I've just spotted a pattern in this card! Your line about "grasping at straws" gave me the clue. I normally associate rods with the intuitive function, and astrologically with the air signs. So the top cup represents the surface—where the life-giving air is to be found. You see the air hoses leading up in the other cup?

K: Yes, yes!

R: O.K., the two middle cups represent the head—center of consciousness—and a flower. We can say the "flowering of consciousness." Now! The three cups below represent the watery kingdom of the unconscious. First of all, a rainbow is composed of water. Light shining through it makes for the spectrum effect. Secondly, if we turn over the card, we see another snake, and this one with his tail in his mouth, traditionally a symbol of the uroboros, or the waters of the unconscious.

K: I don't know that word.

R: Well, one meaning is chaos, in the sense of undifferentiated matter. On a human level, it refers to the psychic state of undifferentiated consciousness when one is newly born from the waters of unconsciousness and the ego is as yet unformed.

K: I see.

R: Therefore, we have these historical associations with the snake, and if you'll notice the one sitting in the cup has his eye intently fixed on the contents of the next cup. Which are?

K: It puts me in mind of a bowl of fruit, grapes hanging over the side, an apple. Is that a butterfly on top?

R: Exactly! Now, here is the really extraordinary thing about the pattern. In some other decks I have seen, this is not a bowl of fruit, but a bowl of jewels, with pearls hanging over the side in the same way the grapes are. This is one way in which the artist of this deck has exercized his poetic license. However, if you were as avid a reader of mythology as I am, you would know that there are many, many myths—all the way from ancient Sumerian to recent Irish fairy tales—in which there is an undersea world wherein resides a great treasure—the treasure hard to attain—guarded by a giant serpent. And as my friend the brilliant mythologist Joseph Campbell has so often pointed out, the treasure is not to be taken literally as material wealth. It is itself a symbol of many things. To the child it would be ego consciousness dwelling in the waters of the unconscious. To an enlightened adult, the treasure might suggest spiritual atonement, the spirit at the core of matter. In Jungian psychology, it is the same golden treasure the alchemists sought to refine from base matter—Selfhood. Furthermore, the butterfly has always been a symbol of man's spirit or soul. I once did a short Japanese-style poem on this.

K: Can you recite it?

R: Most of my poetry I can't, but this one is very short.

> Dusting off snow
> And bearing last year's mummified flowers
> We opened our old friend's tomb:
> Out flew a solitary butterfly.

K: Well, I like that.

R: So you see the incredible grouping of the pattern here. Jung would call it synchronicity in that maybe the artist did not know consciously the meaning of the butterfly, yet it was so "right" for him to place it on top of the fruit/treasure. So to sum up, below is the watery domain of the unconscious, the uroboros, while above is the airy world, perhaps paraconsciousness if we can say that intuition, as symbolized by the Rod, is one of man's four functions that most nearly approaches his highest consciousness. And in the middle we have man the mesocosm. Now here's an added thought. I commented on the man's eyes—they aren't open. I said he looked drowned. Suppose we say that he is asleep, or unawakened. The unawakened state is always a metaphor for one who is *spiritually* unawakened, unaware of his high potential consciousness . . . well, we've gone into this card rather profoundly. This is exactly what persons reading this book should do when attempting to give a reading themselves. Give all of the associations you have. "Read into" the card everything you can. Because that will be the meaning of the card for that reader. My meaning is not his, and his is not mine, but it doesn't matter. The worst thing anyone can do is to buy a book of interpretations and then be bound by that. One can be sure then that he does not have his own meaning. Throw away the interpretation books! *You* are the reader! Excuse me for getting away from the reading, but I get worked up when I think of authors trying to force their interpretations on others. It's like the idea of the One Church, the One Faith, and anything else is heresy!

K: I don't blame you. Am I supposed to be seeing things in this card that mean something in my own life? I mean everyone has flowers and a fruit bowl around the house, but, goodness, I hope I don't have any snakes!

R: Not necessarily. In the cards, the whole is often greater than the sum of its parts. For example, in the SEVEN OF CUPS the strange association of all the objects may add up to a psychic effect. Remember I said earlier that usually when I saw this card it suggested to me unconscious contents overwhelming the conscious mind.

K: How do you mean?

R: Well, if I could sum up with one word definitions—hallucination, fantasy, psychism, maybe even madness.

K: Hmmm.

R: How this fits into the pattern of your own life we won't know until we look at the four preceding cards, which represent past factors leading up to the present. So let's turn over the number one card . . . the TEN OF CUPS. This card is nothing but happiness, fulfillment, exchange of feeling with another. I've just noticed that the cups are arranged in such a way that the blank space at the middle of the card is heart-shaped. This suggests an exchange of love vows between the man and the woman gazing intently at one another at the bottom of the card. How would that relate to a marriage in your own life?

K: As soon as I saw the woman I felt myself to be there in the card! That's the way I used to wear my hair about the time I met my husband. I was married at nineteen, and our 45th anniversary will be next May.

R: Well, obviously after 45 years it must be a happy marriage, and everything about this card suggests it. Let's turn over the next card, and that is the SIX OF CUPS. Here we have floral abundance spilling out of the cups, which connotes fertility, so I would say you had many children.

108

K: Five. Of course, they're all grown now.

R: I don't have any further associations with this card, so unless you see something else worthy of comment we'll go on to the next card.

K: Fine.

R: That is the FOUR OF SWORDS. Well . . . there seems to be a knight lying in state. My feelings are that this represents the death of someone close to you, possibly having profound effects upon you.

K: Yes, dear, that would be my husband. He was my knight in shining armour.

R: Well, the indications of the first two cards are that you had a very beautiful and long-lasting love. Forty-five years, did you say?

K: Next May.

R: Then before I comment further on this card, I'd like to look at the next card, which will conclude the pattern of the past. That card is the TWO OF SWORDS . . . All right, the woman is in darkness—blindfolded. And she holds two swords, which suggest to me two *ways* or paths. But being in the dark, she dosen't have a clear vision of which way to take. She's confused, lost. I think, therefore, that what I said a moment ago about the death having a profound effect upon you applies here. In front of the woman are many barriers, one of them sword-like itself, and to me this means obstacles, problems—probably great emotional turbulence. Ah, now the lightbulb comes on over my head. Remember we spent quite a while discussing the Key I card, the SEVEN OF CUPS, and I said that my first reaction to it was unconscious contents dominating the conscious mind, rising up out of the cups and overwhelming consciousness.

K: Yes, you also said madness and hallucination. I didn't want to say anything then, but I must be honest with you. Since my husband's death I've felt many times that I was losing my mind, and that's why I didn't want you to use my name.

(The recorder continued here, but I have chosen to eliminate the material as it was of a personal nature to the woman given the reading. That her grief was great cannot be doubted, and she was having difficulty coping with it. During this interlude we talked about spiritualism, among other things, and I tried to give her reassurances that all consciousness is continuous and eternal).

109

R: Getting back to our layout, these first five cards lead from the past up to the present. There is an unbroken sequence of total happiness until last year—more than 40 years of marital bliss, so in many ways you have more blessings to count than other people who are not as happy together as were you and your husband. Would you agree with me there—that it was total happiness?

K: Totally.

R: I see you are smiling again, and since the tape recorder cannot register smiles, I want to mention it for the sake of our readers, who I am sure empathize with you, and would be as happy as I am to see you smile.

K: You know, dear, that the one thing that made our life together so joyful was doing things together. We shared all our interests. My feelings recently are that nothing is worth doing— matters anymore—because there is no one to share it with.

R: I imagine he would have felt the same way had he survived you.

K: I'm sure.

R: This reminds me of something the great analyst Dr. Viktor Frankl told one of his patients whose wife had died in a concentration camp. The man was totally bereaved at his loss, and Frankl pointed out to him that had the situation been reversed his wife would have had to bear that cross of grief. So if you can put yourself in his place, you see you are the one to bear the grief and your husband has been spared it. You are bearing it in his stead so you must try to be brave. Incidentally, the man's mental outlook improved dramatically after he began to look upon the tragedy in this new light. In other words his life *did* seem to have a new meaning. By bearing the grief, his wife had been spared it.

K: I never thought of it that way, but it does make sense. I think it is true that every cloud has a silver lining. I just haven't been able to see the silver lately. Seems like my only companion is the television, and not a very good one at that. When I start to enjoy doing something, then I lapse into our old way of turning to one another to share what we are thinking, and then I remember, and the blues start all over again.

R: Why don't you take a trip to visit your children. You must have many grandchildren and I'm sure it would cheer you up.

K: Well, I did visit one of my sons right after the funeral, and they all want me to spend some time with them, dear, but there is something that is keeping me in this area for the time being. Should I tell you about that?

R: Let's see what our next Key card is, and then maybe I will be able to tell you. All right, counting ahead four cards, we come to the first card in the second tier of the pyramid. This is Key II, and the card is the EIGHT OF WANDS. What does it look like to you?

K: Just some sticks flying through the air. (Laughter) Are they supposed to mean something to me? Wait a minute, are they wrapped up with paper flowers?

R: Possibly. I think what you said about flying through the air is the impression I always get, and since this suggests activity, I simply interpret this as meaning that you will be very active in the very near future, and this will probably be the cause of dispelling your blues. In other words, you'll fill up your consciousness with new concerns, so that the old pattern of dependency upon relatedness to your husband will be broken. You're nodding, and the machine can't record nods.

K: Yes, I think that's right.

R: O.K., let's go back and, following the same procedure as before, let's see what cards lead up to Key II and all this activity. First, there is THE MOON. Remember this is not the future but the present. We are pretty much in the same time chronologically as we were in the previous card, the SEVEN OF CUPS. Again to review what I said about that card then was that those things rising out of the cups suggested things rising out of the unconscious mind, which can overwhelm the conscious mind, with obsessions or even misery. So although the moon depicted in the card is very beautiful, my associations with it are not with the romantic moon of tin-pan-alley but with our knowledge of it as rather depressing—barren—empty. Also, it has no light of its own, it merely reflects the sun's light. Now, if you'll forgive me for being blunt, I do see a parallel here between this card and your present state of mind in that you don't at present seem to have much light or brightness of your own. You are still reflecting your husband's light. He was the sun in your sky, so to speak, and your personality reflected his. Probably the same applied to him since it was such a happy relationship. Each was given his identity by the other. Each saw himself through the eyes of the other—as lovers are wont to do. But now that your sun has gone out, you are in darkness and lost—the blindfolded woman in the TWO OF SWORDS. So the problem becomes how to become a light unto yourself. Easier said than done, of course, and I don't for one minute want you to feel that I am judging you. Obviously you *would* like to be happy, and I think I see a little more clearly how very deep the relationship was between you and your husband. Darby and Joan come to mind, and also the idea of symbiosis. In effect, you two didn't need other people, probably found that they intruded upon your relationship. This does not apply to your children, naturally, because they enriched your relationship, possibly because unconsciously you saw them as extensions of yourselves. Well, you have been nodding your head quite vigorously, so I shall stop hogging the stage and let you speak.

K: You have put into words many things that I have thought over the years. I don't know how you do it, but that's precisely how I felt about my husband. And that last point—our children part of ourselves . . .

R: Extensions . . .

K: Yes! For a long time my husband called our daughter little Katherine, my name, rather than her own name. And I began doing the same thing, using his name when the boys were born.

R: Well, I don't want to sound like a minister, but you've pretty much got to tell yourself, "Forty-five years my cup runneth over," and recalling the memory of that, be joyous. I'd like to see you turn your thinking around, and if you are going to dwell on the memory of your husband, then make that memory a joyous one—as was your relationship with him when he was alive. I know anyone hearing me say this to you would want to boot me, because obviously you have been very unhappy and telling you this is like telling a man with a broken leg to get up and run, but sometimes all we need is a new insight into our problems, or a new way of looking at ourselves.

K: Well, I'll certainly try, dear. You know you should hang out a shingle because I find this very good advice.

R: Isn't it always easy for us to give advice to others, but so *damn* hard to do something about our troubles ourselves. I want to say here that you are a very brave woman, and I am most glad

112

and grateful that you allowed me to give you a reading with the cards.

K: Thank you. And if you find the rest of it satisfactory to your needs, you have my permission to use it in your book.

R: Well, I thank you.

K: Of course, you won't use my name.

R: Just Katherine, which you said yourself.

K: That will be satisfactory?

R: Absolutely.

K: Fine.

R: Well, let's get on, Katherine, to the next card. We are still in the present, and the next card is the SEVEN OF RODS. Here I see a man in a warding off or defensive pose. He may be menaced, or he may not be, but he is not taking any chances. Again, I associate this with your present state of mind. If you are to find out that people have anything to offer to you, you must be open to them. The man in the picture is not letting anyone inside his little circle, so he will never find out what they have to offer. I don't have any further associations. Do you have any ideas about this card?

K: No, I guess I'm overly suspicious of people at times.

R: It's not just suspicion. Look at the first two cards of your reading, the TEN OF CUPS and the SIX OF CUPS. Notice how the figures are gazing at one another. A closeness is suggested, a rapport, an openness. The man in this card is fending off others. Maybe they will harm him, and maybe they won't. He will never know.

K: I see.

R: Now the next card is the QUEEN OF SWORDS, and a very lovely queen she is. This could be you, engaging in some kind of intellectual activity. Swords suggest the intellectual function to me usually. Umm, do you have a friend or someone with whom you are associated now who is quite brilliant? Oh, also there is a peculiar thing about the hilt of the sword. It is encased in blossoms, feminine symbols, so although this person is somewhat masculine because of the high degree of intellectuality, the feminine side of the individual is not forsaken.

K: That puts me in mind of my therapist. She is a woman doctor, but I don't think she has forgotten that she is a woman.

R: Well, this is an encouraging note. You are actively seeking help for your depression, and that is the first step in overcoming it. Thus I can see this card blending well with the following Key II card, the EIGHT OF RODS, which we discussed previously, and I had said it suggested activity.

I particularly like the idea of women analysts because my own interests are along Jungian lines. He had many brilliant disciples who practiced and wrote fascinating books about their cases. There was Anelia Jaffe, Esther Harding, Yolanda Jacobi, Marie Von Franz, and my absolute favorite is Frances Wickes, particularly the *Inner World of Choice.* In many ways women make better Jungians because he felt the *square* of consciousness was so important—all four functions. And men have great difficulty with intuition and feeling.

K: Would you write down for me after the reading some of the names you mentioned and their books? I really want to read some good books.

R: Absolutely. How long have you been going to this woman?

K: I began last month. I got so blue I thought I was losing my mind. Do you know, dear, I called four doctors before I found one who had room for a new patient. They say the world is going crazy, and if the psychiatrists are that overworked I'm sure it must be true. But the prices they charge. You wouldn't believe it!

R: Well, I particularly like the vibrations of this woman in the card, and I think she will be a great help to you.

K: Oh, I'm sure she has been already!

R: Fine. O.K., let's follow the same procedure we have been using and skip over the next three cards and turn up Key III. Then we'll go back and look at those three cards. Key III is JUDGEMENT.

K: Oh, I don't like the looks of that.

R: Why not?

K: It puts me in mind of the Angel Gabriel blowing his horn, and you know what that means?

R: Umm, well, what does it mean to you?

K: Why death and judgement day. I guess everyone wonders about their death and when it will come. I think I may be looking forward to it in hopes of a reunion with my husband. When is the time of this card?

R: Key III is at the end of the near future and the beginning of a new turn of events ... Well, I think we can say that this is a card of *new* birth, or resurrection. I see this as the result of a transformation that will take place in you during the period of your analysis. You may *die* to your old miserable self, but you will be reborn again to your former joyous self.

K: (laughter) Well, then, I take back what I said about not liking this card.

R: If we go back now and look at the three preceding cards, we should have a better clue as to what this card stands for. O.K., following our activity card, the EIGHT OF RODS, we have the SEVEN OF SWORDS. This suggests to me that you are engaged in quite a bit of intellectual activity at present. Are you studying something?

K: Yes.

R: All right, let's look at the next card to see if it reveals anymore. The SIX OF PENTACLES. Here is a woman intently regarding a scale, and it is not a scale for weighing abstract concepts. No indeed. Pentacles are often connected with monetary or materialistic concerns. I don't know if this represents a complete departure from the previous card or not. Normally the ways of the scholor or student are not the ways of the world. Let me ask you, do your studies have something to do with material or financial matters?

K: How right you are.

R: O.K., I guess you're studying something that will prove to be self-supporting for you.

K: Perhaps.

R: We can hope. Well, this could be economics, business administration, the stock market. I'd just be guessing. But don't tell me yet, because there are quite a few cards to go.

K: You are doing just fine, dear.

R: O.K., next card, FOUR OF CUPS. Here is something being given—a gift on the side of feeling, since it is a cup. I always like to see this card turn up in a reading. It may sound farfetched, but I always associate the figure beneath the tree with Buddha receiving enlightenment beneath the Bo tree. For you in your own life it may mean the gift of a new feeling like love, or ... Wait! The hand offering the cup comes out of a cloud, so it may not be an actual material gift from a flesh and blood person, but something from the astral or archetypal world which results in new feeling *within yourself.* That fits with what I said about the following card, JUDGEMENT, new birth, new consciousness within yourself.

K: I think it has already begun—through the help of my therapist.

R: Excellent! The feeling may begin as a psychological transformation and end up resulting in a spiritual transformation in your life. I believe that the next evolutionary stage in the development of man will be not on the side of physical change primarily, but a general spiritual transformation of *homo sapiens.* As a matter of fact, I gave a sermon at a San Francisco church on that topic just last month.

K: Why, I didn't know you were a minister .

R: I'm not. It was sort of a voluntary thing, but it took me several days to prepare.

K: I'll bet it did.

R: I spoke for forty-five minutes so I can't go into it all now, but one idea I touched on is that complete physical metamorphosis, that is, larva, pupa, and mature form is limited to the simpler organisms in nature and is not found in animals with highly developed nervous systems, so that nature seems to be saying this is as far as you can go physically. Therefore, the next evolutionary stage—mankind's metamorphosis—may be spiritual transformation.

K: That idea is very appealing to me.

R: All right, let's look at Key IV. This card is the TWO OF PENTACLES. Offhand I have no suggestions as to the meaning of this card, so I'll deal with the three preceding cards initially. The first of these is the WHEEL OF FORTUNE. For me this card usually suggests what is known in occultism as the Law of Attraction, which simply means that each of us has a particular rate of vibration which attracts to us similar rates of vibration. If our rate of vibration is at a high frequency, then generally we live so-called fortunate lives, just as a low rate of vibration tends to attract misfortune to us. However, fortune is not to be interpreted solely in a materialistic sense. A man totally at peace with himself is certainly most fortunate even though he may live in near poverty. I think the man in the TWO OF PENTACLES may be attracted to you—not in a romantic sense probably—but he will come into your world and it may prove fortunate for you as a result of raising your rate of vibration. For example, the blues and depression are a low rate, but with a rebirth of consciousness—as in the card JUDGEMENT—then we may say that there will be a change of fortune on the mundane plane. As in the inner world, so too in the outer world. As above, so below.

Following the last card is STRENGTH and again this is not to be interpreted merely in a material/physical way. It is more on the side of fortitude, or inner strength. This strength comes from being in touch with the life principle that I mentioned a moment ago—the Law of Attraction.

Let's look at the next card, unless you have some comments to make. No? All right, the following card is THE CHARIOT. Well, to get four of the Major Arcana in a row gives a lot of power to the reading. The figure in THE CHARIOT suggests to me rulership, mastery, willful control of self, leading to dominion in the mundane plane. Think of your personality as the vehicle for the expression of the inner Self, or the *real* you in the Jungian sense. Also, your personality is also the expression of the cosmic force and divine will behind all the varied expressions of matter. So what one must do in his own life is to consciously use the vehicle so that one's life is a willful expression of the higher cosmic principles.

Frankly, I can't see anything but a complete reversal of your recent depression. In effect you are starting a new life, and these three cards, coming on the heels of JUDGEMENT, the card of rebirth, leads me to speculate that you will come through in grand fashion.

Let me turn over the card at the very top of the pyramid, Key V, because it is the ultimate card in your reading and it should substantiate what I have just said. That card is the TEN OF PENTACLES. This really is fulfillment on the earth plane. There is a lovely gateway resplendant with pentacles as an entry through a wall protecting a distant castle. I'll come back to this card, but I'm still puzzled about the Key IV card, the TWO OF PENTACLES, so by turning over the cards that follow it I may be able to see a pattern. Therefore, those three cards are THREE OF PENTACLES, EIGHT OF PENTACLES, and KING OF

117

PENTACLES. And, as we have said before, the last card in the reading is the TEN OF PENTACLES. Thus, five pentacles in a row! Undoubtedly you're going to wind up a millionairess.

K: (Laughter)

R: I don't recall ever having seen so many pentacles at the end of a reading or all lumped together like this. There is, of course, a danger in becoming so caught up in material concerns that all else is forgotten. But if you'll remember what I said about the four cards JUDGEMENT through THE CHARIOT, I think you'll remember not to put the cart before the horse, or, we might also say, the vehicle-chariot ahead of the means by which we pull it. In other words, the vehicle is carried along by attention to matters of where the next meal comes from and keeping a roof over the head. But this is a means to living in the higher sense of the word; it is not the whole of life!

K: This is intriguing because of certain future plans on which I have already begun working. You mentioned the studying.

R: Right.

K: I have some feelings about the possible identity of the man in the TWO OF PENTACLES.

R: Good. It's not too logical, but I also have a feeling about him. Is he an architect?

K: How did you find that out?

R: (Laughter) Well, it was just a wild hunch, but the card following the TWO OF PENTACLES, the THREE OF PENTACLES made me think of a stained glass window about to be installed, and about Gothic cathedrals and architecture in general. Possibly the man in the card is a craftsman, or he might be an architect. Actually where there is a lumping of one suit together like this in several cards I think they may all be dealing with the same general concern or endeavor in your future. So perhaps I am justified in thinking that the THREE OF PENTACLES modifies the man in the TWO OF PENTACLES. O.K., I also notice that he has waves or an ocean behind him, and he holds two globe-like pentacles, so does this architect live across an ocean? In other words, is his residence or nationality not of the American continent?

K: True. This is my son, I think.

R: Well, then your feelings about the card when you saw it were to associate the man with your son?

K: Not at first, but after you said I was going to be a millionairess and then warned me about overstressing money matters.

R: Is he over-concerned with material things? Is that why what I said made you think of him?

K: No, he isn't. That wasn't the reason. But he lives in London, so you're right completely about the two continents part.

R: Uh, huh . . . Well, I still haven't been able to define what it is you are studying. You did tell me it was concerned with monetary matters, but it wasn't the stock market or economics, so I'm still in the dark about that. You're not studying architecture yourself?

K: No, dear.

R: Are you hoping for some help from your son in a professional capacity in this endeavor, as opposed to financial aid?

K: Yes.

R: Well, I'd say you're probably going to get it, because you see he turns up here in a Key position. That is, after the first three cards in Key positions, SEVEN OF CUPS, EIGHT OF RODS, and JUDGEMENT, the card that represents him is in the fourth Key position. The Key pattern has been a psychologically unsettled mind, Key I; activity towards a goal, Key II; birth of a new consciousness, definitely a more stable, stronger one, Key III; and then he appears as Key IV, so he must play a big part in your future plans.

K: I certainly hope he will.

R: Well, possibly Key V could be representational of you and your son and the realization of a mutually held dream, because that is the feeling I get from Key V, what with the distant castle and all. Obviously it has something to do with building or buildings, because it is an ever-present symbol in the THREE, EIGHT, and TEN OF PENTACLES. You have already said that you hoped he would help you in his professional capacity as an architect, but I don't see the connection between his role of architect and what you are studying . . . Mmm . . . he would be designing houses, correct, in some mutual venture with you?

K: Correct.

R: Well, I really can't visualize you going into the construction business, but it would obviously have to do with remodeling old buildings, or—I suppose—building and selling new buildings.

119

K: That's it, I'm studying for the state examination for real estate brokers.

R: Well, I don't think I would have guessed what you were studying. Where does your son come in?

K: I own 80 acres of property and I want him to be the architect of the homes that would be built there. The property has been in the family for over a hundred years, and it's just beautiful land— lovely trees and gently rolling hills, and I just could not stand by and see it become a site for tract homes. It's not near any large cities, so the land value is not as great as you might think, but for retirement homes, or as a summer resort area, the site would be ideal.

R: Well, I'm in favor of any endeavor that helps to stem the tide of tract homes. How does the song go, "little boxes and they're all built just the same"?

K: What I had in mind was at least one acre for each house— possibly two. And each of my son's designs for the homes would in some way be different.

R: So no two houses would be exactly the same?

K: Precisely.

R: I think it's a marvellous idea. What does he say?

K: He wants to see the land developed in the same way I do, but so far I don't think he believes me to be entirely serious. Anyway, he has said that he must stay with his present firm a year or two more, then perhaps he might take an extended leave of absence to free-lance on his own.

R: Of course, if you don't get a broker's license you can still sell the property as the owner.

K: However I wouldn't have as much control over the development of it that way.

R: Well, they have colleges for this sort of thing, then. I don't recall any courses along this line when I was in college, but, of course, I wasn't too familiar with what was being offered in business administration, since I was a literature major.

K: Yes, I'm going to a school now. There are other problems connected with my idea, such as the fact that the properties must meet certain code requirements. Roads, sewage, water, electricity all must be provided, of course.

R: I didn't know a broker could sell his own property, but when

120

I think about it, I guess there's nothing wrong with it.

K: Well, the owner must make a disclosure to the buyer that he is acting as representative as well as owner.

R: I see . . . With all the Pentacles at the end of the reading, it appears to me that you will be devoting many years of your life to this. I would say that after you develop your own acreage, you may even branch out.

K: The surrounding property is available. That is a possibility, dear.

R: The penultimate card is the KING OF PENTACLES, and you and your son may form a partnership with another man, perhaps represented by the man in this card. Because of the bull behind him, he may turn out to be a Taurus. Do you know of anyone like that now?

K: Taurus, when is that?

R: April 21st to May 20th.

K: No, I don't.

R: And no other partnership has been discussed?

K: No . . . This is still in the air castle stage, I'm afraid. So many things are still to be worked out. Passing the state exam and obtaining the broker's license comes first. Then I won't do any more until my son is free to devote his time to it. But the main concern is my health. As long as I'm depressed, I don't care what happens. But I do feel I'm beginning to see the light at the end of the tunnel.

R: The reading definitely indicates this. With STRENGTH and THE CHARIOT back to back in your future, there is no doubt whatsoever in my mind that you will come through with flying colors.

K: Thank you, dear, I hope so.

R: I just noticed a very interesting vertical pattern in this spread, reading from the bottom up. The third card from the right—on the bottom—was the FOUR OF SWORDS. That represented your husband's death. Immediately above it was the SEVEN OF SWORDS, which I said was intellectual work. Above it was STRENGTH. So the progression vertically reads this way. Your studying for the broker's exam, starting a new life, in other words, helps you to forget your husband's death, and in the future will lead to a new inner strength.

121

K: Yes, I believe it is helping me.

R: O.K., look at the next vertical pattern. The fourth card on the bottom was the TWO OF SWORDS. The woman was lost, in the dark of depression. Above her is the woman weighing some new materialistic possibility, SIX OF PENTACLES. Again this new step in her life, the effort to find a way out of her depression yields the self-control represented by the card above—THE CHARIOT.

K: Yes, yes.

R: Then another similar vertical pattern. From the unconscious dominating the mind—SEVEN OF CUPS—we came to the card above, the FOUR OF CUPS, and I said this was to be a gift of new feeling from within. This change in your psychology, if we again consider the Law of Attraction, brings your son to you to work with you on your project. Perhaps he hasn't been too enthusiastic about the idea of working with you on this because of your present state of mind.

K: I think that's very true.

R: Then finally, we come from the barren MOON, the sixth card on the bottom, which I said described your state of mind in which you were not self-illuminating, but still reflecting your husband's light, we come from the barren MOON to the card of new birth above it, JUDGEMENT, to the THREE OF PENTACLES, which suggests the hard work of your project. All in all, there is a definite change for the better in each one of the four vertical patterns I have mentioned.

Incidentally, for the sake of a person new to Tarot reading, the vertical way I have just read this spread is not part of the normal order; however, whatever pattern a reader may see in a spread is completely valid if the reader feels that it helps to reveal additional insights.

Katherine, I don't have any more to add, and unless you do, I think we can conclude this reading. I am most happy you allowed me to read for you. And please—in the coming months—keep the spread in mind, and remember that your own will can make the good things shown come true a lot faster for you.

K: Thank you, very, very much.

122

123

fter following the usual shuffling, reversing, and cutting procedures, the readee returns the cards to the reader, who then deals from right to left a row of seven cards, representing the readee's past. Above it another row of seven is dealt from right to left. This row signifies the individual's present life. Indicating the future, a third row of seven is dealt from right to left at the top.

R: The date is November 17, 1970, and this is a reading for Arthur. First of all, I'll name the cards of the bottom row, representing your past life. They are STRENGTH (Key 8), THREE OF RODS, TWO OF PENTACLES, SEVEN OF SWORDS, reversed, TEN OF RODS, PAGE OF PENTACLES, and THE DEVIL (Key 15). The cards of the other two rows I shall leave face down until I come to them in the reading.

Our first card, STRENGTH, portrays a man who appears to be the very embodiment of that quality, not only in the physical sense, but also in self-reliance and sense of purpose as well. We may say these were your innate gifts at birth. In the next card, the THREE OF RODS, I think the same theme is continued. The three rods in the picture form a kind of gateway, and I get the impression of a youth crossing a kind of threshold, or *about* to cross a threshold. Did you leave home at a very early age?

A: Moderately early, by the standards of those days. Many kids were working at age twelve.

The Three Sevens

1. Strength
2. Three of Rods
3. Two of Pentacles
4. Seven of Swords (Reversed)
5. Ten of Rods
6. Page of Pentacles
7. The Devil
8. The Wheel of Fortune (Reversed)
9. The Tower (Reversed)
10. Nine of Rods (Reversed)
11. Eight of Swords (Reversed)

R: Well, you didn't actually leave home bodily at age twelve?

A: No, no, I was fifteen.

R: O.K., you see how the figure has his back turned to us, so it suggests to me facing in a new direction, making a new start in life. Since it is only the second card of our reading, the implications are that you started out on your own very early in life.

A: Yes, yes, I agree with that statement.

R: O.K. Now the man in the third card has before him two large pentacles, incidentally the card is the TWO OF PENTACLES, and whenever I see this one the phrase "two different worlds" flashes in my mind. Also, the waves in the background make me think of oceans crossed–travel in general. When you left home at fifteen, did you go to another country to work?

A: Yes, yes, I did. South America. I went to New York, hired on as a swabbie on a tramp to Venezuela. It was the first time I'd even been on a ship. I loved it, didn't get seasick at all, and slept like a baby in a hammock. I thought I'd like to go to sea for my living, but in those days there wasn't much chance for advancement.

R: Well, the next card is reversed, upside down, so you may have had many setbacks initially in connection with your new job. I get the impression of purely menial tasks from the figure carrying the swords in the SEVEN OF SWORDS. It looks like a hard life.

A: It was, believe me!

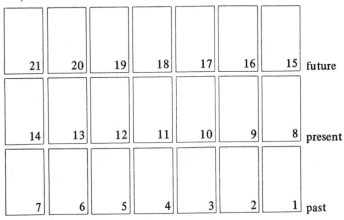

21	20	19	18	17	16	15	future
14	13	12	11	10	9	8	present
7	6	5	4	3	2	1	past

12. Nine of Swords (Reversed)
13. Six of Pentacles
14. Death
15. King of Swords
16. Three of Swords (Reversed)
17. Queen of Cups
18. Page of Cups (Reversed)
19. Temperance
20. Two of Rods
21. The Emperor

125

R: The interesting thing about the TEN OF RODS, the next card, is that it's almost a duplication of the previous card. That is, the accent is on carrying a bundle, or burden—in one case the swords, and here rods. It's rather unusual for two similar looking cards to fall next to one another like this, and I think what it means is that this same kind of life pattern went on for a very long time. You see, ordinarily one card will stand for a certain period in the life, and perhaps for a certain type of activity. This strikes me as unusual because it looks like you were doing the very same thing—some kind of manual labor—for a very long time. Although one point is different, this last card is not reversed, so towards the end of this period you probably began to progress in your work. Well, that is a very inane remark on my part, because there probably isn't any job in which a person wouldn't advance if he had been there quite a few years. Normally I try to be specific when I give a reading, because all kinds of general observations may be made which will fit practically any life or situation, and to me this is just hedging, so whenever I make a remark like that last one, call me up short on it.

A: All right. I think you've been specific so far, except for that remark. The time span is right—twenty years of hard labor with oil companies and construction outfits. At the beginning, when still in my teens, I had to take a lot of crap from the older guys. Had to work longer and harder for less pay. If someone pushed me too far, there'd be a fight, and as the newcomer I'd always get canned. That's why I wasn't getting any place at first. Boy oh boy, I still get mad to this day thinking about some of those guys—they were real bastards! Luckily there was always plenty of work waiting with new outfits. In those days, new labor came by slow steamer. You just didn't pick up a telephone and have men hop on a jet and fly out from the States. Wouldn't trade my experiences for the world though. I wish I was a writer and could get them down on paper. It sure would make a corking good book.

R: I once saw a film called "Wages of Fear" about life in a South American oilfield. There was a big fire and in order to stop it they had to blow it up with nitroglycerine. One guy takes the job of driving a truckload of it over a long bumpy road to the oilfield. It was very exciting.

126

A: Well, if you thought it was exciting as a movie, you should have been in one of those fires. I was in tougher deals than that. Floods, earthquakes—the bunkhouse split right down the middle! When things happen fast like that, you don't have time to be scared. Afterwards you start shakin' all over. My worst time was when we were crossin' a river and the boat hit a stump and sank. I wasn't afraid of drowning because I was a good swimmer. I was afraid of being eaten alive because the river was infested with piranha.

R: Wow! What happened?

A: We all made it except for the old native man, who was steering the boat. He couldn't swim very fast. From shore we lassoed his head and hauled him in. He was a skeleton from the neck down.

R: My god!

A: He probably wasn't in the water more than five minutes. That was all it took them.

R: Have you ever thought of trying to write some of these experiences yourself. I think "True" magazine would be a natural market for you.

A: You know, I only got through the eighth grade in school. Maybe I talk O.K., but I still can't write worth a damn.

R: Something along those career lines might turn up in the future cards.

A: I doubt it.

R: Anyhow let's look at the sixth card, the PAGE OF PENTACLES ... To me this means that you finally made it financially. All the years of hard work eventually paid off. The perseverance and determination present in you from the beginning—STRENGTH, the first card—enabled you to realize your goal. As a matter of fact, the figure of the Page bears a striking resemblance to the man depicted in STRENGTH. The moustache is the same.

A: Let me see that ... Yes, yes, it looks like the same man shown in profile!

R: Right. So tell me a little about how the success eventually came about?

A: Nothing spectacular. After twenty years I realized I'd worked at every job connected with oilfield operation from foreman down to cook. Same applied to the construction business.

Thought of starting my own company, being my own boss for a change. Of course, for a long time it was only a pipe dream—I needed a backer. That kind of thing takes more capital than what I had saved up. But a backer finally did come along and we became partners with the understanding that I run the show. He put up some money and just took profits, which was fine with me because there was more than enough profit for two of us. We were in construction of housing facilities—mostly for Americans and their families who had come down to South America. I suppose you could say I got very rich by the time I was fifty. I married a Spanish girl, and that is one of the best things I've ever done. She is the kind of wife you read about in books.

R: Great. One thing, when you were in South America, you didn't get mixed up in a black magic cult of some kind, did you?

A: Me?! Voodoo? Why do you say that?

R: The next card is THE DEVIL. Let me ask you a few questions here.

A: Sure.

R: Since you returned to the United States . . . well, let me express this idea another way. Notice that the Page in the previous card is holding onto the pentacle and gazing at it very intently. Also, he faces to our right, which in the scheme of the cards is towards the past, correct?

A: Yes, yes, I see that. But what does he have to do with the Devil?

R: Outwardly, probably nothing at all, but inwardly he is enslaved, just as are the two figures in the fire shown in THE DEVIL card. Bondage to materiality—in all its many aspects—is really what that card is all about.

A: The Almighty Buck, you mean.

R: In part, yes . . . I don't know how to phrase this exactly, because your life has been much tougher than mine, but I can see that this may have worked against you in the long run. In other words, you had great perseverance and determination to get what you wanted—realize your goal, but when you achieved it your life kind of stopped because you wanted things to stay just as they were, and this is contrary to the nature of life, which is constant change and development, or the result is stagnation and death.

A: But I didn't have any more dreams I could realize. I was

married to the one girl in all the world I wanted, and I had all the money I could ask for—and more—so wouldn't it have been greedy for me to look for anything more?!

R: Hmmm. I see your point. I have to answer that two ways. You're right in one respect; however, what I'm talking about is change outside the field of materiality. Your life for so long had room for nothing else but making a living, so it cramped you somewhat. This card generally appears when the person has become a prisoner of his own self interests.

Let me sum up these first seven cards. You see, the youthful vision in card two was too narrow of field, and the labor of cards four and five was too long and in some ways dehumanizing in that only one side of human life was fulfilled. Therefore, the desire in card six was to hold on to what had been gained (represented by the pentacle), and to live out the rest of your life desperately grasping the pentacle. This made THE DEVIL spring up. You see what I mean though, Devil is a concrete representation of what is really an abstraction—enslavement to the flesh in that all other considerations of human endeavor are forgotten or forsaken.

A: Well, I never was much of a churchgoer. I think most of them are deluding themselves.

R: Anyway, let's turn over the seven cards dealing with the present. They come up as Key 10, THE WHEEL OF FORTUNE, reversed unfortunately—no pun intended, Key 16, THE TOWER, also reversed, NINE OF RODS, reversed, EIGHT OF SWORDS, reversed, NINE OF SWORDS, reversed, SIX OF PENTACLES (straight up and down!), and Key 13, DEATH. I don't think I've ever seen so many reversals consecutively! Well, beginning with the first card of the series, have you had a setback in fortune?

A: I think so.

R: Don't you know, or would you be giving away your question if you told me any more?

A: Hard to say. It may not be a setback but it *seems* like it at this time.

R: I understand . . . Next, Key 16, THE TOWER. When this card appears, there is generally a force at work in the life—it may *appear* to be working outside of the life—to break down the old ways and patterns so that a new, more dynamic force can restructure the life. It's comparable to the influence of Saturn in the zodiac. Whatever is going on in your life now, even if it seems to be a setback, is fracturing the Devil power, that is, the hold that materiality has had on you.

A: If I'm thinking of the same thing you are, I don't see how that can be true.

R: Well, we haven't as yet turned over the future cards, so wait till I come to those before you judge the reading.

A: Don't get me wrong, everything fits so far, but the situation that has come up, which my question is concerned with, doesn't seem to be connected with my interest in money.

R: O.K., we might come back to that point later. The next card is the NINE OF RODS. Here I get the feeling that you are being hemmed in, a feeling you've never had to cope with before in your life.

A: That's right.

R: I don't know what it could be that causes this, but your mind goes around and around this barrier, looking at all the possibilities, and finds nothing comforting, nothing of solace to reassure you. I see the next two cards as being in the same general vein. Indecision, uncertainty, inability to resolve a crisis, that is what I get from the EIGHT OF SWORDS. It's all these reversals coming one on top of the other. It's been rough on you, very rough. Then this NINE OF SWORDS—despair, misery. You know, I don't think this is a financial setback that is causing the trouble, because your nature is such that you would almost be willing to hop on the next freighter to South America and start all over again.

The next card is upright, and I think here you are weighing the possibilities. The woman sits in front of a scale, and obviously *she* is concerned with money matters, but my eye went right to the scale, and the concept of weighing various factors flashed in my mind. In other words, about this time in your life you are attempting to make a decision that will resolve the suffering from uncertainty depicted in the two previous cards. Incidentally, that upright card I just mentioned is the SIX OF PENTACLES. Have you come to a major decision in your life?

A: Well, I've been putting it off, but I can see it clearly here. I have to do it, that's all.

R: All right, the next card is Key 13, DEATH. You're not thinking of suicide?!

A: (Laughter). No, no.

R: Thank God for that. When you said, "I have to do it," I detected an almost fatalistic tone in your voice . . . This card is not just death *per se*. It can also be a transformation of the individual, so that it seems like a death in that it is so radically different from the previous life. I mentioned something along those lines in connection with THE TOWER.

I just had a flash. Has your worry and uncertainty been about death, either your own or someone close to you?

A: Yes, yes.

R: Hmm. When I looked at the SIX OF PENTACLES I felt it wasn't money you were worrying about, even though I almost always interpret Pentacles as connected with material things. My eye went to the scale and also to the number six, which in astrology is the house of health matters. It's really funny the way I'll get the same card in two different readings, and each time my consciousness will focus on whatever there is in the card that holds a clue.

Let's turn over the cards in the top row standing for the future of your question. First is the KING OF SWORDS. That looks good. Then the THREE OF SWORDS, reversed. Followed by the QUEEN OF CUPS, PAGE OF CUPS, reversed, Key card 14, TEMPERANCE, TWO OF RODS, and finally Key 4, THE EMPEROR.

The KING OF SWORDS could be you facing the future, or it could be someone on whom you rely in this matter, someone of strength. You don't have a son, do you?

A: No, no—no children.

R: Can you think of anyone this can be—someone you have great confidence in?

A: I can, yes.

R: Hmm. Normally I associate the Swords suit with intellect, but I don't think an intellectual solution is what will help to resolve your situation . . . You're looking for this figure in the card to fulfill a role—do something for you that will resolve the problem?

A: Yes, yes.

R: Hmm. Let me look at the rest of the future cards . . . There are a lot of puzzling figures here, pages, queens, emperors—even an angel in TEMPERANCE . . . Well, it's obvious. If you're worried about death, it's a health concern. Is it your heart?!

A: Yes, yes, how did you know?

R: I'm looking at the card the THREE OF SWORDS. The three swords are piercing a heart!

A: (Laughter). I don't know what I'm laughing about, that card looks like the operation I'm worried about!

R: Then the man in the KING OF SWORDS is a doctor—no! not a doctor—a surgeon?

A: Yes, yes, that's who I was thinking of.

R: All right! Now we're getting somewhere. That's what you meant when you said you've been putting if off, but you had to go through with it. The operation?

A: (Laughter). Yeh, I wasn't going to kill myself.

R: Then your question was about how the operation will turn out. Right?

A: Yes, yes, and what the future holds in store afterwards.

R: O.K., let's look at the post-operative card. (Laughter). Here is the beautiful QUEEN OF CUPS . . . I think you are going to take a turn for the nurse.

A: (Chuckle). I think that card represents my wife. Haven't said anything to her about the possibility of an operation because I didn't want to worry her, and I didn't know if I should go through with it.

R: Why not?

A: Well . . . open-heart surgery is dangerous, and there would be a possibility that I would be a burden on my wife if the operation wasn't a success. I wouldn't want that.

R: There may be some complications connected with the operation, because the card is reversed that seems to represent it, the THREE OF SWORDS, with swords or scalpels cutting into the heart. Then we have your wife, bringing to you love—the symbol of the chalice—as well as expert care during the recovery period.

A: There is no finer woman anywhere than my wife. She is Spanish and all I can say is every man should have a Spanish wife. No matter how poor a man may be, they always make their husbands feel like kings.

R: Marvelous. Now let's look at the PAGE OF CUPS. I really

don't know what to think about this card in connection with your life. Maybe this represents self-reflection, long overdue in your life. In other words, for the first time in your life, instead of looking outwardly to the world as a means of fulfilling yourself, you are gazing inwardly.

A: Not sure I understand exactly.

R: Well, we talked before about the hold of materiality on you. It looks like your illness and the operation will be a means to the end of turning your attention within. You may get to know yourself—something you probably never had time for before.

The next card, TEMPERANCE, suggests this also! I think there will be a tempering of your aggressive, outward-seeking personality. You will have to adapt to a new way of life which you can make every bit as rewarding as your early life. The early years fulfilled your adventurous nature, and led to material enrichment. How old are you now?

A: Fifty-nine.

R: Well, the time has certainly come to redirect your thinking inwardly to concerns of the inner world. Just as there was gold to be gained from the outer world, so there is wisdom's gold to be gained from the inner. I think TEMPERANCE shows that you will be adaptable to this change in orientation.

A: Does it look like a full recovery, or will I have to take it kind of easy for the rest of my life?

R: It doesn't look like you will be going back into business as such. I really feel you will find the rewards of getting to know yourself even more enriching than your former active life.

A: Hope so. Just not used to thinking along those lines.

R: The next to the last card is the TWO OF RODS, and to me this means that an entirely new adventure will begin for you; this card is similar to the second card in your reading, but there the young man set out on his own with nothing at all. Here he looks to the future, carrying with him a kind of sun globe, which may be the sun of Selfhood. Ahh, in the last card, the EMPEROR, he holds a similar globe. I believe this symbol traditionally stands for the earth, so what is meant is dominion over the world, but in the case of what I have described in the three previous cards, I think it means *inner* dominion at the end of your life. You *will* become familiar with your inner world, and you will find it just as exciting and challenging as the South America of your youth. (Laughter). I just thought of something in connection with this— the personal unconscious also has piranha infested waters! But the sense of strength and stability which I get from this card suggests that you will be able to swim in these waters safely.

A: You mention strength. Notice how this card is like that card (indicating the first card of the reading, STRENGTH).

R: Yes, the reading has come full circle . . . And we also mention- ed that the second card is like the next to the last card. For the sake of clarification I'll read them. They are the THREE and TWO OF RODS. Although all four cards are similar, the last two are different in one small way, which is nevertheless extremely important to the sense of your reading. Do you see the object which makes them different?

A: The ball?

R: Yes, the globe of dominion which I take to mean that you will achieve psychic integration . . . Hmm. I'm following along this idea of comparing the first card and the twenty-first, *et cetera*, and I notice that while in the third card, the TWO OF PENTACLES, you were learning to master a new world, South America, in TEMPERANCE the same thing applies, although on a different plane of being. But in both cases you are becoming master of two worlds.

This works also for the fourth card and the fourth from the last! See on the bottom row—the past—your total concern is mundane and material. In the SEVEN OF SWORDS it is manual labor represented, but on the top row—the future—inner self- reflection. The PAGE OF CUPS! And so on with the other three cards at the end of the past! In TEN OF RODS, further menial tasks, but its opposite above is the love gift from your wife in the card the QUEEN OF CUPS.

A: That would be about the time I first met her. We did get married before I was successful—before I had my own business.

R: Yes, that comes in the next card of your past, PAGE OF PENTACLES. So where you first have material good fortune, the opposite is again shown in the top row where the THREE OF SWORDS represents the setback of the operation, which as I said before is probably only a temporary physical setback, but its result will be to redirect your energies on a whole new course in

134

life.

Here's something of further interest. In connection with the last card of the past row, THE DEVIL, you remember I said it signified bondage to materiality. Now its opposite number, the first card in the top row, KING OF SWORDS, is also a figure of power, but he is indirectly a means to freeing you. We can infer that with his sword he severs the ties that bind you. In between these two cards there has been the illness and the anxiety over it. In a way, therefore, he cuts you off from the restricting past so that—after your recovery—you can begin a new life. To me it's really enlightening to read your life pattern in this way. There are similarities between each card and its opposite number in the two rows, but the differences of the two rows are really incisive. Can you see it?

A: I can. Naturally I don't see as deeply into the cards as you, but I can see it.

R: Well, may I use your name in the reading?

A: Only one problem.

R: What's that?

A: I haven't told my wife about my heart attack and I haven't told her about the prospect of an operation. Not yet at least. I think she would resent my not confiding in her, particularly if she read about it first in a book written by a stranger.

R: Well, before we started the tape, and when I first mentioned what I wanted to do, you said it would be all right to use your reading in the book.

A: That's still all right, but I didn't think this kind of thing could go so deep.

R: As yet I haven't had what I would regard as a bad reading.

A: That's good. Could we compromise and just use my first name?

R: O.K. You shall be known only as Arthur . . . I want to thank you for letting me read your cards, and if you do have the operation I wish you the speediest of recoveries.

A: Thank you, thank you. Can you jot down the name of this deck of cards so as I can buy them?

R: Be glad to.

T his is a reading for Howard Malby given February 21, 1971. First
of all, Howard, I'll deal seven cards that will stand for the past of
your life . . .

The gifts that you are born with are mostly on the side of
intuition and feeling, which as Jung defined it is a judging/evalua-
tion type of function in the individual. Among the first seven
cards, four are of the Cups suit.

H: I drew a lot of cups, didn't I.

R: Yes, I would expect that in the spread of a psychic or sensitive
person. I'll talk first about the formative years. QUEEN OF
CUPS, the first card, signifies harmony with your unconscious
feminine aspects, which harmony as an heritage should yield
visionary and spiritual qualities in your later life. It's rapport with
the water side of yourself, which the cup symbolizes. The stem of
the cup has a blossom, which suggests flowering of imagination—
creativity. The lightning bolts, or what appear to be lightning
bolts, radiating down from her crown, suggest an interplay
between higher mind and the unconscious. I feel she is wearing a
crown of individuated spirituality. She projects a feeling of
harmony between inner and outer levels of being. So this is kind
of like an heritage card for you at the moment of birth. A very
beautiful beginning.

H: As a matter of heritage it is paralleled by a numerology
analysis I had when I was eighteen years old, so it is no surprise to

The Three Sevens

1. Queen of Cups	12. Seven of Swords
2. Page of Rods	13. Six of Swords
3. Temperance (Reversed)	14. The Empress
4. Two of Cups	15. The High Priestess
5. Nine of Cups	16. Knight of Rods
6. Knight of Cups	17. King of Pentacles
7. Eight of Pentacles	18. The Moon
8. Ten of Rods	19. The Hierophant (Reversed)
9. Ace of Rods	20. The Star
10. The Magician	21. Ace of Cups
11. Ten of Swords	

me. What you said is almost exactly what the analysis put forth.
R: Now the PAGE OF RODS. I've had that come up quite often
before. That signifies the servant of the rod, and the suit Rods I
associate with the Jungian function of intuition. And the head-
gear is over the eyes because the individual relies more on inner
sight than on visual seeing.

Now we come to TEMPERANCE, reversed; this is the only
setback in your formative years. Reversed like this, it suggests
intemperance. In other words, kind of a wild life.
H: (Laughter). No way. Wish it had been. At least I feel that I
followed all of the patterns of the good little boy doing what he's
supposed to do, etc. I suppose my folks would say I didn't, but as
a matter of anything gross, I mean like drinking, smoking, sex,
cars, gambling, running away, or stealing, they just were not in
the picture, if that is what you mean by intemperance.
R: I am off the beam there, obviously, with that card.
H: Could that have to do with an intemperance of inner feelings
relative to the QUEEN OF CUPS? Or an excess of idealism?
R: I suppose an excess of idealism might be regarded as . . .
H: . . . As a form of intemperance?
R: Yes.
H: I think that if there were any one thing that I could dig out of
my consciousness it would be that kind of thing. You know as all
children do in high school and so forth, daydream—I can recall

21	20	19	18	17	16	15	future
14	13	12	11	10	9	8	present
7	6	5	4	3	2	1	past

daydreaming about sort of a knight in shining armor, except up-dated to the western cowboy with the black boots and "heigh-o, Silver," shooting up all the bad guys and helping out all the people who needed help. You know with black hat, black boots, black gun, black horse sort of symbology; idealism about love and the man-woman relationship. As I look back, I think these things were out of focus for my age group and temperament. Now whether that would be considered intemperance—it would be the nearest I could reach for you.

R: I can say this: earlier depictions of this card had shown the figure of the angel pouring water from one cup to another. She has one foot on the land and the other in water, which suggests a rapport with the unconscious and is interpreted often as dynamic exchange or replenishment of the conscious being through an exchange with the waters of the unconscious. With the reversal there on your card, if we again refer back to the history of this particular card, we come up with a suggestion of an imbalance on the side of the unconscious world through fantasy and day-dreaming.

H: Would this also perhaps be introversion?

R: Oh, yes, that's what I'm driving at.

H: Well, all right. I was seriously introverted with an inferiority complex which was overcome by a sheer consciously directed extroversion to compensate. Perhaps I may have overcompen-sated, but of course these things are difficult to evaluate in one-self. Lots of people do this; it's a very common thing. I was in college; I was having trouble in ROTC—well, I wouldn't say trouble; I got the best drill soldier award, but in officer relation-ship one of the army majors came to me one day and said I would never succeed in any military activity and probably in life, if I didn't stop having an inferiority complex that manifested itself in my commands to the men. He said you shape up and get rid of it, that directly and that bluntly. I think he did me a great favor. So maybe that's what it is . . .

R: Yeh. Very often when a card is reversed, it is interpreted by many as a change of the energy of the card from outer directed to inner directed. It's often called a setback on the mundane plane in normal interpretation of the cards. My readings are being done in a way that will probably infuriate occultists in respect to this deck. But the purpose of this book is actually to enable people to read the cards themselves, and they cannot do that if they are hamstrung by having to refer to books of interpretation for each card. They should open up their own psychic sides and see what they see in the cards.

I think the idealism towards love, Howard, is represented by the TWO OF CUPS here. It's one of the most idealistic cards in the deck, and this can be rapport again, if we refer back to things happening mainly on an inner plane for you in the early years. It can refer to a quest for what Reverend Becker used to call the soul mate or the inner beloved. In Jungian terms it is the anima that we search for in the outer world, which is a flesh and blood representation or projection of our own inner archetype. So that can be interpreted that way, or it can mean your first marriage, which may have been too idealistic to survive.

H: No, it was a rebound affair. The idealistic love preceded that. This is, say, up to age 20?

R: It could be.

H: I mean in the whole reading, talking about the heritage?

R: This represents the past—the first seven cards.

H: Well, there was definitely that involved, but not with a marriage.

R: This might be your marriage with Helen, which has survived— how many years now?

Helen: Fifteen.

H: Now, this situation is separate—another entity. We both know this.

R: All right. Why don't you talk about it for the sake of the readers. I know that this is embarrassing . . .

H: No, it's not embarrassing. I was in love with a girl named Martha in high school. We never got together, and my first marriage was on the rebound from that affair—not affair but love; it was not an affair. It was a chaste love, very much idealized, and when I spoke of idealizing, in that case it was perhaps the persistent example of over-idealizing to the extent of having nightmares about not being with her throughout all my adult life. She is dead now. I would say that was a case of idealization relative to love and to a given person.

R: Right. O.K., the next card represents a surfeit of feeling, perhaps, since there are nine cups in the NINE OF CUPS. This may have been the result of what you just talked about, or it is often interpreted as material well-being. This card is kind of the "fat cat card." It may refer to financial success at some time in the past.

H: No. Historically speaking, then, that would refer to feelings, because I have always been told I was too intense. I presume that is what you would classify as over-feeling?

R: Yes—nine cups.

H: Well, I have been told this throughout my entire life. Everybody has asked me why I am so intense.

R: I would think that probably the feeling function is your superior function. I think that has been my superior function too, and I think I compensated for that by overdeveloping the intellectuality. You may have done that also in your life.

H: I think I came to the intellect not by overcompensation, but by social and parental influence. Where I would tend to do things by intuition and feeling, I was trained that education and college were the road that society and man had to follow. If everybody would go to college, this would be a peaceful, wonderful world, and so I should go to college. Of course, I followed this throughout my business career with science, and have only recently recognized that this is a terrible conflict which had to be resolved. The intellect or feelings—one had to dominate. So now I am in the process of getting rid of the domination of the intellect. To what extent the intuition and feelings did affect it in the past is hard to see.

R: The next card, the KNIGHT OF CUPS, suggests someone seeking feeling fulfillment, being a face card of cups, further substantiation of the feeling function within you. It has been very operative in the past.

Then this is the card of hard work, the EIGHT OF PENTACLES. It is pretty much work on the mundane plane, actually. There is a distant goal, of course; we know that from the work you have been doing. But the necessity now is to try to get the work out of the way on the mundane plane, so that you will be able to function on the higher planes by using your feeling function.

Now we are going to go into the present. It is a duplication of the EIGHT OF PENTACLES, the TEN OF RODS, continuation of the hard work.

H: Yes, that has been the picture most intensively since, what would you say, Helen—1959? I wasn't hitting it quite so hard before I went East, was I?

Helen: No.

R: Well, I think the intuition is flowering now. This next card is the ACE OF RODS. The feeling and the intuition are working together in you and have been all along; we haven't yet had a card of intellectuality or strife. I interpret the Swords suit as either the intellectual function or strife, conflict and negativism in the life, and we haven't had a single Swords card come up yet. It has been all smooth sailing for you. Suppose I lay out the next five cards that deal with the present. (*Laying out the cards*).

H: (Laughter). What's that you hadn't seen yet? (More laughter). What were you just saying?

R: The last five cards for the present are THE MAGICIAN, TEN OF SWORDS, SEVEN OF SWORDS, SIX OF SWORDS, and THE EMPRESS.

Now to have the ACE OF RODS and THE MAGICIAN together suggests influence from the astral plane. As the number one card of the Major Arcana, THE MAGICIAN stands for constructive will and powerful initiative, probably coming to him from the infinite plane. Witness the symbol for infinity over his head. He is using his high consciousness to attain dominion over his own four functions and also over the four elements of the earth plane. Witness the four symbols for these on the table before him. But above all he has made himself a channel for forces higher than his own.

H: That's a good description of what I am trying to do now.

R: The next card is the TEN OF SWORDS, and this is definitely a card of hard karma. Evidently there has been some tragedy, strife, or unhappiness present in the life. I would think that if it isn't something that is occurring right now, then it happened within the past year—do you have any associations with this?

H: Yes. There are a lot of things happening and that have happened that would fit that completely, wouldn't you say, Helen?

Helen: Yes, very much so.

H: In fact, the situation got so bad that year before last there was a period of time it was doubtful I would retain my sanity. And it's still going on. So this is very definitely true. Are these three Swords cards sequential??

R: Yes.

H: I think I am over the TEN OF SWORDS experience, and I think probably now I am over to the SIX OF SWORDS experience. How are these cards usually interpreted?

R: The SEVEN OF SWORDS really represents a setback, but not in the nature of the total defeat of the TEN OF SWORDS. The man is trying to recoup his losses; he is trying to make a new start. But there has been a battle, and there has been a lot of suffering. In the SIX OF SWORDS there is a new beginning. He is perhaps fleeing from his difficulties with a journey over water. In part it is fraught with peril; this may be the waters of the unconscious that he is passing over. What this may mean, Howard, with so much in the way of cups and the feeling side—and we also talked about the intemperance and introversion—is that the feeling side may so dominate that it kind of overwhelms the consciousness. So those waters might be the waters of the unconsciousness fraught with peril; the boat with the swords might signify that kind of anxiety and strife. The swords almost seem to pierce right through to the bottom. It's a difficult journey.

Helen: Well, I think you are going through that journey right now.

H: Why don't you talk about it then? Well, yes, I can understand this.

R: The end result I'd just call the love vibration in spiritualist terms. THE EMPRESS, with the symbol for Venus on her shield, and the sheaves of grain, and the symbol for rulership on the earth plane, I think will represent autonomy on the earth plane and a real balance of the feeling side of yourself, which Venus may stand for. She seems to be a balancing card, appearing here at the end of the present, to the Queen of Cups, which was your very first card. They both are rulers, and THE EMPRESS seems to harmonize with the Queen of Cups and to bring you hope and stability after the unhappy experiences represented by the three Swords cards. The Queen of Cups stood for your inherent traits; THE EMPRESS is someone whom you earned, or perhaps qualities that you consciously gained.

142

Summing up the first two rows of your spread, the EIGHT OF PENTACLES and TEN OF RODS back-to-back represent a period of long hard work. Two cards with the same theme like that are pretty unusual; usually one card will stand for an entire theme in the life, or a whole period.

H: That whole period of hard work, when I had my coronary, was part of this whole picture, to give you some background—and I guess this will be helpful for your book. When we went East in 1959, I was with Celanese Corporation, and in the first year we were there we had four weekends that I didn't work on Saturday and sometimes on Sunday, as well as a full week's work. I was traveling all over the country.

Helen: At ten hours a day.

H: This went on and got so bad with Celanese that finally I left that company and went with Chevron back East, and I stayed there. I built a laboratory, and the building of the laboratory was the acme of a dream. In my field as a chemist and as an engineer, my dream along my whole career and learning was to have a laboratory of my own, which I couldn't afford to build and run myself. So then I was given half a million dollars to build anything I wanted, buy anything I needed, and hire all the people that I needed to build and run a laboratory. By the company's own admission I was hired because I knew more about plastics than anyone else in the company. Sure, they had people looking over my shoulder from the standpoint of money management, personnel, and all of these things. But when it came down to what was supposed to be about plastics, especially in the practical application field, not even in their whole Chevron Research Corporation arm did they have anybody that had the level of experience in plastics that I had. So I was given *carte blanche* to do what was needed within the framework that I just mentioned. So I hired and had working for me about forty people—engineers, technicians, machinists, the whole staff. In six years of operations I only had two technicians leave me; all the engineers and everybody else I'd hired stayed right along. And then the company decided to get out of the business, and I was brought out here and given orders to terminate the employment of all the personnel I had hired, break up the laboratory, sell off all the equipment, do away with everything that I had built that was the acme

143

of my scientific career, and move to California. We have been this way ever since, so I think this started with that situation there; the hard work was the buildup for it. So I can see much that is involved here—it makes a very clear story, don't you think, Helen?

Helen: Oh, yes, I can see it.

H: So that was some of the background for the defeated man in the TEN OF SWORDS. Actually what happened was that the defeat finally became sufficient that I had to decide if I should take all of my life apart—business, personal, every aspect of it, and tear it up by the roots and start all over again. I would interpret this as the man defeated—I was defeated. I had come to the acme, and then everything was chopped off. I think perhaps I should add one other thing. Helen, what do you think? Do you want him to know the whole picture for his book?

Helen: Of course. I don't think that he is going to get the true facts unless he does. Go ahead.

H: Oh, all right. The reason I have been hesitating is just for Helen's sake . . .

Helen: Oh, no, no.

H: When I was talking about the TEN OF SWORDS, what I hadn't said was that at this time I had fallen in love with another person; that was a sort of catalyst, and our marriage now is breaking up. All this period of time was a re-evaluation of this situation, so we are in a critical problem area, and that is also part of this. In other words, this defeated man has been defeated in every realm you can name, excepting the spiritual. Is this all right, Helen?

Helen: Oh, of course it is.

H: This whole picture has so much accuracy that it's fantastic. I think for the value of your book, and for your sake, that you should know that this was an intense level of work here in the Eight of Pentacles, Ten of Rods, and The Magician, coming from the background and all the way up to the present and through the present. But all the way along, intuition prompted me to tell my wife in 1966 that the company wasn't going to make the grade and I should leave the company. We went so far as to go to a personnel agency, and they assured us that they could get me a $35,000-a-year job as the vice-president of some small company if

144

we would retain them. We talked about it, and Helen felt that things would probably work out, and I wasn't sure . . .

Helen: I didn't like the man that was talking to us.

H: Anyhow we decided not to do it. The sequence of events then went on not only from that, but from the fact that one small thing after another went wrong within the division of the company and it was broken up. They decided not to be in the plastics business any more. I had to terminate the laboratory that I told you about. They then brought us out here and said they were going to stay in the fiber business. A few months later they terminated for early retirement, whether he liked it or not, my immediate superior and general manager of the division, brought a new man in, and one year later they offered me termination. At the time that they terminated my superior I became aware of the fact that I had fallen in love with another woman who got married and removed herself from availability.

Helen: That was another form of rejection.

H: So within a twelve-month period, there was defeat in every phase, and at that time I became aware of a problem in our marriage that had been smoldering for some time without either of us being aware of it. So I discovered at that time defeat in love, in business, in marriage, and . . .

R: Well, you could name off ten of them, probably, because there are ten swords in the defeated man, or ten nails in his cross.

H: I probably could. And I had been aware that there was something brewing intuitively for three years, but I was unable to put my finger on it and specifically to do anything about it. Now on a spiritual basis, I believe that all of this was in divine order and that this was definitely divine plan because I was supposed to have done something 'way back which I didn't do. Then this is when I decided on my own, without discussing it with Helen, that instead of staying in my field of plastics, where I could go out and get another good-paying job, that I would undertake some kind of new work (pointing to the SEVEN OF SWORDS) that would be compatible with spiritual activity and have a support to it, so that I could do spiritual things without having to lean on any kind of church for its dollar/mundane support. This is where I made the decision to go into chiropractics, to go back to college for three years, six hours a night, five days a week, to become a doctor of chiropracty. I see the SIX OF SWORDS with the boat going over the water to new shores—the risk is to become a chiropractor and to become successful and to find some kind of feminine balance (pointing to THE EMPRESS), love balance, in life. The Empress comes apparently at the end of this. So now I think you see that the story is more accurate than you had any idea on looking at the cards. When you talk about the present connected with the seven swords, I assume you mean a period of about ten years ago extending up to this year.

R: I think that's the way it's shaping up.

I just noticed something about THE MAGICIAN. Do you see all the paraphernalia on the table in front of him—that reminds me of a laboratory. They are symbols for the four elements: earth, air, fire, and water. You know, I started to see this at the time but didn't let it come through; I let the traditional interpretations bind me too much. But when I saw THE MAGICIAN it reminded me of an old-time Magus, but what I wanted to say was alchemist.

H: And I was chief alchemist.

R: Right, absolutely.

H: I could run my own show—in modern language we had oscilloscopes, computer hookups, shared-time computers; all my engineers learned to use it, and I called the shots on the work and the kind of thing that was done. Your interpretation of that card fits exactly.

R: You know the interesting thing, though, is that the previous card, the ACE OF RODS, represents the flowering of some inner principle. The alchemist was always supposedly trying to make gold, but this is what the people who weren't highly evolved thought. The gold that he was making was called in Jungian terms Selfhood, or we might call it the realization of the spiritual self.

H: Well, that was going on throughout all this period—my struggle for self-realization and unfoldment, which culminated with Reverend Becker's class, where I met you. No, I shouldn't say culminated because it is still going on through all of this.

R: But you became very conscious of it at this time, as I did too.

H: Well, I was before. I would sit and meditate through all the years; this started 'way back in 1959. We would hold our own church services, Helen and I, in our study. We would read the

Bible, and then after a few years, after we had read through that, I would read books like the "Betty books," by Stewart Edward White, and other spiritual books. From them I learned a way of meditating, and I would spend a few minutes every day and an hour every Saturday and Sunday morning meditating in an effort to reach unfoldment. So this was going on throughout all of this period.

R: O.K. Let's have a look at the future cards now.

I'm not going to refer to this card, THE HIGH PRIESTESS, as representative of a flesh and blood figure, because when this comes up in a man's reading it is a card of psychic abilities. This veil behind her is the veil between the other world and this world, which has to be rent and opened. I feel that, if nothing else goes right for you on the mundane plane, what will happen is that the sought-for psychic ability will come through with great, great power because this is the card of subconscious psychic receptivity. THE HIGH PRIESTESS suggests impressionability and occult knowledge.

H: This could be both mundane and psychic?

R: It could be, but the Major Arcana are kind of archetypal figures, and I usually refer to them as changes of consciousness on the inner plane. Now it could be, in mundane terms, that you will say to me in a year, "I met this girl who is a medium." Who knows? But I think it is on the side of inner spirituality.

Now the KNIGHT OF RODS comes up; you have the KNIGHT OF CUPS and KNIGHT OF RODS, PAGE OF RODS, and QUEEN OF CUPS. The KNIGHT OF RODS is right above your ACE OF RODS card, so there will be more flowering of the intuition and spiritual powers and further quest for intuitive unfoldment. I think you are going to have a return to success on the mundane plane; the KING OF PENTACLES really means the king of the mundane plane. It's as if the EIGHT OF PENTACLES and TEN OF RODS were the hard work cards to attain the position of the KING OF PENTACLES. I don't know if you are going to have your own laboratory again—but again it is over the laboratory card.

H: (Laughter). Would you believe my own clinic or hospital?

R: No, but you would.

H: As a chiropractor with my own clinic and hospital. Just last

147

week one of the younger fellows at school wanted to know if I cared to join with three or four others interested in the possibility of building a chiropractic hospital, of which there is only one in the country at the present time, in Denver. Whether this comes to fruit or not, or something like it, I have the strong feeling that is the direction all of this is tending toward. I will be in business for myself as a chiropractor, and of course if that is successful then I gather that that is what the KING OF PENTACLES represents.

R: It does. Howard, when the HIGH PRIESTESS came up, I was about to add that along with THE MOON it was the card denoting psychic ability. And now we have THE MOON in your spread. THE MOON is a card of spiritual illumination and is associated with mediumship. As does the moon, a medium utilizes forces and energy other than his own, which he then transmits as a passive channel for the forces of the other plane. In the same way, the moon passively reflects the active light of the sun. So through meditation, the receptive state in which you placed yourself, symbolized by THE HIGH PRIESTESS, now at this future point in your life represented by THE MOON, the spiritual illumination which you showed all your life is forthcoming. THE MOON and THE HIGH PRIESTESS together indicate that the reversal of the past will be turned around. I think that the Swords cards represented lessons that were being driven into you.

H: I'm sure they were.

R: In the TEN OF SWORDS you are actually nailed into the ground by this hard karma. But above this card now is the shining light of THE MOON.

Now the next card is reversed, but I don't think it represents a setback. I am definitely going to relate it to the other reversed card, TEMPERANCE, because we learned a lesson in connection with the interpretation of it, that it represented the introversion. Now we have THE HIEROPHANT, reversed, often called The Pope, and he is seen as a traditional religious figure. Whenever this card comes up for me, I see it as someone who mediates between the two worlds, something like a card of mediation or shamanism. There are the two kingdoms; he holds the keys to the two kingdoms, the mundane plane and the astral, psychic world. For you to have THE HIGH PRIESTESS, THE MOON, and THE HIEROPHANT for your future cards tells me that there definite-

148

ly will be psychic unfoldment and mediumship for you. I think what is going on here is this: in order for you to attain the thing you most want, service of mankind through your psychic gifts, all else that you may hold dear must be sacrificed. It is a very hard lesson; it's almost as if God is saying, "Do you love me enough for all this to be taken from you?"

H: That's right. This is the way I feel about it. I feel that it is distinctly required of me that I have to show this, that I have to give everything away and lose everything that I hold dear, and that He is taking care of it and it is just a matter of lessons. I feel that the requirement in love is to be able to love without expecting anything in return at any time from any person; and I am speaking now very mundanely as well as spiritually. I don't see any difference in kinds of love; I see love as a feeling which asks nothing and receives nothing. I have a very strong intuition that I am supposed to do something very specific and that all of my life has been a lesson and preparation. Purely and simply I have missed the road many times, sure, but nevertheless it's been a matter of lessons for this thing that I am supposed to do which has not yet been revealed to me.

Helen: Well, I think as far as the past and present are concerned, you should know everything, Richard. You see, actually Howard and I are not battling; we aren't fighting.

R: I understand that.

Helen: We aren't fighting at all; but we are talking about divorce, primarily because Howard does want to make a new start in life. I'm still not quite able to accept the whole thing, and he is being patient with me. But he is so far advanced beyond me. It is something I am trying desperately to understand. I feel as though no human being should have a hold on another person, whether it is material or otherwise. I'm trying to let him go; I'm trying to let him do his thing.

H: Anyhow, THE HIEROPHANT could represent this mediumship, the mediator between the two worlds, which I am sure will come to pass.

R: It's so much like the TEMPERANCE card, for which my first and fallacious interpretation was intemperance. Then you said you were doing all the things a good little boy should, and then you called attention to this introversion.

149

H: How would you have interpreted the reversed HIEROPHANT without considering what we learned from the reversed TEMPERANCE?

R: Well, THE HIEROPHANT reveals sacred truth which comes to him from the spiritual plane. Therefore, he is the medium of the message. Since the card is reversed, it may mean that you are going to have a difficult mediumship, although I really feel that the reversal of the card indicates inner direction rather than outer. There is always a chance that forces that you wouldn't want working within you might try to take over. There is that danger whenever anyone goes into that field.

H: That's just a point to be aware of.

R: In that sense we could talk about a setback or reversal in connection with that particular card.

The next card may qualify that somewhat. This is THE STAR, and I just was dealing with this card yesterday. It is in Jungian dream interpretations, in dreams of evolved persons, representative of kind of becoming a light unto oneself, becoming kind of a sun consciousness. It is a symbol for the Christ spirit or the inner spiritual light coming out from within, shining in your own life, the fully individuated person of higher consciousness.

H: Would that be the perception of oneself being a part of God?

R: Oh yes. There would be no sense of a separation. Here you would be doing that divine will in the form of THE HIEROPHANT, whether it be through healing or mediumistic service. I have a friend, Jack Schwarz, who resembles you somewhat; he's pretty evolved. He worked as a masseur out of his own home; he charged only for the massage, but actually he was giving healing vibrations.

H: This is what I have hopes of when I do my chiropracty, that when I go through the motions of the chiropracty I will develop the healing capability to help them.

R: And I can see also, Howard, with the intuition so fully in flower and with your great gifts on the side of the feeling function, you will be able to feel or intuit what the real cause of the illness is. You may discover it to be a psychosomatic thing; and when you have done that, you can begin to treat it on another plane than just the physical. The healing will take place on all levels of the personality. That is a good place to end the life, of

150

course, but this reading ends up on a setback of some kind because I can tell from the back of the card that the card is reversed. Oh, no, no, this couldn't be a setback. (Laughter). I just have to laugh at this, Howard, because . . .

H: What does it mean?

R: This is the ACE OF CUPS. I said it's a setback because it's reversed, but it's turned back into the unconscious or the spirit world, personified by the water. The lotus on top represents the Eastern orientation—the jewel of unfoldment, the jewel of the spirit, is in the lotus. The card stands for the Holy Grail, or the Silver Chalice; as such it represents an abundance of spiritual enrichment and inspiration, divine love.

H: What is the meaning of it reversed, in the sense of a setback? I don't understand how that card can be a setback.

R: It isn't. That is why I said, oh, no, it's not. It is a change—a going within, inner orientation and fulfillment rather than on the external mundane plane.

H: What if it were the other way around?

R: It could then represent, on the mundane plane, a success, happiness, maybe sexual love. I think this is going to be pretty much a solitary journey for you for the rest of your life. You will hope for relatedness on a close human level; I don't think this is an impossibility, even though you are in such a rarified atmosphere here. As Helen said, you are so far advanced that it is going to be difficult to find anyone to relate to you on that level. We can talk on this card extensively. On a psychological level, the sun shining out of the cup is the sun of Selfhood, the same thing that is represented by the light of the star in THE STAR. It means a fully individuated man with all four functions mutually supportive and operative. On a spiritual level, it is of course Christ consciousness, cosmic consciousness, the inner spiritual light shining out as a beacon to the world. On the mundane plane or day-to-day life, it would be human love, earthly happiness.

H: Oh, I see what you are saying—that card really can't be negative because any way you look at it it's got to be right. It is either love and a personal relationship of a higher level, or it is God consciousness and spirituality turned within. These two things are really the same thing; it doesn't matter whether they permeate the entity.

151

R: Uh-huh, right. There is an incredible amount of psychic and spiritual power manifested in your last seven cards. The lowest level of card there is the KNIGHT OF RODS. We said that that was a continuance of the theme of the flowering of your intuition, the service of your own intuition. We had the KNIGHT OF CUPS earlier; there you were serving feeling in the earlier part of your life. THE HIGH PRIESTESS and THE HIEROPHANT are cards of psychic ability, and so is THE MOON. I could show you the other cards of the twenty-two Major Arcana, and you would see that these are the three most psychic cards.

Helen: Hmmm!

H: Hmmm!

R: And then THE STAR and the ACE OF CUPS have the same theme—this shining forth of the inner light.

H: Would this be perhaps that which I am supposed to do, that all the rest is a lesson for it?

R: Well, I think that all the rest is what you are supposed to do, and it is going to be done. I don't know what orders the cards—I say psycho-kinesis, but again we talk about divine order, and I would say that row of cards is divinely ordered.

Helen: That's interesting.

H: Yes, it's amazing.

Helen: It's interesting to see the change from the present problems to the higher level of the future.

H: And all of these swords right below it; and this man with all the ten swords in his back.

Helen: I can think of ten. (General laughter).

H: Fantastic.

Helen: You see, Richard, actually with Howard going through all this, it has affected me tremendously because Howard and I have been very close. So by his climbing his mountain of transfiguration . . .

H: . . . Dark Night of Soul.

Helen: . . . I've gone through this with him also. Sometimes we both look at one another and wonder how we can stay sane. Howard and I have always had fantastic rapport in feeling. Just one night last week I was very down, and Howard sensed this 400 miles away in Los Angeles and called on the phone. We've had this rapport for . . .

152

H: . . . Years!

Helen: . . . I can be away from him, but he always knows my feelings and will call if there's anything wrong. That's why it's difficult for me now because we do have this fantastic rapport that many other married couples don't have.

H: And yet with all that going for us, here with these three cards, the TEN OF SWORDS, SEVEN OF SWORDS, and SIX OF SWORDS, it became necessary to sacrifice everything.

R: It reminds me not only of Job and the way his faith was tried, but also Abraham had to sacrifice his son.

H: Yes, at least he had to be willing to.

Fundamentally it is the lack of perception of our Godhood within that causes us to see it as an unhappiness at the time it's happening. If we did so fully understand ourselves and our unity with God and with each other, there would at that moment be no unhappiness within us, or that which we call sacrifice.

R: You may remember my speaking about *The Hero With a Thousand Faces,* by Joseph Campbell, which is my bible. In this book he says, "Every inability to deal with a life situation must in the end be laid to a restriction of consciousness." If we could see the situation with opened eyes at the time, then . . .

Helen: Those are the thorns.

H: It's a thorn because we don't see clearly or perceive clearly.

Helen: Are these all of the cards?

H: Yes, that is the end of the reading.

R: Yes, past, present, future.

Helen: Isn't it interesting that it ends up with the Holy Grail. From the way you interpreted the cards, the worst seems over.

R: Yes, Howard says that he is here at the SIX OF SWORDS now, and this represents a journey to a new shore.

H: Well, I assume I'm there.

Helen: I would say the SIX OF SWORDS myself.

R: O.K. Howard, do you have any further comments?

H: Well, I think the reading and the sequence of the cards and the explanation of them is absolutely fantastic in its reproduction of the past and present. Naturally I hope that the future turns out as spiritual and as fulfilling as is predicted in the cards representing the future.

R: Amen, brother.

153

One of the shorter arrangements of cards is the Yes-No Spread. After shuffling and reversing some of the cards during the cutting process, deal five or seven cards horizontally from right to left. The middle card will have a value of two, the others each count as one. The combination of upright and reversed cards count as yes and no in answer to the question posed by the readee. Furthermore, the sequence of the cards, and the story that sequence tells, may prove to be as relevant in determining the yes or no answer as the number of upright or reversed cards.

R: For this reading, utilizing the method known as the Yes-No Spread, we desire the answer to a specific question which has already been revealed to the reader. That question is: will there soon be a new female in the life of the readee Larry Collins? In this case, we are shortening the reading to five cards instead of seven.

First of all, our spread of five horizontal cards includes no inverted cards, so we have six yes answers, the middle card counting as two. Reading from right to left, the first card is the TEN OF CUPS, so in effect we may say that "your cup runneth over." Really, Larry, the resolution of your question couldn't begin with a more auspicious card, unless perhaps the Ace of Cups. The suit Cups is associated with the feeling function, as you have heard me say before. Now since your question falls into the category of

The Yes-No Spread

what they called in Victorian times "an affair of the heart," the interpretation of so many cups would have to be total fulfillment of the emotional side of your nature. The rainbow is universally a symbol of happiness, joy, and attainment of whatever the heart desires. The rainbow comes after the storm or rain, and in your case you mentioned the tempestuous and negative emotional relationship you were just undergoing with a rather unstable girl.

L: Right. Well, suppose the following cards contradict the happy outcome you see.

R: They can't, because none of them is reversed. They can only qualify the success as to the character of the girl who will come into your life, and the nature of your relationship with her.

L: I see.

R: O.K., the next card is the NINE OF CUPS, and if we look at the expression on the face of the man in this card it is one of satisfaction and contentment, so we have further substantiation of the happiness and fulfillment which will be yours when this girl does come into your life.

L: Far out!

R: Now the middle card of the spread is the PAGE OF RODS. I associated the suit Rods with the intuitive function, and since this figure is a Page, perhaps we can say that he represents a *servant* of intuition. Now during a day a great number of young ladies come in and out the door of your bookstore, but I would say you're

1. Ten of Cups
2. Nine of Cups
3. Page of Rods
4. The World
5. Six of Rods

going to know it when she comes in because of your strong intuitive function. Would you say it is probably the strongest developed of the four functions in your psyche?

L: Yeh, probably it is.

R: Notice that the hat covers the figure's eyes, as if to tell us that he does not rely on what his eyes see—the sensing function—as much as on his *inner* vision—the intuition function.

L: Yes, that's a very good point.

R: Now for the cards of the future. First is the 21st Key card, THE WORLD. The associations I have with this card are very similar to those of the TEN and NINE OF CUPS, happiness, attainment, and, since we have a full circle or cycle surrounding the woman in the card, completion is also suggested.

Also, this is the last card of the Major Arcana, and probably also the last card in the deck, so I feel that self-completion is stressed in the divinatory meaning. She is depicted as one of the Graces or Muses of mythology, as if drawn by Rossetti, so I get strong feelings of self-completion on the side of relatedness to your own anima.

L: My feminine ideal inside?

R: Exactly. So interpreting this figure at the center of the wheel in a psychic or psychological way, we have a sense of wholeness and balancing within you, an integration with the yin or feminine elements of your psyche.

L: That really relates to what I'm looking for.

R: I see. . . . I just saw another parallel here. The Latin name for soul is *anima,* and this card is titled THE WORLD, so what comes to mind is the Biblical phrase, "What profit a man if he gain the whole world and lose his own soul?" Therefore, a word of warning in connection with the seductive anima figure at the center of the circle. She supports the wheel, keeps it turning, and in that sense she is the Indian goddess of illusion, Maya. It may turn out that the girl bears an anima projection from your own unconscious. Such relationships are more intense than the ordinary, because one holds before him a mirror of the idealized woman within. Generally in such a relationship one does not see the flesh and blood woman as she really is. One has thrown the mantle of the goddess over her, so she has taken on the *mana,* or divine power of the goddess. So in that sense there is a parallel to Maya, the goddess of illusion, because it is this polarity of masculine and feminine, yang and yin, positive and negative, which keeps turning the dynamo of life and the world. But if the projected anima is too illusionary or destructive, then the real world may be lost to the man. In which case we can then rephrase the Biblical line to read, "What profit a man if he gain his own anima, yet lose the whole world?"

L: Right, right. I understand. . . . Aren't those the four fixed signs of the zodiac at the corners of THE WORLD?

R: Yes, Taurus, Leo, Scorpio, and Aquarius. And they are also symbols of the four apostles.

L: I think you've gone into what I'm seeking very deeply. In other words, it is someone who will help to draw out the feminine principle within me.

R: Excellent. . . . Now the last card, the SIX OF RODS. The rider holds a laurel wreath on high, and again this is a reiteration of the persistent theme throughout your reading of triumph, success, happiness in the matter. Also, the wreath is a symbol associated with the muse, the goddess of inspiration, and this concept again leads us back to the ideal woman within the unconscious. It may not be that you will attain the relationship that you desire with a flesh and blood, mundane type of girl. It may be the inner relationship to the anima. This will result in some kind of gain or victory for you—as depicted in the card. The victory may be on the side of feeling and an opening up of your intuitive power. The muse is always inspirational; therefore the victory may be a personal conquering of those elements within yourself that you desire to master. There will be a gain on the side of feeling and inspiration.

L: I always have thought that in searching for the perfect woman, as in Hermann Hesse's *Narcissus und Goldmund,* that the perfect woman is a part of every woman, so that actually you never find it in what you are looking for outside yourself, but you find it inside yourself. If you can find it first inside yourself, then it is easier to find it in anyone outside yourself.

R: Exactly, exactly!

L: Then you don't have to worry about who is coming into your life and who isn't. (Laughter)

R: Only whether or not *you* are there!

157

his is a reading for Carol Krueger; the layout of the cards is the Yes-No Spread. Today's date is February 28, 1971, and I shall allow Carol to state the question to which she desires her answer.

C: I would like to know if I should go back to school this summer in Indiana to get an A.B. degree in zoology.

R: The past is represented by the ACE OF CUPS and the KNIGHT OF RODS, and the card that leads into the present is THE DEVIL; the immediate present is represented by the KNIGHT OF PENTACLES. The card that leads into the future out of the present is indicated by JUDGEMENT, reversed, as is the KNIGHT OF PENTACLES; and the future is represented by the TWO OF PENTACLES and DEATH, reversed.

The first thing that comes to mind is that the background of the question is concerned with love—the ACE OF CUPS is present—love and a beautiful state of consciousness. This suggests that there is a love concern that would make you wonder if you should go back to Indiana. So I'll let you talk about that. Incidentally, the going back to school involves leaving this area, so it suggests that there is someone in this area that you would not want to leave.

C: That's right. It's the guy I'm living with; I have been with him for a long time, and I met him right after I quit school before. In my own mind I don't think it's so much this one person; I think it's the whole idea—going to school and being a full-time student,

The Yes-No Spread

or being in love with someone. Being in love is a full-time job; it's a total preoccupation, at least for me. But school, or the idea of having a career, is also a full-time preoccupation.

R: And the situation now is that he is not able to support you so that you can go to school full-time.

C: Right, and he wouldn't want to either; he would be jealous of the school because I would throw myself into it so heavily. I'm doing that with the music school now, and he is jealous of the music.

R: What are you studying?

C: I am studying music in general, and I play the piano. So I go to school and work during the day, and practice piano in the evenings. I don't know—maybe there would be someone sometime who wouldn't resent that in me, but as it is now I think I'd have to choose between the person and the school.

R: The next card is the KNIGHT OF RODS. Because of the winged headdress, I get the impression of Mercury. And Mercury of course is a messenger in the zodiac, and it suggests that this whole question came up because of the recent arrival of some sort of message. Is that correct?

C: Yes. It was a letter that I got. I knew that I was going to get some kind of information because I wrote away to the school. But it was really weird that when the letter came it just changed my whole outlook, more than just receiving some kind of infor-

1. Ace of Cups
2. Knight of Rods
3. The Devil
4. Knight of Pentacles (Reversed)
5. Judgement (Reversed)
6. Two of Pentacles
7. Death (Reversed)

mation that I'd sent away for would do. I couldn't think about anything else for the next two days.

R: The next card is THE DEVIL. This occurred in the Yes-No Spread of Karen Allen, and it was kind of the key to her solution. My remarks were at that time, I believe, "Whatever your decision is in the matter, it should not be dictated by material considerations at all or material expediency," because THE DEVIL is often called bondage to materiality. I note also that the two lovers are shown in the Devil's thrall in the fire, and obviously they got themselves into that situation because one or the other of them was excessively preoccupied with the things of the mundane plane to the detriment of the evolvement of the individual. In other words, psychological and spiritual growth must also be taken into account, and if you are going into a field simply for money and status, you are doing yourself a disservice.

C: There again there are two sides of it because if I start going back to school now, I'm going to be poor for a lot longer. It would be a big financial loss for me to leave this summer because I would have to leave behind a lot of things and would have to go back to living in just a room. I would have to sell my piano. But then, when I got out of school, it is likely that I would be able to get a much better job than I could now.

R: In music or zoology?

C: Either. I could be a teacher.

R: The present of the matter shows that it is pretty much a materialistic concern. Oh—here's something that shows the relationship to the previous card. Our card at present is the KNIGHT OF PENTACLES, reversed, which indicates two noes because the middle card counts double. Knight suggests questing and looking for the answer, and Pentacles suggests material solution. Essentially yours is a love for which you would like to find the material solution so that it would be a tenable love, a position for you that would not be in jeopardy, really.

C: What do you mean by that?

R: Well, it would secure the love if it were possible for it to seemingly have some kind of future.

C: Oh, yeh, sure.

R: The way you talk about it now, it doesn't seem to have a future.

C: Right. There's another thing about that—I have dreams of getting married some day; I'd like to get married. This is partly because I'd like to be able to explain what is happening to my parents so that they can understand what I'm doing—I want to come back into the fold of the family. Bob doesn't believe in marriage, but I do. I want to be able to see some kind of future in our relationship, and I just can't right now because of this.

R: O.K. There are two points connected with this card. On his sleeve the Knight wears the pentacle, symbolic of his suit, and since the card is inverted it makes an inverted pentagram, which is what we have on the forehead of the Devil. The pentagram is the symbol for man, with the one point at the top, the two arms at the sides, and the two feet. The five points also stand for the five senses, and it is through the five senses that man measures everything. So symbolized by a five-pointed star, man is the microcosm of the universe. In black magic ritual, this symbol of man is turned upside down, which suggests a subservience of the mind or will to the lower senses, to the higher will of the Devil or to the Devil's bidding as such. In other words, man gives up his own will to become a servant, in effect, of the lower forces. The KNIGHT OF PENTACLES here is in a reversed position; he is looking to the next card, which is JUDGEMENT, and JUDGEMENT is associated with what other people think. This involves of course the judgement of the family, the judgement of the peer group, and maybe the judgement of society generally, in that you recognize that you have talents along two lines, zoology and music. This card, reversed, indicating negative judgement, shows a fear on your part of disapproval from family and society.

C: Oh, yes, that is really strong in me. We were talking about Leos, about when I was little and realized that people didn't like me—I think then I developed a really strong fear of having people think I'm not doing the right thing. On the one hand it is a fear of my parents' disappointment in my not finishing college, and on the other hand of having my peer group now think that I'm hiding in books and that I'm placing myself in—not a hidden world, but . . .

R: Ivory tower?

C: Yeh, sure. A university is very strange community. The people that you have around are people that are nice to have around.

161

R: (Laughter). It used to be that way before the riots started!

C: Well, yes, that's true. But you can keep away from that.

R: But how does the poor professor keep away from that? (Laughter).

Since JUDGEMENT, reversed, shows fear of disapproval, obviously this provides one of the negative answers to the background of the question, which is concerned with love and with the whole fulfillment of your feeling and emotional side, represented by the ACE OF CUPS, which is a very beautiful force within you. Yet the talent side is also there, and you are really on the horns of a dilemma.

C: Mm-hmmm.

R: I think the next card indicates a kind of solution—the next two cards really. The TWO OF PENTACLES is right side up, and we have the two pentagrams that are now right side up like two globes, suggesting two different worlds to me. I think that our reading has been about two different worlds.

C: That's really true.

R: The ivory tower world, perhaps, and the day-to-day nitty-gritty of a love relationship. I think what will happen in you involves a change of consciousness, shown by the next card, DEATH. It will be in the nature of an interchange because it is inverted, directed back towards the side of the unconscious. Your change in consciousness or transformation will enable you to do something that I spoke of just a few moments ago, that at the level of the problem there is no solution. If you get off the level of the problem, if you become a different person, then the problem isn't there anymore.

C: Oh, yeh. I thought of that myself. I thought that my purpose in life is to advance spiritually—I guess it is for everybody, but . . .

R: You really feel that yourself?

C: Yes, oh, yes. I feel like that is what I am really supposed to be doing. My question right here is what should I be doing on the side—should I be running a household or should I be a professor. I guess it will answer itself if I just keep going on.

R: Yes, this indicates that if there is a change in consciousness, then we reappraise the entire reading and start looking backwards. The TWO OF PENTACLES suggests an exchange between the two worlds. It suggests that there is the possibility of having a career and also having the family life, being a wife, and having a love relationship. What has been indicated so far is that the one with whom you are presently involved is not attuned to this. He may change his consciousness in time, grow enough to permit you to fully realize your talents outside of the immediate relationship with him. Or you may change yourself in such a way that it is possible for you to continue the relationship even as he is and to pursue the career. Or, as a third possibility, you may abandon the relationship with him because of the oppressions and may at some time in the future find someone else who understands that your own individuality is best manifested by your doing something with the talents that you have. Then there would be an exchange between the two worlds as shown in the TWO OF PENTACLES. As far as an answer to this, we can see that we remain on the horns of the dilemma; there are four yeses and four noes, which . . .

C: Which I dreamed about last night.

R: Oh, you dreamed that the spread was perfectly balanced?

C: Yes. I didn't see the cards like that—they were pieces of toast, and I didn't see exactly seven pieces of toast, but they came up yes, then no, then yes, then no . . .

R: Well, this is a reflection, of course, of your own indecision in your unconscious. As I have said before, the shuffling process and cutting process is the method by which the unconscious conveys its wishes to the deck of cards so that they can be read by the reader. In all the readings I have given, there were clear answers, so the person was probably decided on the unconscious level, and the conscious mind wasn't convinced yet. This indicates that you really should not do anything now. Usually making no decision is a negative thing, but this spread, with the middle cards being THE DEVIL, the KNIGHT OF PENTACLES, and JUDGEMENT reversed, indicates that the decision would be based on expediency of materiality and judgement by society. These would not be your own decisions at all.

C: I just thought of something else. If I go back, my father will pay for it.

R: That is shown by the KNIGHT OF PENTACLES. He has the power of the purse there.

C: I think if I wait another year, I could not really ask him to give me the money to do it. But if I wanted to do it, I'd find a way.

R: Well, this spread indicates that you shouldn't do anything. You will continue to find yourself and to keep your ultimate goal of spiritual development in mind, and keep maturing on a day-to-day basis so that as you evolve you will leave the problem behind you. You may leave behind you the others who would continue to make it a problem for you, but your own consciousness will grow to the point where the answer to the question will not really be needed.

C: Yes. If the time comes when I am supposed to leave Bob behind, if the time really comes it won't be such a big pain because it will be time.

R: You will have changed. Obviously it is holding you back now. Your past needs at any rate are on the level of requited love . . .

C: Oh, yeh!

R: . . . shown by the ACE OF CUPS.

C: Could this be interpreted not only as a person, but as the concept of having to love someone, and that I may grow out of having to have someone around all the time?

R: Yes, it doesn't represent a person as much as this need of yours for fulfillment. This is a beautiful card, and it suggests a fulfillment through love. The card at the very end of the reading, although inverted, I don't look upon as representing mundane death or a literal death. I look upon it as interchange because the card is inner-directed, and that would be a transformation of consciousness that would perhaps free you of those who would be too possessive of you in love and who would be too demanding. When you are evolved to that higher level of consciousness, then you will attract those who are on a higher level and can love without possessiveness. So those two cards at the beginning and the end are very highly charged.

To sum up, the second card suggests the message that arrived and offered you the opportunity to return to school . . .

C: Yes, with the flower on top of the rod . . .

R: Good news. And this good news immediately suggested the separation of the lovers, shown with their backs turned to each other in THE DEVIL card. The role of the father is suggested in the KNIGHT OF PENTACLES, an imposing figure who also bears

164

on his sleeve the pentagram of man turned upside down in bondage to material concerns. In part, you would be pursuing this to please the father, and this is like putting your head upside down and putting your conscious needs and will second. Those are topsy-turvy for you, as shown by the two reversed pentacles.

C: Could the pentacle mean, not only financial gain, but status? I think I am more after status than money, when I think about my bad points. Could that be considered material things?

R: Yes. That would be a concern of the mundane plane; it would be a material concern definitely.

C: It's just satisfying my ego.

R: If you want to go into it in regard to Leos—they desire approbation from others more than any other sign of the zodiac. In most cases they are very worthwhile people, and they are very well qualified to lead and to have status in the society. They know this about themselves, so it's very difficult for them to get off an ego trip, and to be self-effacing, and to pursue an inner orientation and a spiritual orientation. I would say generally Leos aren't very spiritual because whenever you go on the yellow brick road, spiritual path of life, you usually do it alone as a quest. Therefore, you don't have any followers to go along and give you reassurance in what you are doing. It's a covenant between yourself and God. The card JUDGEMENT is also connected with resurrection and new change of consciousness, so we can look at it on two planes. On the mundane plane, negative judgements. The reversal of the card is one of the things that you are concerned with here. And on the higher level, the spiritual level, being turned upside down suggests being turned towards the inner world, where judgement or a resurrection of a new consciousness will enable you to see the solution to the problem. This is the same card in spirit, really, as DEATH. Whenever I see them I think of transformation of consciousness, and the fact that they should both appear in the spread suggests that this is what is going on. As it goes on, you will be able to harmonize the two worlds, as shown by the TWO OF PENTACLES. There will be a rapport between them. As a matter of fact, the symbol that binds them together there is the symbol for infinity, and so there is an exchange—the one world will help the other. If you put love that you attain in a personal relationship into your work as a teacher

165

or an artist, it is projected to the people that you are associated with.

C: That always happens. Just being in love makes you happy.

R: So the two should reinforce each other, and there should be exchange, almost like the exchange between the conscious and unconscious. There shouldn't be a separation in your mind between career and love. No reason why you shouldn't have both of them, and your job is to transform yourself so that that becomes tenable; you will probably have it, if not with whom you are involved now, then someone who is on the same plane as you are.

I think the cards are very much to the matter of the question, and I am almost sorry that I knew the question in advance because the way they are, they read almost like a simple short story. I think I have told you about all the same elements.

C: That's what it is. What's been said here is almost exactly what has been going through my head.

R: The cards indicate that making a decision when you are not sure is worse than making no decision at all.

or this reading, R denotes the author/reader, K stands for Karen, the readee/querent, Ron is her husband, and C denotes Carrie, a mutual friend.

R: The date is October 10, 1970, and this is a reading for Karen Allen. She has kindly consented to the use of her name in this book, so to further establish her identity I should like to ask one more question. What kind of work do you do?

K: I'm a social worker for the State of California in Vallejo, California.

R: All right, this is the Yes-No Spread.

K: Before we begin, may I ask a question?

R: Absolutely.

K: Is the reading dependent upon the way the cards fall, or upon what one reads into them? In other words, I have a question in mind that I have been trying to work out myself, but I seem to have one part of myself feeling one way, and another part another way. Now in the reading, how much will depend upon my projections onto the cards, and how much in the fate of the way the cards fall?

R: That's a very good question. Normally the reader is the one who interprets the outcome for you. I as the reader will project my associations about the cards, and then ask for your association. The other point is do the cards themselves have magic? What

The Yes-No Spread

I think occurs is a kind of psycho-kinesis. Are you familiar with that term?

K: No.

R: It means the mind moving matter. They try to demonstrate this in the laboratory by making a very lightweight object move by concentrating on it. I think the unconscious of man is in touch with all knowledge, so in effect when you shuffle the cards you know the order, even though you have never seen these cards before. Therefore, after you shuffle them and they are dealt out, psycho-kinesis has arranged them—unconsciously of course—into an order that is meaningful to your situation or question, and perhaps will give an answer to it.

K: What is the probability of chance in a Tarot reading?

R: That's another good question. I don't know that chance is a factor. I'd have to say it is 100% or nothing. It depends on how we interpret chance. Do you mean chance in the way that the cards fall?

K: Yes.

R: No, I don't think that is chance.

K: You think that is predestined?

R: Not predestined by fate, but predetermined by your unconscious. I have done readings in which I picked out the cards for the person—from the face down pack—and then told them what was their wish. In that case we could say that my unconscious

1. Two of Swords (Reversed)
2. Nine of Rods
3. Queen of Cups (Reversed)
4. The Tower
5. The Devil
6. Temperance
7. Ace of Rods

was attuned to theirs, in an intuitive way, and the psycho-kinetic effect controlled my hands enabling me to select a meaningful order that would throw light on the question involved. Any further questions?

K: Does Tarot answer all questions? You can't probably ask it does God exist. Should it be a question that relates to me?

R: It is best to ask the kind of question that will have an outcome in your life, because Tarot will delineate the future. Can your question be answered by a yes or no answer?

K: Yes, it does have a yes or no answer. Are you allowed to know the question?

R: I think it's better that I don't. I haven't known so far in previous readings, and we have had pretty good results.

K: Can the cards show one more about his or her real self than he may be aware of?

R: Definitely. I read an article in a magazine recently in which the author said the cards showed her more than they should and they frightened her. It was obvious from the way that she was speaking about Tarot that she was discussing her own unconscious. Certainly it was a frightening thing in her case. But she did not realize that what came out in the cards was a projection of herself.

All right, let's get started. This is a demonstration of the Yes-No Spread. We are using seven cards, dealing from right to left. The middle card will count twice the value of other single cards. In large part, our answer will be determined by whether or not reversed cards dominate the spread. A majority of these, as against upright cards, will indicate a negative answer . . .

We have two cards reversed, the rest are straight up. I shall read them. TWO OF SWORDS, inverted, NINE OF RODS, QUEEN OF CUPS, inverted, THE TOWER, THE DEVIL, TEMPERANCE, and ACE OF RODS. This adds up to six yes and two no, counting the middle card, THE TOWER, as two.

K: When I was concentrating on the cards, I was asking, "Should I do *this*?"

R: That does give us a definite answer then—you probably should do it. We will proceed from right to left. The first three cards represent the past of the matter, the middle card the present, the last three the future. The first card, TWO OF SWORDS, suggests to me two paths, two ways of going. Because the woman is blind-folded, she is in the dark as to which way to choose. Perhaps this reflects your own confusion on this question. There may be strife connected with one of these paths, or difficult times.

The NINE OF RODS suggests a fence or barrier of some kind.
K: The reason I asked the question is that I foresee certain barriers to my plans.
R: Do you feel in some way kind of fenced in, and this feeling makes you question whether or not you should go through with your plan?
K: Yes!
R: That's good, because we have first the two possible paths, and the woman in the dark as to which to choose, and then the feeling of being fenced in, totally enclosed by the Rods in the second card.

Now the QUEEN OF CUPS is subject to interpretation on three planes. First of all, in the realistic sense, the figure may represent someone who may give you help—not necessarily in a financial way—but in a supportive role, buoying you up. The first flash I had on the card was that this may be your mother. In the second level interpretation, psychologically the figure may stand for the woman within you, the positive feminine principle within, who perhaps has been a help to you in your life. You perhaps would not be aware of this figure except through dreams. Let's be hypothetical. Let's say you had a dream in which you were blind-folded and holding two swords, and you were walking along a precarious way—maybe it was like walking between blades—and you came to a fork in the road and had to choose between the two paths. Now there is great danger if you make the wrong choice. This is, of course, a symbolization of a situation. But can you recall a dream similar to this in which a helpful female guide appeared and showed you the way?
K: Yes, one just like the one you described.
R: On a third level, this figure is the Queen of the Grail. As such she is protector and preserver of your spiritual powers.
C: Maybe she could discuss some of those dreams.
R: That would be interesting. Have you had any dreams that you might be able to see as a symbolization of this particular situation you're asking about in connection with the cards?

K: Yes, this one, the TWO OF SWORDS. One dream that recurs is that my grandmother, mother, and myself are in a concentration camp, and I have to choose which one will die. If I don't, both will die. I agonize over which one to spare, and I can't make any decision, then suddenly this religious figure appears and I no longer have to make the choice. She kind of looks like the Virgin Mary, long, flowing robes, and a very kind, compassionate face.

R: Well, then what happens?

K: The dream ends—as soon as she appears.

R: And you say the choice is between your mother and your grandmother?

K: Since I've been married the decision demanded in the dream is between my husband and my mother, or my husband and my grandmother.

R: I think your dream is an excellent example of your inner feminine principle as a saving grace. Now the card that involves the present is THE TOWER. Oddly enough you have just talked about two figures being sacrificed, and this card is often depicted with two persons falling from the top of the tower. Here we have the tower on fire. Without making it too heavy a trip, the card generally means a shock of some kind that can potentially result in transformation of the individual subjected to this shock. You don't have to say anything about this at present. I'd like to go on to the future cards and come back to this card.

K: This is spooky, it really is!

R: (Laughter). The next card, THE DEVIL, has given me a little clue as to which of the two paths you should take. Notice that the devil holds two figures in bondage. These two persons are Adam and Eve, or the lovers of Key 6. That card is often called the Two Paths. Now with the first card, I suggested that there were two paths. Whenever I see THE DEVIL I think of material bondage, so whatever path you choose be sure your choice is *not* governed by material considerations. Whichever choice would yield the greater financial security, reject it and take the other path. This is what the cards say.

K: Hmmm!

C: I wish you'd be more specific.

K: In answer to my question that's very specific! Because what you said about the NINE OF RODS and my *barrier* relates directly to this bondage card and what you said about *it*!

R: Now if we go on to TEMPERANCE, we see an angel, a winged figure. O.K.! Then the way over the barrier is through temperance, that is, tempering your desire for material things. This will lead to a happy resolution of the matter in the future. One other point on this card. The angel is often shown pouring water from a stream onto land. This is the idea that the feminine water must intermingle with the masculine land, and the two principles will enrich one another. The exchange of the two is important. I don't know how that fits in with the question you want answered, but I see your face is lighting up like a Christmas tree.

K: That interpretation answers my question! Completely!

R: Finally, the last card is the ACE OF RODS, and I often take Rods to be a symbol of the intuition function, and thus this card suggests that if you will turn your thoughts inward, your intuitive side will provide a solution that defies logic, and you will know inwardly what is right, and you will get a kind of substantiation and support in your choice from this psychological figure—the QUEEN OF CUPS—representing the feminine principle within you. Possibly also in the outer, mundane world your mother may provide links that will help you to make a choice.

K and C: (Laughter)

R: Let's sum up. Card one—the horns of the dilemma, the querent in the dark. Then the NINE OF RODS—a feeling of being fenced in. Then in the third card, the first hint of a way out by looking to the inner female. Then THE TOWER, suggesting that a shock in the life will lead to a transformation. THE DEVIL—bondage to materiality impeding you. TEMPERANCE—conveying an idea of tempering the material desires, and an exchange between masculine and feminine elements. Finally the ACE OF RODS, a card of great intuitive power, suggesting that an inward turning to your intuitive side will provide the answer you seek.

Would you like to comment on the spread and on what I have said?

K: Well, I really don't know what to say! But the reading has answered my question for me.

R: Well, why don't you tell us now what was your question.

K: My question was should I bear children? Would I be a capable mother? Should I bear children because of my own reservations about bringing a child into this world?

R: I see! Well!

C: Do you want to do the reading over again?

R: No! No, I'm very happy with what I said! Because I said look to the inner feminine principle! And that's the whole answer! Obviously one of the reasons why you have hesitated about having children is that you are concerned about a feeling of being fenced in. Also the material considerations. "Are we in a position now to have children?"

K: It's not a question of now, but five or ten years from now would we be in a financial position to have children?

R: Also, what I said earlier about the exchange of masculine and feminine principles in the TEMPERANCE card! If you didn't have children you wouldn't have fulfillment of your feminine principle on its deepest level.

K: Was that a good kind of question to ask?

R: I don't see why not. What is a good question?

K: The reason Carrie and I were laughing when you said my mother might provide hints that would help me to make a choice or decision is that she is always after me to have a baby. It's almost to the point now where she is nagging Ron and me about this. Carrie knows this, so when you said that it was really startling.

C: Before, when I mentioned your doing the reading over, I didn't mean that it wasn't accurate, I just wanted you to elaborate more.

R: Oh! I don't think I can elaborate any more. I will, however, say something more about THE TOWER. I think I said it was the card of transformation. Right? I gave a sermon a few weeks ago on transformation. Another word for transformation is rebirth, and for you it would be a process of birth.

K: Or death?

R: You mean death in childbirth.

K: Umm-hmm.

R: It's dangerous for you—you've been told that?

K: It could be.

R: As I said before, this is a card of shock, and you can see great turbulence here, so there are suggestions that this may be a difficult process for you.

174

C: I thought of it as a personality transformation.

R: Yes, I think that is what I said first. This literal interpretation as birth is a retrospective analysis in view of the fact that we now know the question.

K: The series of the cards seems to have almost an exact progression of the situation surrounding my question.

R: Yes, we can say probably that more light was thrown on the question by means of the progression of cards than through the six yeses and two noes.

Let's look at the middle card again, THE TOWER. The transformation of an individual is never accomplished without some kind of shock to the personality. I mentioned in my sermon that the problems in our lives are actually the means to growth, but if we had it to do over again, we would just as soon skip the problems—we'd rather not go through them again. But they are a means to growth, and THE TOWER is a card of turbulence and transformation, potentially at least. So it may be that the future answer or decision you will make is dependent upon the present personality change. And what you have to avoid is considering only the material side of the matter, whether or not it will interfere with your living in the style to which you are accustomed, or, projecting your sense of materiality even onto the unborn children, what you think they ought to have in the way of worldly goods, which may or may not be happiness for them. We have seen this in our own decade, whereby the most revolutionary of the young have been the ones who had the most affluent parents. It may be that giving the child all he wants, or trying to make up for what one didn't have as a child, is not the answer to the family situation, and by logical extension, not the answer to the world situation.

I think that the last card will hold the answer. After the personality transformation has taken place, the intuitive function within yourself will provide the sought-for answer. At some future date you will say to your husband, Ron, I have made up my mind and this is it.

R: (to Ron) I think your mind is made up and you would like to have children. Yes or no?

Ron: Yes.

R: (to Karen) All right, I think at some point, maybe some morning out of a clear blue sky, after one of those dreams in which the helpful female figure has appeared to you in the dream, you will just say to him, "Well, I know the answer, without any ifs, ands, or buts about it anymore. It will be all right." So I think it is a really beautiful spread, and it does seem to have a nice sequence to it. . . (To Carrie) What are you beaming about? (General laughter).

Ron: (To Andy, his very large poodle) Down! Down!

R: Let's pick a card for Andy. (Laughter)

This will be the first time that a card has ever been picked to match the personality of a family pet—as far as I know. Actually some occultist will come forward to say that he had a pet monkey, given to him by an ancient magus in India, who actually gave most of his Tarot readings for him. (Laughter). All right, I'll cut a card from the facedown deck . . . Andy, this is your card . . .

Ron: Speak, Andy! (Laughter)

R: That is the SEVEN OF RODS. And that fellow has a dogface. (Laughter) Now I'm getting something here that is really interesting. (Laughter) No, really, really! (To Karen) You told us earlier why you bought this dog.

K: Oh!

R: Why?

K: I wanted a dog because I'm lonely and Andy's a companion for me. Ron's gone a lot at night to architectural school, and I'm much more comfortable when Andy's around.

R: Comfortable in what sense, late at night?

K: Secure.

R: Uh, huh. Look at what that fellow's doing in the card! What's his posture?

K: Erect?

R: Yeh, but I mean . . .

K: He's holding one of the Rods out in front of him.

R: Exactly! I would say this is a defensive stance. A protective posture! He is fending off the other six Rods. So I think that's a good card for Andy. (Laughter).

K: Yes, that's why I got him really.

R: The more you get into these cards, the further out it gets, believe me!

176

T he date is October 10, 1970, and I am about to give a second reading for Mrs. Karen Allen. Her first reading was the Yes-No Spread. I have decided to use a second layout of cards because during the first reading I was aware of an excellent rapport with this readee, and this is certainly one of the most important factors contributing to a good reading.

All right, I won't go into great detail about the format of my Jungian Spread because it is explained in detail elsewhere in the book. Earlier your husband, Ron, had inquired about the meaning of the snake with tail in mouth, and I had said this was a symbol of the uroboros, the creative matrix of the universe. And in deference to the fact that no realistic depiction can represent this principle, I place this first card face down in my spread, equating it with the Zero Key card of the twenty-two Key cards,

The Jungian Spread

1. Facedown Card
2. Justice
3. King of Swords
4. Queen of Swords
5. Four of Swords
6. Ace of Rods
7. The Empress
8. The High Priestess
9. The Magician
10. Knight of Swords
11. Page of Swords
12. Eight of Cups
13. The Fool
14. Judgement
15. The Sun
16. Five of Pentacles
17. Queen of Cups
18. King of Pentacles
19. Death
20. Six of Cups
21. Five of Cups
22. Two of Pentacles

and this spread has twenty-two cards to it.

The second and third cards represent the pairs of opposites within the archetypal world of the individual. First, the feminine principle within, and then the masculine principle, or animus, as Jung calls it. These two cards are JUSTICE and the KING OF SWORDS.

I asked you in the previous reading if you could recall any dreams in which a helpful, feminine figure appeared in difficult situations. You cited the case of the concentration camp dilemma. If you look at this card closely, you will notice that Justice holds a sword in one hand and a balance in the other. To me the dream situation is suggested here. The sword—the means by which people are put to death. The balance—the weighing of lives, lives held in the balance. There is such a similarity between

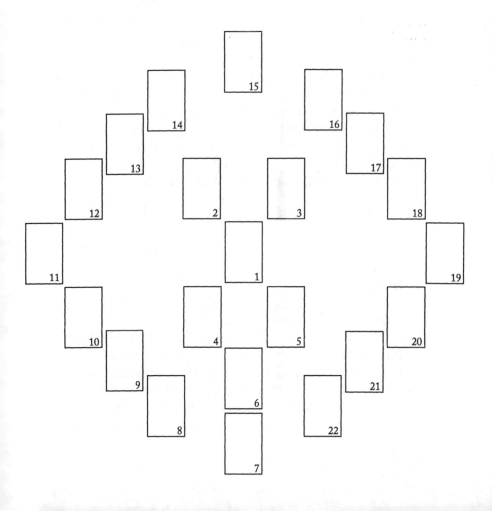

the figure depicted in JUSTICE and the saving person of your dream that I find it quite staggering. I cannot think of another card in the entire pack of 78 that could better represent what you said, so again I think this proves what I said earlier about psycho-kinesis operating on the unconscious level.

Then we'll go into the next archetype in your unconscious, the animus. We have a similarity here between what I take to be the meaning of this card and the reading for Barbara Skaggs. She is a person of great feeling and intuition. Through the animus, who came as a kind of prince, there was an awakening of the potential for conscious reflection and differentiated thought. This card, KING OF SWORDS, again suggests such a figure. I think that the fact that you had Sun and Mercury together at the moment of your birth makes for intellectual brilliance. The capacity for ordered, logical thought is part of the animus' function. The fact that this figure is a king leads me to infer that you will have strong support from the masculine archetype within you.

Now we are going to move to the cards depicting your parents. Just as the archetypes are determinants of what we may become in our lives, so also are the parents. QUEEN OF SWORDS is in the position of the mother. Again, I associate the Swords suit with the intellectual function. This rational power is nearly as great as that of the King of the previous card. I can see that the QUEEN OF SWORDS applies to your mother because I remember your saying that most of her friends were poets and writers. I find this interesting because there are very few women like this, particularly of your mother's generation.

K: Among her friends were Tennessee Williams, Clark Mills, and Clark McBurney—people like that that she went around with in St. Louis in the 1930's.

R: The interesting thing about the sword the Queen carries is that it is garlanded by roses; thus I find your mother—the way you have described her—immensely appealing to me because in my own life I have always wanted a woman who was interested in the intellectual function and cultivated the creative element in the male. With this card we are now in your Freudian territory. The blade is the phallic masculine principle, yet the hilt of the sword is immersed in blossom. It's kind of a marriage of the feminine principle, as symbolized by the floral motif, to the masculine

180

principle, as symbolized by the sword.

Now when we come over to the card representing your father, the FOUR OF SWORDS, I note that this card came up last week in a reading I gave for an elderly woman whose life was remarkably placid and fulfilled for about fifty years. Because I have already discussed this card in connection with her reading, I can first ask for your associations without seeming to equivocate about the card's meaning. What does that represent to you in regard to your father?

K: His death. He died at a very young age.

R: Absolutely. It's a funeral scene. A knight lying in state. When I showed her this card she said, "Yes, he was my knight in shining armor." And she's beginning a whole new phase in her life at the age of sixty-four, which suggests a second meaning of the card— regeneration of energies after rest and recovery.

K: That's amazing that this card would come up here!

R: When I saw this pattern I thought that it dovetailed perfectly with just the seven card reading that we gave you earlier. Oh, I forgot to ask you, do you want to say anything more about your mother in regard to what I said about the previous card?

K: Only that she is an avid reader and supporter of writers and poets. It's part of her basic "gut."

R: The thing that stands out in this card is that the blossoms are covering the hilt, and if we associate the blossoms with the female, and the sword with the male, it seems that her relation to these writers is not in the role of a financial patron of them . . .

K: No, no . . .

R: . . . but she kind of takes them under her wing as a woman and says in effect, "I admire what you do, and in my role as a woman I shall attempt to make you feel as much a man and as fulfilled as you can possibly be."

K: I think her aim was to inspire. Not in a conscious way but in a very unconscious way.

R: In a very feminine, muse-like way.

K: l don't know.

R: Maybe that's just as well, but if you should read her memoirs some day . . .

K: I've read a poem that was written about her in *The World's Greatest Love Poetry*! There was one written by Clark Mills and it was called "Catalina." I was shocked!

R: Well, if she ever comes up to visit you, I would like to present her with an autographed copy of my collected poems.

K: I told her about you, and that I was coming for a reading, and she is going to write you with Clark's address in New York.

R: I'd appreciate that . . . Well, let's get on with the reading. This is a really beautiful first four cards. I can't say much more except that in Jungian terms, your own feminine principle is in part formed by the model of the feminine that your mother presents to you, so it is interesting that the card in that position, JUSTICE, contains a figure who holds a sword just as does the Queen of Swords. Further, the debt your feminine principle has to your mother is also perhaps expressed by the scales or balance which Justice holds. I'm sure in her own life your mother psychically weighed these poets' lives against those of many well-to-do businessmen she may have met.

K: No-no.

R: In what sense no-no?

K: Well, I don't think she . . . Wait a minute, you may be right! Because she was in contact with *very* well-off businessmen, but she never was romantically interested in any of them—never found anything in them. It was always the rather poor but poetic and *gifted* person whom she found stimulating.

R: Right. This is the formation factor involving your own concept of the feminine. This is all very well, but if your masculine principle, the man within your unconscious, were operating in a negative way, you would have great difficulty in consciously utilizing the feminine side of yourself. As it is, however, the KING OF SWORDS suggests an animus conducive to great intellectual development. Because I associate swords with the thinking function, and because this is a *king,* it suggests intellectual power.

Now the sixth card is the one I place between the two wheels symbolizing the inner world and the life from birth onward. This is a real mind boggler. Do you remember what I said about the ACE OF RODS in your "Yes-No" spread?

K: You said it represented the intuitive side of myself, and if—when I come to a decision—I will let my intuition guide me, I shall be better off for doing it.

R: Uh-huh. Each of the first six stations of the cards defines the

182

meaning of each card. And this position defines the way in which you relate to the outer world.

K: It's right then. Exactly.

R: The intuitive function. Just give me a quick concrete example from your own daily life as to how you find this approach most valid in your dealings with people.

K: Well, part of my job is to try to diagnose problems that people have. We have all kinds of tools, and I've had all kinds of training in how to use certain skills in tuning in on a person's problems, but they are methods and techniques, and I find that if I want to get to the essence of the problem it is not by using these skills that enables me to do so, but by allowing my intuition to guide me—and then I always hit it right on the nose! It's uncanny with me! I can go in and within a matter of two minutes know exactly what that person is feeling.

Another example of this was the first time I saw my husband. (To Ron). Do you mind my telling this? I walked into a room and saw him, and I knew right away that he was the person. It sounds silly, it sounds romantic, and all the logic was against it because he was engaged to another girl, and was about to leave the country. I mean every logical odd was against it, but my intuition was very strong. No girl would get involved in the kind of situation I got involved in. It was just ridiculous, but my intuition was so strong that I pursued it against everything, and it *was* right!

R: I would like to tell a little story about that regarding my mother, who evidently had a very intuitive waitress in her restaurant, because the first time my father walked in she turned to my mother and said, "That's the man you're going to marry." So I think perhaps the intuitive function is the highest function in man in that it seems to go right to the heart of the matter.

I think I use intuition much more than intellect in Tarot reading. A card may come up and I'll have a feeling that I should say a certain thing in connection with it, which I may not say next time for a different readee even though it is the same card. On this point, I want to caution the readers of this book. They should not take my interpretations for their own. Again, the point of the book's being written is that they see whatever they want to in the cards, and that will be the meaning of it for them.

For example, if I gave you this deck and you gave readings for your friends, I know with your great intuition and feeling you would do a beautiful job at it. But in no way should you say when JUSTICE came up, when the ACE OF RODS came up, Roberts said that they meant *this*. That would be wrong, self-defeating.

O.K., we're going to continue now with the wheel of life for Karen Allen. The moment of your birth. A very, very beautiful card. THE EMPRESS. My associations with it are with the feminine archetype within you—with the Queen of Cups which we had in your "Yes-No" spread, with JUSTICE, the card representing your feminine principle in this reading, and with the QUEEN OF SWORDS, the "Mother card" of this reading. Generally speaking, this is the card of the Eros principle, as opposed to The Magician, which is Key I of the Major Arcana, and represents the Logos principle. Again, it is really impossible not to refer back to your question about whether or not you should have a child, because this EMPRESS card *is* the card of childbirth. Notice on her shield the astrological symbol of Venus. Venus is the patroness of art, love, and all beautiful things. She is the feminine principle *made* manifest, and as such she is a sponsor of fertility, birth, and growth. You see, this marvellous feminine potential you had *before* birth (represented by JUSTICE and the QUEEN OF SWORDS) was only a potential because we were dealing with the inner world—whether archetypal or unconscious or both. It was a *virgin* potential, therefore. This concept is perhaps best summed up by the meaning of the card that precedes THE EMPRESS in the normal Tarot order. Key II is the High Priestess, and she is a virgin, her whole orientation directed inwardly to subconsciousness, Platonic ideals, and psychism. But the Empress is fertile. She holds dominion over the earth. Her feminine subconscious has been impregnated by the masculine logos from the animus, represented for you by the King of Swords. So here in your birth card, THE EMPRESS symbolizes the generative, life-giving function of the impregnated subconsciousness. It is difficult, very difficult to talk about these concepts because we are really talking about states of mind, and words can never really fix that shifting reality. It is easy enough to give people readings when the questions they ask are limited to the surface of life—money, jobs, things like that—but the Jungian spread is geared to

184

capturing the spirit of the whole individual—inner and outer worlds. So when I speak about your inner state of mind I must, for the most part, speak symbolically.

K: I understand.

R: I must refer back again to your question of the previous reading, "Should I have children?" This card in effect says that this would be the fulfillment of your life. You have considered this question so seriously that you are not going to undertake child-bearing in the usual matter-of-fact way that the ordinary mother does. You recognize the full significance of it in the mythic sense, and what it means to the racial heritage, the *future* consciousness of mankind.

K: That's exactly right. I can't believe it.

R: Free associate with this card, Karen, and see what she means to you—colors, symbols, or anything that you see in it.

K: I see her as a symbol of quiet strength—very together. I see her at peace, in control of herself.

R: Yes, if the race is to go on it will be because of her as the Mother-Empress of the world, symbolic of the generative power. Any other association?

K: I'm most taken by the strength of her natural background.

R: Oh, yes, the rock and the water.

K: Whenever I am out of harmony with myself I look to hills or mountains and suddenly I am renewed. THE EMPRESS is in front of these mountains, and that is where she gets her strength.

R: It also reminds me of what I said about Temperance in your "Yes-No" spread—the exchange of masculine and feminine symbolized by earth and water. This is the whole relatedness principle coming to the fore. It is the idea that the Word must be made Flesh. The Word comes out of this face down card that we cannot see. It must take a material form, be made manifest. She is the agency for the appearance of the god-principle in the world. Or perhaps she is even the third principle, offspring of the virgin High Priestess made pregnant, not Son but Daughter of God. Maybe that is why she is number three, or Key III.

Now we shall proceed around the wheel.

(Laughter). I was just contrasting The Empress with the High Priestess, and now THE HIGH PRIESTESS appears as the second card of the life wheel. As subconsciousness, not yet impregnated by the Logos principle, she is symbolic of inner reflection, the dream state, fantasy, and psychic activity. When you were a very young girl—two, three—was there a great deal of fantasy and psychic experience—more so than usual with a child of that age?

K: When I was between two and three my father died. At that point there was a lot of fantasy about him because although I never really knew him, he was my father and now he was gone. So the fantasies revolved around where he had gone, since I was not told until much later that he was dead. Also, at age three I had many, many imaginary companions.

R: You see at an early age, one is still close in consciousness to the inner unconscious; hence one is much more open to psychic influences than later when the ego has been erected as a kind of membrane to screen both inner and outer effects.

Well, with the HIGH PRIESTESS to go with The Empress, Justice, and the Queen of Swords, your feminine legacy is that of goddess—manifested on the earth plane.

K: Wowww! I'll come back *anytime*.

R: Now your next card.

K: Before you put that down, does it have anything to do with the masculine side of me? Because I want to tell you that it wasn't until about four years ago that I even wanted to be a female. And all through my schooling I was a tomboy and I didn't relate to women at all. I only related to men because they were the only people I could talk to, or who seemed to understand my thinking, and I still don't understand women. Does that have any relationship to the card?

R: Absolutely! Out of the face down "zero" card, comes card "one," the card of being and spiritual essence. In short, the creative Logos principle. So this is your card, THE MAGICIAN, Key I.

Earlier Ron had asked me about the meaning of the figure eight symbol above his head. Mathematically it is symbolic of infinity.

Ron: But you had another term for it relevant to the "zero" card.

R: Yes, the uroboros or creative matrix out of which comes being. And I never noticed this before, but placed over his head as it is, he stands in the same relation to it as does Key I and Key zero. "Something from nothing never yet was wrought." Probably the zero card does not represent "nothing," but instead non-being. Also, the symbol of the uroboros is reiterated by his belt; hence it encloses or surrounds him.

Without a doubt, this is the most masculine card in the deck, in that it is a conscious symbol of the Logos. It takes form and is defined out of the World Stuff represented by zero. The Magician has on the table before him symbols of the four suits, signifying dominion over the elemental world of Fire, Earth, Air, and Water.

I'm very glad you stopped me to ask if this card had a relation to the masculine side of yourself because the creative principle was looking for a way out. In other words, a woman is like a circle, an egg, and she needs in some way to break out of the circle of containment.

K: There have only been two women in my life that I could admire—my mother and my grandmother—outside of an unreal figure which is the Virgin Mary. I've always been disappointed in relationships or friendships with girls or women. I have never been disappointed in a relationship with a male.

R: Incredible.

K: Never.

R: I say incredible because practically all people bad-mouth the opposite sex because of previous experiences, but you have such a wealth of femininity to offer that . . .

K: I guess I'm in a sense afraid of it. Because it's so strong, and tied in with my own intuitiveness, I almost have to compensate to preserve some stability.

R: I agree with you. You must strike a balance in your life between the two principles. We have to harmonize yin and yang in ourselves.

K: Right, this is probably why I sought the masculine—carried out to extremes.

R: Well, this would probably be in your teens, according to the chronology of the cards.

K: Right. Sixteen, seventeen.

R: Let's look at the next card . . . Well, this always happens to every young maid. Your knight comes along.

K: Yes.

R: And since I didn't live your life for you, I'll let you talk about who was the KNIGHT OF SWORDS.

K: He was my husband—my present husband.

R: You had no loves before him?

K: None. He was the first person who made me want to feel feminine. I was roving around with boys, and getting as drunk as they were, and as obnoxious, until I met him, and then suddenly I wanted to be a girl. I'm finding it's kind of nice.

It's funny this card would fall after the other one, because it's right in the order. This is really phenomenal.

R: Incidentally, we could have a knight of one of the three suits, but I do associate Swords with intellect.

K: I think my husband does have a strong intellectual curiosity. In fact our whole beginning was on an intellectual basis, not at all on a feeling or sense basis. It was his thoughts that I was drawn to.

R: He passed the test of fire. In the card Justice, associated with your feminine principle, in one hand is the scale, and there is the weighing and the judging. In the other hand, the sword. Also, the figure for your masculine principle also carries the sword. So what I was about to say, he passed the test of fire, or he passed the test of the sword. You put him to the test intellectually.

K: (Laughing) Yes. Definitely.

R: And you found he was not wanting; therefore, the female in you said, "O.K., I've found you, now I'm ready to be a woman."

K: Huh!

R: Am I right?

K: Yeh! You are, you are . . . Huh! O.K.

R: As they say in soap operas, the plot thickens. We now have a new character coming on the scene. Whereas the husband faced to the East, here comes the PAGE OF SWORDS facing to the West. Any associations with him at all?

K: (Laughing). I'd have to ask my husband to leave the room . . . Yes. Let's say I had a brief encounter between the time I met my husband—maybe several encounters—and the time we married.

R: And he had similar intellectual qualities to Ron. You suddenly found it very exciting that the world could hold two such persons. This is the speech of Prospero's daughter in *The Tempest.* "Oh, brave new world that has such creatures in't," and Prospero replies, "'Tis new to thee." Of course it was marvelous for you with *two* men like that, but think how it would have been if you'd met me at the same time! Typist, cut that line!

188

K: I don't like your cards. They're too real.

R: Well, now in the EIGHT OF CUPS a change of some kind is indicated, perhaps your first setback because it is reversed. In some way are you at present turning your back—like the figure in the card—on some aspect of your previous life to strike out on your own. You see this passage over distant mountains. Physical elevation is often associated with spiritual height. Also, above the mountains is a sun and moon united, which suggests a psychic integration within, a unifying or fusing of your masculine and feminine sides. Maybe the reversal of the card indicates that the energies are directed inwardly—an inner change.

K: The only thing I can think of at this point is renewing my spiritual journey. I'm still very occupied with philosophy and theology. I have been all my life, but it's really become almost an obsession.

R: O.K. The next card should throw a little more light on this . . . Oh, well (Whistle) . . .

K: Oh boy!

R: Actually when this card comes up we should all go around the world—room—world/room—blowing noisemakers, dancing, behaving non-rationally! The reason this card is face down in the middle of the spread is that it is in the natural position of the "zero" card, THE FOOL, which has just come up. Nothing can represent it. I take this to be an holy fool, a fool for Christ, one who has made the breakthrough into cosmic consciousness. This follows right on the heels of your discussion of your own spiritual quest. In my opinion, there could not be a better foreboding that you will attain the higher consciousness you seek.

At times the card may have the value of a simply foolish person, but that would be in the case of someone who comes to a reading and asks a question like should I buy a new Cadillac this year. Given the sequence that we have here, it suggests the nothing, evolvement beyond concern with the things of the material plane to higher development.

Next is the card of spiritual resurrection and new birth, JUDGEMENT. Do you have associations with it?

K: Only death.

R: There is a card called Death, naturally enough. And again Death probably may represent on a higher plane transformation.

One dies to the world in order to be reborn to the spirit.

In JUDGEMENT we have the sun rising, and blossoms flowering, which we saw earlier in the feminine principle which you brought over to this life, and Gabriel blowing his horn . . .

I just noticed this about the previous card, THE FOOL. The two O's in the word are intertwined, which makes what kind of a figure? Your figure for infinity, again.

Now let's look at the meridian of your life. (Whistle!).

K: What's wrong?!

R: Nothing could possibly be wrong with your reading, Karen. Ron, you asked me a question before we started the reading about the relation between the birthtime of a person and the position of his Sun in the chart. I gave you as an example a person born at noon, who would have his Sun placed at the very top of the chart. (Laying down Key XIX, THE SUN).

K: How about that?!

R: At the height of Karen's life we have THE SUN. And in astrological and in Jungian terms, I take the Sun to stand for the inner higher Self, capitalized, whereas the ego is the lower case self, and the Moon is the persona, the changing face we show the world, but not the face that was ours before we were born. The Moon casts a reflective light, changing its aspects "inconstantly", as Shakespeare said. The Sun is the immutable fire of the regenerated, resurrected divine Self, reunited at last with the cosmic Father. Actually, reunited is a bad word, because in her consciousness here she would know herself to be One with the Father, and always had been, only her earlier restricted consciousness made her think that she was separate from God.

K: Wowww.

R: In Jungian terms this is Selfhood, fulfillment of what you came to individuate, total at-one-ment.

K: That's what I'm working on very hard.

R: Well, you see if you're working on it—consciously aware of it—then that's half the battle. The man who is unaware of this is truly the fool, in the mundane sense. Any general associations with THE SUN?

K: The Sun to me means light.

R: This is a good point. Then Moon would represent reflected light, masked light (the changing phases of the Moon), and the masks we put upon our faces when we go into the world, because we can't show the world too much of our real selves. Yet the highest holy fools have no masks whatever. They show themselves just as they are, and the world cannot . . .

K: . . . understand or accept them.

R: Absolutely, absolutely . . . Now we begin the downward path from the meridian of your life. FIVE OF PENTACLES. My immediate associations are with the Flight into Egypt. It suggests that at some future time, after you have attained Selfhood, and I feel that this will happen with Ron's help—that together you represent a yin and yang principle . . .

K: We do.

R: . . . going through life beautifully, and when this Selfhood is attained, there may be a desire for a change. You will turn your back on your whole life as you have known it heretofore. You may say, "Let's get a little cabin up in the woods somewhere. We have a little money saved. Or why don't we sell the house?" Or Ron might say, "Why don't we go up there and you have the baby there?" Something like that.

K: Hmm. That's very interesting because Ron and I talk a lot about going back—after we get our education—to where I was really together, and that was in Sweden. I've talked about not wanting to have a baby here, but having it there.

R: Isn't that what Mary said? "We can't have the baby under Herod. We have to flee."

K: That's wild. Because the whole thing about the politics here, the assassinations, the riots, the impending fascism. We've talked often about leaving when I get ready to have the baby. (Laughter). That's wild!

R: Next card. Oh, wow! Now you see this Flight into Egypt is a crucial situation. I said Mary didn't want to have the baby under Herod. The next card is a card that you had in the previous reading, which we *did* associate with the Virgin Mary because she represented the feminine inner principle as she appeared to you in dreams. The QUEEN OF CUPS. There she is again to sustain you in your hour of need. Joseph Henderson has written of this in *Thresholds of Initiation.* When we encounter a crisis in our lives, then these archetypal figures rise up in our dreams, and even if we have no conscious knowledge of it, these figures are true to myth-

191

ology, functioning as guides and supports from the unconscious to buoy us up, give us inner strength to see the resolution through on the mundane plane.

Well, we have talked about her before, so I don't think we have to say any more.

K: No. It seems to fit in very well with what Ron and I have talked about and planned—or considered doing, rather.

R: Now the next card, KING OF PENTACLES, reversed. This may indicate some kind of set-back for you. I think you are going to be tempted in the desert.

K: The financial advantages of remaining in this country.

R: Yes, here's King Herod portrayed by the King of Pentacles, and behind him you see the golden calf.

K: He could by my stepfather as well.

R: Does he try to exercise an influence over you?

K: Oh, very much so. He tries to influence everyone, and he has a bull-like way of doing it.

R: O.K. . . . Now we come to that point on the wheel of your life where the sun has dropped below the horizon and we are in the last part of the life. This card is DEATH. (Whistle). I'm trying to whistle as I pass the graveyard.

K: I knew it! I knew it would be early. But I wish the card hadn't come up.

R: I'm glad it did, in the sense that even if you have been believing that you would have an early death, this card is not necessarily a confirmation of that. DEATH may mean change, transformation, or possible spiritual renewal. You're shaking your head.

K: My intuitiveness says it's not physical death, but mind says the opposite.

R: Well, look at the sequence of the cards. There has been a definite preparation for another transcendent card. The Fool, Judgement, and The Sun are all cards of higher consciousness. None of these was interpreted literally by me. Furthermore, the immediate pattern preceding the Death card is one of beginning a new life—what I called the Flight into Egypt, and you qualified this as your desire to leave the country and reside in Sweden, where you might have a baby. And I said you would be sustained in this by your inner feminine archetype—symbolized by the QUEEN OF CUPS—and would meet opposition from an antago-

192

nist, **KING OF PENTACLES.** So the logical sequence is that the stage is set for a new phase of your life—the death of the old life, the old ways, making room for a new beginning. Let's take a quick break here and recommence momentarily . . .

K: While you were out of the room, Ron and I were talking. We don't know what the other cards in the deck are like, but we were just amazed at how close you have come to my life. What amazes us most of all are the five cards in the center standing for my inner life. Really that is me.

R: The inner world of Karen . . . One, two three, etc. I was just counting the cards in the outer wheel to see how many more I needed and I see that DEATH is the thirteenth card, and thirteenth is its natural position because it is Key 13.

K: This is sounding really weird, but this is true! (General laughter). Do you know that always on the thirteenth something weird happens to me. And I'm very superstitious.

R: The thirteenth of the month?

K: Yes, or things happen to me in sequences of thirteen. I can verify it! That's why I'm superstitious—or intuitive, if you want to call it that.

R: All right, let me suggest something to you. You had said that while you were shuffling you were really concentrating.

K: Right.

R: And I think this is very important. You are supposed to fix your vibrations . . .

K: On the cards!

R: . . . on the cards.

K: That's what I was doing.

R: Now I want you to think about the Christ consciousness. Our whole Western religion is based upon the victory over death as exemplified by the resurrection after the crucifixion. Obviously you have a hangup about death, but there is no reason to have this. Given the first five cards representing what you bring into life, and what transformations have already taken place in you on the wheel of life, don't go through life saying I'm one who is going to have an early death. Say instead, I'm one who is going to encounter at an early stage a trial or opportunity for transformation when I shall either fail, and die on the physical plane, or succeeding, I shall become more than what I was before, and my wishes fulfilled and all things given unto me.

K: That is dependent upon the next card.

R: Yes, the SIX OF CUPS, in which the cups are full of blossoms. Blossoming means new life to me, and I think it was very perceptive of you to say that the kind of death of the previous card would be qualified by the following card. So I think that greatest trial of your life will prove to have a felicitious outcome.

K: That's lovely.

R: Isn't that a beautiful card?

K: It is.

R: They're like wooden cups in which I suppose they have earth and water, and the flowers live also on the air and the sunlight. Any personal associations with that card?

K: Growth. Plants and flowers mean to me growth. That's why I'm going through a thing now of loving to plant flowers because I see life and I see growth, which I just get ecstatic about.

R: This is your empathy with The Empress and the High Priestess, goddesses of regeneration and natural mysteries symbolic of your at-one-ment with your own feminine principle.

Next is the FIVE OF CUPS. When this card has come up before, it represented an entirely new beginning for the individual. This may not be true until thirty or forty years hence, but it suggests your life pattern may take you beyond Ron. I hate to say this, but people outgrow relationships. I don't mean this in the sense of putting you down, Ron, because as a surfer (laughter from Ron) you are one with me, but this girl has such a heavy spread of evolvement that she almost may leave mankind behind.

K: I wish you wouldn't say that because many times I have thought of joining a religious order.

R: I don't think it would be in that sense. I think it would be into a new marriage. In the same way that you met Ron at an early point in your life, you may undergo a new intuitive experience where later in life you meet someone who will also be on your new level of evolvement. What we'll have to do next time is to give a reading for Ron because he will be panting to keep up with your evolutionary pace.

K: That's funny because my mother is intuitive and she has already said that would happen.

R: But she likes Ron very much?

K: Oh, she adores him.

R: You see how far you go. The great crisis will be at the Death card, and you may die to your own self. Because you die to your old self, your old life may not fit anymore. It will be worn out.

TWO OF PENTACLES. I see a new man coming now from across the sea.* Did I hit something there?!

K: Nooo.

R: O.K. Someone who if he is not of the European or Asian world beyond the mundane plane, may be more of the spiritual world, and, therefore, understanding of the vast changes that had occurred in you and easily able to relate to you. He may be master of the two worlds, master of the mundane and spiritual planes. I can't do much more with him.

Now finally I sometimes will turn over the face down number zero card, particularly in a reading like this in which the cards have been so propitious. In your beginning is your end, and in your end is your beginning. The point of the tail in the snake's mouth, things come full circle. The card is the FOUR OF RODS. To me this is a gate of four rods, comprising what is known in Jungian psychology as the quaternary—the square of consciousness, all four functions working effectively. This is a card of fulfillment, realization, attainment. The floral festoons on the rods suggest victory on the earth plane. This was your cosmic inheritance, and this is what you ultimately return to. The flowering of yourself, individuation, Selfhood. God bless you.

K: You've told a beautiful Tarot for me. I'm very happy.

R: Well, you obviously have brought this consciousness to the reading, so you have earned it. Ron, get a golden key to that house in Vallejo and lock her up, because you have a jewel.

(General laughter).

---

* At a later date, Karen Allen revealed that she did not want to discuss the man I had described until first mentioning him to her husband. My two main points were corroborated, his residing in Europe and his evolved spirituality. She confessed to a personal inclination towards him because of his empathetic understanding of her.

T his is a reading by the Jungian Spread for a psychic named Georgiana Sagee. Today's date is February 5, 1971.

G: Don't pull punches with me.

R: The first card represents the Unmanifest, that which we come out of, and that which we know nothing about. That's why I keep it face down, because no card can bear the symbolical weight of representing it. Originally the name of God was never pronounced, and profanity was born when someone did. The same concept applies here.

Now I use two cards for the feminine principle and masculine principle as they exist archetypally within the individual, and also two cards for the Mother and Father. Therefore, these four cards stand for the pre-conscious heritage. The card signifying the feminine principle is SEVEN OF SWORDS. For the animus the

The Jungian Spread

1. Facedown card
2. Seven of Swords
3. Strength
4. Three of Swords
5. Knight of Cups
6. Six of Rods
7. Ten of Cups
8. The Moon
9. Three of Rods
10. Knight of Swords (Reversed)
11. Nine of Swords
12. Seven of Pentacles
13. Two of Swords
14. Nine of Rods
15. Nine of Cups
16. The Devil (Reversed)
17. Temperance
18. Death
19. The Hanged Man
20. Justice
21. Ten of Rods
22. The Lovers

196

card is STRENGTH, Key 8. The Mother card is THREE OF SWORDS, the Father card is KNIGHT OF CUPS. So on the side of the relationship to the Father and to your own masculine half, I get an impression of Logos power and loving affection.

G: That's right, I was very close to my father.

R: What STRENGTH really stands for is an interplay between the higher consciousness and the animal awareness of the individual—maybe the intuitive side because we know that animals are naturally psychic. In much older decks a woman either opens or closes a lion's mouth—occultists aren't sure which.

The KNIGHT OF CUPS represents the actual father in life. Cups became the Hearts suit in present day playing cards. So in this case there is great emotion, feeling, and love radiating from the father. Were you aware of your psychic gifts when you were

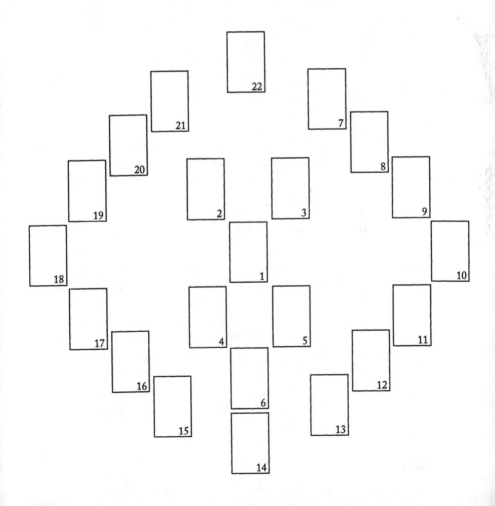

young? I'm sure you must have been because you were born with them.

G: I started very young, and I was aware of it.

R: Now these two Swords cards suggest separation and sorrow in connection with the mother, and perhaps unfulfilled love from the mother.

G: Well, I lost her when I was eleven.

R: Eleven. Well, I think the THREE OF SWORDS may portray that very well.

G: So you see there was a loss.

R: The SEVEN OF SWORDS is on the side of the feminine principle within, and one aspect of it is known as the shadow, or that part of the individual that has not yet been brought to full consciousness. Sometimes this archetype can cause disruptions in the personal life. Here the figure's face is averted, so I do have an impression of the negative side of the feminine principle, the shadow. I think the Logos principle is better developed in you. The relation to God is more important to you than say the relation on a family level. I could be wrong there.

G: My family's always been very close, but I've always been very conscious of God. Not on a church basis. I'm a rebel.

R: I am too.

G: I built my own religion.

R: Yes, yes, that is an important thing to do.

G: And I always did. I rebelled when I was a kid. I didn't accept any of them—went to all of them.

R: This card, the SIX OF RODS, is the card that shows your relation to the outer world, and I think it kind of symbolizes in many ways what you just said. The man mounted on the horse carrying the laurel wreath suggests someone who has decided to make himself higher than the ordinary churches, the ordinary religions. It is a card of victory. The six rods also represent great intuition, because I frequently associate the Rods suit with the intuition function. Of course there is no doubt that you have that, or you wouldn't be in this line of work, but I think a Rods suit card would represent you well here.

What we are doing really now is to show how this inner world is projected into the outer circle that will be around here. The SIX OF RODS is kind of a card of completion. It is two threes, like two trinities. Well, we might come back to this later. But now we will start with the outer circle.

The TEN OF CUPS is your heritage at birth, and that is a card of great fulfillment. You did mention that you lost your mother at eleven; probably there was a great deal of love and rapport in the family at about the time you were born.

G: Oh, very much. My folks were very much in love. They'd been married ten years when they had me; they thought they'd accomplished something.

R: You notice that the cups at the top are arranged in the figure of a heart, with the rainbow and the loving looks between the two people.

G: Yes. It was a very beautiful time.

R: I can see why the THREE OF SWORDS represented such a loss.

G: Very much so.

R: O.K. This card, THE MOON, suggests to me your psychic powers coming through at a very early age. It is a symbol of femininity and psychic receptivity. There isn't much more to say about it.

G: I am a moon child.

R: Are you? Uh-huh, uh-huh.

G: Yes, I'm a Cancer.

R: O.K. These first two cards represent a very beautiful beginning.

The next card, the THREE OF RODS, suggests someone who is about to cross a threshold and go out into life on his own. I hope I'm not generalizing too much about psychic people in general; I am sure it is true, though, that there is certain separation between your playmates and yourself, because as soon as you are cognizant of your gifts it makes you see things that they do not, and it makes you aware of areas that they are not conscious of.

G: That's right; I never had close playmates.

R: Well, that isolation is suggested there, and it also suggests the beginning of your concept of becoming your own church, since you are about to go through this threshold and make of yourself a complete world. The three rods plus the man equal the four quarters or the square of consciousness in Jungian terms.

Now we come to a reversal here. This is the KNIGHT OF

SWORDS. Of course all these cards can function on three levels, on the mundane, on the astral, and on the spiritual. On the mundane this KNIGHT OF SWORDS may represent someone who might have been your first love. Since it is reversed it would suggest a certain amount of unhappiness, some setback there for you.

G: There was. There was a divorce, and he has since passed. I was very much in love with him.

R: Was he a fire sign?

G: No, water—Scorpio.

R: They say Cancer and Scorpio should get together.

G: We were very, very much in love. It was during the Depression and we had monetary problems; but I loved him very much and always did, until he died many husbands later.

R: The separation following was very heart-rending for you and full of grief.

G: Yes, lots of problems in it . . .

R: . . . As portrayed by the NINE OF SWORDS.

G: Yes, very much. Lots of good in it too, but the very process of maturing was difficult.

R: Next card is the SEVEN OF PENTACLES. I have a completely unique association with this, which is based on a poem which I like very much, "Leda and the Swan," by Yeats, in which Zeus has assumed the form of a swan, and he brings the logos principle to the female. This represents that to me, that marriage with the bird, and I think what sustained you after the grief of this separation and divorce from your husband was a return to an inner awareness of your own inner strength connected with this logos principle. It means really your relatedness to God. You had some work to do in life and you got to work on it.

G: That's right.

R: Then I wonder if about the same time you didn't have a choice of taking two paths. I suppose we all have this some time, but was there ever a question of doing something else? That is represented by the TWO OF SWORDS. Do you want to talk about those two alternatives briefly?

G: It was minor. It was just following in the restaurant business and the entertainment field, or going into the psychic realm.

R: It's interesting, my mother had a restaurant in Summit, N.J.

G: I followed in the restaurant business whenever I got tired of psychic work. If I felt the need to get into something else, I would get into the restaurant business. My people were hotel and restaurant people.

R: Now we are going to have sixteen cards in the outer circle, and we have seven, so this is the midpoint of the life. It is positioned not quite below the SIX OF RODS. the psychologist Carl Jung talks about four functions in the human psyche. What I said about the SIX OF RODS is that your way of relating to the outer world is through the intuition function. There we had six rods, or two threes; here we have nine rods, or three threes, and the card is the NINE OF RODS. Another trinity is added, so you really developed well your intuitive heritage, the heritage which you were born with and which you brought with you from the astral plane. You are really now getting to work in it, and I think you are reading well, psychically speaking.

G: Well, it's my life now.

R: Yeh, yeh, I know that the way people speak of you around the Abraxas Bookstore, by the way your appointment book is filled, that you are very good.

G: Thank you.

R: NINE OF CUPS represents a certain amount of fulfillment and happiness. I see this as a kind of reaping the fruits of having chosen the right path.

G: That's right.

R: It's matched with the TEN OF CUPS that you were born with, and is a return to that beautiful state at birth.

G: Very true.

R: Well now, this card is always difficult to interpret when it comes up; it is THE DEVIL. It's easy to interpret when it comes up in a businessman's reading, because it can represent enslavement to material things and to the body. I mentioned that I gave a reading Thursday for George Hernandez, and this card came up in his reading. Of course, he is a very spiritual person, very much like yourself, so momentarily it was a puzzle to me as to what the card represented. He suggested that when one opens oneself to the psychic forces, very often forces come through that are negative in quality.

G: That's right.

201

R: And they try to use you for their own means.

G: That's right; you have to be careful.

R: I think this is perhaps what is represented by The Devil, and the pentagram of man turned upside down means man upside down as the devil attempts to subjugate him. This might be interesting for the book if you can tell us if you had a hard battle with a certain force that was evil or negative that you can remember.

G: Well, I gave up psychic work completely—turned my back on it. Not that I disbelieved in it, but I just gave it up and went into the bar and restaurant business. Of course I was around a lot of drinking, and of course I was drinking myself. I went through that period; I didn't feel qualified to read for people. I wouldn't say I was possessed or anything, but it was a period I had to go through. That's 'way past now, 'way, 'way past. But I got into the bar and restaurant business, and first thing I knew I was wound up in that, and of course that doesn't go with the psychic realm.

R: Would this have been around the age of 35?

G: That's when it started.

R: That matches the life chronology in the cards.

G: I started through the menopause and I was restless; I didn't want to sit home and wait for appointments. I'd make appointments and then never keep them, and I was abusing my gift, and I have always respected my gift. So much so that when I decided I was abusing it I decided it was time for me to do something about it. So I gave it up, went to San Francisco, and went into the bar and restaurant business. All I did was work hard and have a ball. At least I thought it was at the time. I went over to Reno and I ran restaurants and made chef, and drank up a storm, gambled up a storm, and played. I completely left all of this; I was interested in it but I never touched it.

R: How long were you away from it?

G: About ten years, a little longer than that maybe.

R: Let's see what the following card shows . . . (Laughter). This is really beautiful. The name of the card is TEMPERANCE.

G: I would never be drunk because somehow liquor doesn't get me that way, but I drank enough for ten people. I married and divorced and married and divorced, and I just had a ball. I just saw life as it was. The spiritual then wasn't entered into it at all. I didn't hurt anybody intentionally, but I lived very much on a

202

materialistic plane. It was something I had to go through.

R: This card, THE DEVIL, Georgiana, is often called bondage to materiality . . .

G: It was.

R: Or it might be bondage to appetites.

G: Oh, yes, it was.

R: And I think it's really beautiful that it's followed by TEMPERANCE, because here we have a winged angel, and this again suggests the astral plane coming to visit you, but it can't unless you temper your appetites.

G: It saved me—pulled me out before I got too far. In fact my forces almost broke me in business until I had to get out.

R: How?

G: Well, they put me into a place; the last place I was in was Calistoga, where you couldn't have possibly made a living because there were about eleven bars to a town of a thousand people. And I got my money tied up in there and I had to stay until I got out. I had to stay against my will. I had been doing everything as I chose; if I didn't want to stay I didn't stay—just packed up and left. But I had money tied up there where I had to stay. I always say it was my six years in jail, because I hated the town, I hated the people, and I hated the business. I hated being tied there, but if I'd have walked out I'd have walked out not only on myself but my sister. Everything that we had invested would have gone down the drain. If it had just been me, I would have locked the door and walked out, because material things don't mean that much to me. But with her involvement and her finances involved, why, I stayed.

But I learned a big lesson. I was mighty glad to get back into this work, mighty glad.

R: Well, this next card represents complete transformation in you.

G: It was.

R: As we know it on the mundane plane we sometimes call it by the name of death; it represents a deep psychic change, the death of the old person.

G: That's right; I'm not the same person at all. All the things that were important aren't important now.

R: The death of the devil power through temperance leads to a resurrection. The sun is rising in this picture, I think, rather than setting. The card is called DEATH.

G: That's exactly what happened.

R: The next card is THE HANGED MAN; it hasn't come up for me in a reading before, but to me it suggests illumination. Very often in traditional decks the head of the man is shown with golden rays around it, and I think that at that point in your life you began meditating again.

G: I did; that's right.

R: This card suggests to me suspended mind such as in a state of meditation, because the root word for "man" and the root word for "mind" is the same in Sanskrit. I think when the Tarot deck was first brought from a culture different than our Western Christian culture, the concepts that didn't fit were modified both in word and symbol. Meditation was an Eastern discipline; it had no application to Western life. Thus came about the change from an abstract concept (suspended mind) to a concrete, literal situation (hanged man).

Then I think what happened in your life was a complete harmonization and balance of the forces between the two worlds, psychic and mundane.

G: That's right.

R: As the young people say today, you had it completely together at this point. There was exchange from the psychic realm into the mundane plane, and you were about to contribute to others also. You were helping others and helping yourself too. This is implied in the card JUSTICE. Now the intuition is really gathered together here into an entire bundle. We had the SIX OF RODS, the THREE OF RODS, and the NINE OF RODS; we have had multiples of three, and now we have the highest number of rods we can get, the TEN OF RODS. What this means to me is that all your forces now are channeled together. Your intuitive powers, as symbolized by the rods, are gathered together, and you are reaping the heritage of your psychic powers.

This last card represents the end of your life. It is a beautiful card, THE LOVERS, an exchange of love vibrations between yourself and the people of your atmosphere. The harmony of JUSTICE has a love vibration added to it. It is really a returning to the world of the love that was your heritage in the TEN OF

204

CUPS at birth. I can't say much more. I have never had a spread that had so many of these key cards, or Major Arcana, which are cards of great power.

G: Yes, I have love vibrations around me now, of course, with different people, but it is the same inner contentment that I enjoyed as a child.

R: Well, we had only two reversals, the KNIGHT OF SWORDS, who represented the disastrous first marriage, and then this setback period in your life represented by THE DEVIL. I think as the only two reversed cards, they are probably the only two times you would have thought of yourself as representative of these two setbacks.

G: That's right. The rest of my life has been more or less devoted to other people, but the divorce from my husband was mainly concerned with my child. He wouldn't work where my son could go to school—our son. And then that was the beginning of disastrous marriages; I never had good luck in marriages. In this period I went into the restaurant and bar business; I was successful in it from a monetary standpoint, but it was a constant fight, and I hated it. But I learned many things.

R: Tell me, do you have anything you want to add to this; tell me what was your general impression of the overall accuracy of the reading?

G: It was very good in telling what my life was like.

What are you going to call your book?

R: *Tarot and You,* because it will be the first book on the market of actual readings given people. All of the books now are books of interpretations, and I think that this is like the old church, in that one tries to force his interpretation on someone else. I tell the reader to just gaze at the card and say whatever comes into his mind.

G: That's the way I started to read. I'll show you a funny little deck of cards that I started reading with. I was in the hospital; I had a ruptured appendix, and of course years ago that was it—you were lucky if you pulled through it because they didn't have penicillin then. I used to read for the nurses. Did you ever see these?

R: No.

G: They are Tueila cards. These are 35 years old. I started reading

205

the regular cards until somebody went by and handed me a book on card reading. I knew I was psychic because as a child I had heart trouble and I used to play with spiritual friends and have wonderful conversations. Of course, my folks thought it was all my imagination; they thought I had a terrific imagination. I know it wasn't; I went to school under psychic power and got my classwork from it.

Anyway, I started reading the regular cards for the nurses in this hospital and things started coming out; I was there for three months and when I left I had quite a little business established. And then I got in with a group that used to have materialization seances; we were living in Denver at the time. I know now that we were all so ignorant; I was only seventeen or eighteen at the time. It's a wonder we didn't get killed at those seances. My husband was working with this little fellow who gave the seances; he was a cement contractor on a small scale. It was during Depression days and during those days they used to build a little cellar and live in it until they could build a house. Anybody that was in middle class means, all the boys would get together and help each other until they'd get the house built. The little fellow used to have these seances and they were really something—lights and voices and the trumpet, and tables and heavy desks floating around— why it's a wonder we weren't killed. Nobody knew how to handle it; nobody had studied anything. We had no idea what we were doing. Nothing good came of it; nothing bad came of it, but it was terrible forces. And of course everybody went to every fortune teller, we used to call them, we could get to. I also went to some spiritual meetings; my folks were the average Methodist-Baptist type people.

I had an aunt, by the way, who was a very famous astrologer—she worked with Evangeline Adams—and she got me into concentrating on psychic things. I'd threaten people when I was a kid; I'd tell them things, I'd say this is going to happen, and then when it did I'd be scared to death. So that's how I started, absolutely unknown to what it was all about, absolutely vague. It's a wonder things didn't go worse then they did. But that's how I got started in Denver . . .

And then I started a tea room there, reading tea leaves. I didn't know how to read tea leaves, but I told them whatever I saw. I had quite a reputation. Finally I had to leave Denver; my ex-husband was giving me a hard time over the boy and my folks were always butting in, so I came out to California and I followed it out here—worked out in Hollywood in the old days. I have a book here full of the stars' autographs. Read on the lot. I went into Hollywood greener than grass; it was the first time I'd been in the really big city—from Denver to Hollywood, you know. I didn't know the time of day; I didn't even know how to charge. A guy would give me a tip and I'd run after him to give it back—oh, it was really weird, it was really something. But I read for all the top ones; I have, oh I guess, three hundred signatures here. And then I kept it up all those years. I went to Phoenix, back out here, and then I settled in San Francisco, worked the Fairmont eight years. Of course now I have gone into it deeper than ever.

I joined this church in Hollywood back in '36, and I worked and studied and got my Doctor's degree in it, and I didn't follow through with some of their beliefs and they were going to take it away from me. We had a little court battle and I won; I have never been baptized, and when they found that out they were going to take it away from me.

R: (Laughter).

G: But mine was kind of a mixture of beliefs, as the cards showed. I am a complete believer in reincarnation; I'm the only one in my family that is . . .

R: I am too.

G: . . . And I pick up past lives lately. I'm very anxious to get with someone who works with hypnotism; I think I can regress now, and go into past lives. I never wanted to before, because I figured what the hell was the difference, but I do want to now. I feel it has a strong influence on what is around us now. I am very curious about it, so I'd like to go into it. I had the feeling when I walked in the door here that we have been connected in some previous life. I know I have never met you in this life. I am getting those conditions, I think, as I get older, because after all I am in my sixties.

Now let me give you a reading. I won't use the cards or anything, but I'll try to tell you a little bit about yourself and what you are going to do in life.

207

In this reading the reader will give his interpretation first, and the readee will not comment until the end. This is a reading by the Jungian spread for a woman who shall be known only as Frances.

The first card has been placed face down as the Unnamed Namer or World Navel. The second card represents the archetype of the feminine principle within the individual. This is a very nice card, the QUEEN OF PENTACLES. The woman is gazing at a large globe which contains a pentacle. It seems to suggest an inward turning, as though an inward turning will sustain her in later life. The third card, the archetype of the animus, is KEY CARD XIII, DEATH. The fourth card, the FOUR OF RODS, represents the mother; and the fifth card, the THREE OF RODS, represents the father.

Before I talk about the animus card I would like to talk about

The Jungian Spread

1. Facedown Card
2. Queen Penticles
3. Death
4. Four of Rods
5. Three of Rods
6. The Lovers
7. Ten of Pentacles (Reversed)
8. Six of Rods (Reversed)
9. Seven of Rods (Reversed)
10. The Sun
11. The Tower
12. The Devil
13. Four of Swords (Reversed)
14. Five of Swords (Reversed)
15. Page of Cups
16. Page of Swords
17. Three of Pentacles
18. Knight of Swords
19. The Moon
20. The Star
21. The Fool
22. Seven of Pentacles

the FOUR OF RODS, because I see a definite contribution there, an interplay between it and the QUEEN OF PENTACLES. The card representing the mother shows a kind of gateway covered with garlands, and in the distance is a kind of ideal castle surrounded by a moat. It suggests completedness and the Jungian concept of the square of consciousness. In modern terminology one would have to say that the mother had it all together. The floral motif embellishing the rods suggested to me a very rich feminine consciousness. Such a mother would have a deeply positive effect on her daughter. They say that, in part, the archetype of the feminine principle is formed by the mother; so I think the FOUR OF RODS contributes to the QUEEN OF PENTACLE'S being a positive feminine principle. A queen suggests royalty, someone of a regal nature. This is royalty on the side of inner

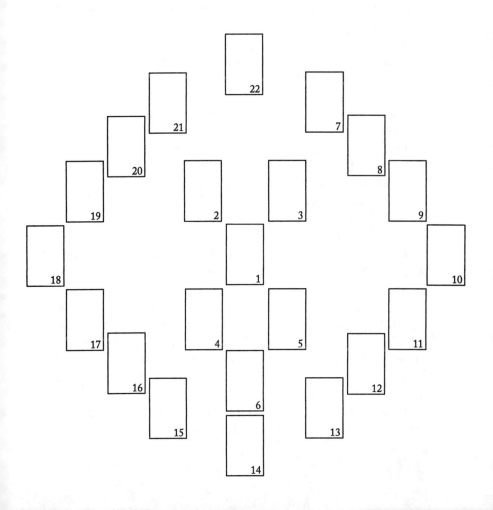

consciousness. The robe of white suggests purity, and the black spots on it suggest the yang principle which the individual will have to deal with in her life if she is to have feminine fulfillment.

The card DEATH suggests to me an animus that is very negatively constituted. In literature one thinks of Bluebeard, Heathcliff, and dangerous figures such as that. Again, there seems to be a contribution between the father card, the THREE OF RODS, and the archetype of the animus as represented by DEATH. The THREE OF RODS shows a figure whose head almost completes another quaternary in the sense of the four quarters, the four sides of consciousness, which are represented by the opposite mother card. But the figure's back is to the reader, and it suggests to me a classic case of the "absent parent" syndrome. If the parent was not actually physically absent from the home, it was a relationship in which nothing was contributed in the way of affection and feeling to the child. I think what this means is that the departed parent will be sought throughout the rest of the life through the next card, which stands for the individual's approach to life, the way she relates the inner principles just discussed to the outer wheel of life, her outward form of expression.

That card is THE LOVERS, so I see a quest through life for the absent father, the negatively constituted animus contributing, probably, to destroy most of the relations. Returning for a moment to the card DEATH, I am almost compelled to say that I feel that the father died at an early age, and this is why he is depicted with his back turned in the THREE OF RODS. This is what is conveyed to me through the card DEATH. So an early death contributed to the negative constitution of the animus.

Returning to the card THE LOVERS, standing as it does between the inner psychological world and the external world (cards 7 through 22), this card represents the means by which the individual communicates with the world. The card may be regarded as moving around the inner edge of the outer circle as the life moves around the circle from station to station from one to twelve o'clocks. The expression of the Self reaches its most meaningful depth in this individual's case through love and through relating to others.

I have laid out the cards VII through XXII so that we have the entire wheel before us. The first thing that comes to mind is that the first three cards are inverted. They are the TEN OF PENTACLES, the SIX OF RODS, and the SEVEN OF RODS. This inversion suggests to me that the individual's early life was probably more difficult than is normally the case. Reversal of a card may suggest that the energies associated with it are working not for but against the individual.

The TEN OF PENTACLES conveys a kind of idyllic scene similar to that depicted in the FOUR OF RODS, so it looks as if there was some good fortune in a material way. If the card were straight up, it would probably mean you had been born very wealthy. The TEN OF PENTACLES reversed might qualify that to the extent of meaning that you were at least very well off. But the figure of the child is looking back over the shoulder, as though looking right back toward the inner world of the archetypes and particularly toward the negative animus, DEATH. I get a feeling of great unconscious fears in the childhood.

The SIX OF RODS is a card that is normally associated with triumphs, but again, reversed as it is, suggestions that come to mind are of a kind of yin/yang type of success. You may have had a lot of opportunities and advantages in a material way, but the unconscious working on you may have made you a little more miserable than you should have been in your circumstances.

The SEVEN OF RODS suggests a man in a defensive pose, and my associations here are with the word contention. Again, I think it is contention coming from below, from the psychological state of being. The SIX and SEVEN constitute thirteen RODS, and this added to the THREE OF RODS for the father and the one rod that supports the banner of DEATH, makes me continually refer back to the concept of the negative animus at work in the life. All these rods suggest, phallically, the power of the animus exercised negatively. I am really drawn now to all of the phallic symbols in all the cards. I am not a Freudian, but the two towers on either side of the round sun suggest the Indian symbols of the sex organs, the yoni and lingam. Then the towers in the TEN OF PENTACLES look extremely phallic. So it seems to be an orientation toward trying to encounter one's opposite in the lifetime, and in trying to find fulfillment through peace and at-one-ment with the opposite sex. In effect, this is what THE LOVERS says and what all the rods and the phallic symbols suggest to me.

211

Some time, probably in the teens, we have the appearance of Key 19, THE SUN. This could be the first love affair, because I am aware now that the rays of the sun look phallic to me. Or, it could mean the intellectual birth of the individual; that is, "seeing the light" or "comes the dawn." These phrases one associates with a change, a new phase of consciousness.

The next card, THE TOWER, conveys an idea of illumination from above through the lightning bolts. In some cases this makes the previous patterns of life orientation completely outworn. It shatters the whole structure of being. It is generally a card of psychic cataclysm of some kind. Followed as it is by THE DEVIL, where the lovers are shown in bondage, it suggests to me an impending dark night of the soul which the next card, the FOUR OF SWORDS, further strengthens. It is interesting that these three cards proceed downhill toward the nadir of the life. It is like a step from brief sunlight down to the underworld, THE DEVIL, and the figure of the knight lying in state. As a matter of fact, the Devil does stand for the underworld kingdom of death and, of course, Pluto rules here. This is, I think, a projection onto the outer world from the inner circle that we saw. The Key Card DEATH dominates that inner circle. It is a very powerful card, and often when it appears in the outer circle, I call it transformation; but as an archetypal card there is nothing to be transformed. The archetype is IT.

So, in your attempts to find the sunshine, to find the sunlight of love in your life, the negative animus has been projected outward from the inner circle of consciousness so that it affects the outer life. The lovers are held in bondage, and the fault is not so much external circumstances as it is within the individual, within the archetype. This is, of course, why we place faith in psychoanalysis today, because we recognize this truth.

In the FOUR OF SWORDS, the three swords that hang above the knight suggest to me three loves which will come in the lifetime. For you, in view of the pattern we have seen established, the love is always going to be a traumatic experience. It is going to be a double-edged sword, as we see in the swords hanging like the sword of Damocles. The sword underneath the knight suggests your own masculine principle, which may sustain you at some point in your life. For this to be positively constituted the animus will necessarily have to be transformed.

You have been in the belly of the whale, depicted in THE DEVIL and the FOUR OF SWORDS. Now at the very nadir we have the card the FIVE OF SWORDS. This card, like the FOUR OF SWORDS, is reversed. When the darkness of night is greatest, then its power must begin to break and the first new light appear.

This is a difficult card to interpret, but I associate the three swords that the figure has collected with my prediction that there would be three loves in the life. These are the three swords that previously hung above the figure in a Damoclean manner. Now they have been collected and they are no longer so menacing. The figure is no longer wearing a suit of armor. In the foreground are two swords that are crossed. They remind me of the card Two of Swords, which often suggests two paths to be taken in life. Also, it is directly below the card THE LOVERS, which in earlier medieval Tarot decks was called The Two Paths. So, by a strange bit of synchronicity here, at the very nadir—in the belly of the whale—the individual is faced with two choices. It reminds me of the ending of the film "The Savage Eye." In this film the individual has gone into the depths of despair. After an automobile accident she is in a hospital receiving transfusions, and in a dream sequence she recognizes two choices: "sleep and the abyss, or the shock of the living sea." Then we see her as a child on the sandy beach, running into the water, and naming the waves. In effect, her life begins again.

The FIVE OF SWORDS really represents for you the two paths. At this particular point in your life you may have either contemplated suicide, or for a time have forsaken the will to live. Two paths faced you, and you embraced the path of love. You went into the battlefield, as did the figure in the FIVE OF SWORDS, to quest your own knight.

I think the first love appears in this next card, the PAGE OF CUPS. To me, you are the figure of the fish emerging from the cup. You are coming out of the underworld, coming out of the unconscious world, and the Page is looking upon you with compassion and tenderness. His hat has some ribbons or embellishments that suggest wings like those of Mercury. He is really, through his presence and his love, announcing a new world and a new life to you. He may be a water-sign man, because he is holding a cup and I associate cups with water signs.

Then the second love, depicted in the PAGE OF SWORDS, was probably an intellectual, because the sword is very prominent and his gaze is very steadfast. I associate swords with the function of the intellect as defined by Jung in the four functions. I get a feeling from him of perhaps too much attention to his work of the mind and not enough attention to you. He is not the same type of man as the PAGE OF CUPS. Probably the man of the PAGE OF CUPS needed some of the objectivity and some of the intellectuality of the PAGE OF SWORDS. The man of the PAGE OF CUPS may have been too emotional, too much like yourself. The man of the PAGE OF SWORDS is steadfast and self-sustained, but from the sky behind him I am getting feelings of trouble from his own unconscious. The sky suggests to me an astral level (which is psychological or unconscious) of great turbulence, and disruptions or changes that have influenced him. He has set his work up, symbolized by the sword of intellectuality, as a way in which he approaches life and attempts to gain self-control; but there is a great turbulence on the astral plane that suggests that he may be no more master of himself than the man in the PAGE OF CUPS.

The effect of all this on you has been to drive you to the wall, as seen in the next card, the THREE OF PENTACLES. Very often in dreams the consciousness, or mind, of the individual is symbolized by a building or by a house of many rooms. The most famous example is Jung's dream about being in his family house. He had explored the upstairs and the downstairs, when he discovered steps leading down into the cellar and then even deeper, where one could penetrate to previously unknown levels. This dream led him to postulate the theory of the unconscious.

Here, in the card the THREE OF PENTACLES, I think you are very aware of your own need to work on your unconscious as symbolized by the structure. The structure of the psyche is your concern. You are aware of the fact that it needs some shoring up and some sustaining. You are now facing outward on the circle, perhaps for the first time. It seems to me that all the other figures have been related to the inner circle, that is the pre-conscious state and especially the negative animus. Here I get the impression that you are facing outward to the world and you recognize that

this work on the consciousness, this repair job, must be undertaken if you are to go any further into life with any kind of
resolution of the problems.

The next card, the KNIGHT OF SWORDS, who is also facing
outwards, suggests to me someone who may be helping you at
this time. The man to help you, of course, would be an analyst,
and he would use the sword of the intellectual function to
analyze what you bring to him and to help you to resolve the
inner turmoil. In this sense he is like the knight who frees the
maiden from the dragon. The encircling dragon in this case would
be the personal unconscious which gobbles everything that comes
to the individual in the lifetime. So, the analyst will slay this
dragon, or a least reconstitute it, through the sword of analysis,
chopping it up into little bits so that it can be put back together
magically in a more positive and less self-fixating form.

I have said that there would be three loves in the life, and we
have had two pages and one knight appear in the subsequent four
cards after I said that. So I would have to suggest here that
positive transference has taken place and the absent father
(absent in the sense of the non-positive animus) and the absent
love have been channeled now into the figure of the analyst, and
he is receiving the individual's love. I am not implying hanky-
panky between analyst and patient, but only the fact that transference has taken place. This is necessary, for if he is to free the
maiden fully, he must have her cooperation and her love as well.

That is the nine o'clock position on the wheel and it seems to
me that that is roughly the present stage in life.

The next four cards are rather positively manifested on the
wheel. They are THE MOON, THE STAR, THE FOOL, and the
SEVEN OF PENTACLES. One pattern is particularly apparent
here. That is, in the first part of the wheel down to the nadir we
had five inversions; and besides the five inversions we had THE
TOWER and THE DEVIL which are rather catastrophic cards.
The only positively constituted card was THE SUN. I suggested
before that that may have been the intellectual birth of the individual, or some transcendental moment that changed the outlook
and gave the first rays of the star of Selfhood which would be
sought on the journey. The rest of the following cards match this
path, because when this illumination strikes in a person's life

215

there is a threshold crossed even if it is only in a psychological, not a material, way. The person begins to live life no longer as a child but as a young seeker in the world. There is a separation from the family and from security. This is perhaps what THE TOWER means as well. It is a fracturing of the old accommodations in life, a movement downward into the belly of the whale. In this journey, the underworld probably symbolizes the unconscious of the individual. Perhaps every myth that has dealt with the underworld has been a description of the descent into the personal unconscious of that seeker.

After the nadir the upward path has been to seek through the three knights the yang part of the consciousness which was so notably absent in the inner circle. It seems to me it almost makes one believe in karma here, because when one has seen this kind of an inner life one would say she would have no choice but to seek for the other side of her own consciousness. She must seek that which is lacking, which is symbolized by the THREE OF RODS, with the figure whose back is turned, and by DEATH, which represents absence and departure. It seems to be a very clear pattern of the need to quest this in life. The last four cards, representing the latter part of life, suggest to me that this will be attained, but not necessarily as a material or mundane solution—that is, finding the actual knight—because none of the figures of the outer world can ever live up to what we seek in the inner world. We make a kind of truce with our archetype of animus or anima and agree to live in a less rarefied atmosphere of day to day living.

The card THE MOON suggests to me the persona of the individual, perhaps also the ego. Ego and persona may be depicted in one, because there is the moon shown at the full and the moon shone in profile. Its phases suggest aspects of the same thing. I think what this means is that you will come out of your analysis with the persona reconstituted, the ego mended and repaired, and you will then be giving the reflected light of the sun of Selfhood which was prophesied so early in the card of THE SUN. You will be giving this light to the world and projecting it outward.

The next card is THE STAR. I associate this also with Selfhood. I see it as another manifestation of THE SUN, the two working together. It seems this has been your higher purpose in

216

life. This is what was to be attained once the lost love of your masculine principle was found to be residing not in the outer world at all but, like the Bluebird in Maeterlinck's work, in your own backyard. One morning you may throw open the blinds and look out and the Bluebird that you had quested all over the world will be right there. In the card it is a lovely peacock with iridescent feathers, a symbolization on the earthly plane of the cosmic star shining above. The star has four main points, or four quarters, which suggest the integration of consciousness which was your heritage from your mother, as shown in the FOUR OF RODS. The feminine principle in you was so strongly developed that it sustained you throughout all of your journey in your quest for its opposite, the yang side of your consciousness.

Now we have the Zero card, THE FOOL. In effect, the card that we first placed face down in the middle of the wheel is the Zero card's natural position. It means, really, getting off the wheel. He stands in the middle because he is not part of the dance. The dance moves around him. He is the still point of the turning world. In view of the fact that in your wheel THE FOOL follows directly after THE STAR, it means more than an interpretation at its lowest denomination, that of foolish conduct or over-concern with material things, or trying to get on in the world. Such would be the real fool in life, who doesn't recognize the divine principles within and does not attempt to fulfill them. All of your pattern has been the opposite of this. It has shown an awareness of high consciousness. Furthermore, for THE SUN to appear at such an early point in the life suggests an unfoldment of the spirit and a beginning of the heroic journey. THE SUN at an early stage suggests a person of high consciousness. So, this FOOL is off the wheel, and you at this stage in your life are finally off the wheel. You have been doing a lot of karmic spinning and there has been great anxiety connected with it. I empathize with it because I am in many ways, though your opposite in sex, in character and unconscious temperament your double in makeup.

THE FOOL suggests an awareness of the cosmic life. THE STAR suggests that too. THE MOON is the reflection of the inner life of the Self being projected now out into the world through the persona.

The SEVEN OF PENTACLES is the last card on the wheel,

but it is a card of new beginnings more than of endings. I see it as a reaping of the harvest. The tree almost suggests a Christmas tree and the idea of the Christ principle. It also suggests fertility and abundance. The bird motif suggests again the peacock of THE STAR. Often I see it associated also with "Leda and the Swan," because when I look at this card I am always reminded of the Yeats poem. In that poem Yeats expresses beautifully the idea of the impregnation of the female principle, Leda, by the logos principle, Zeus, in the guise of a swan. It is a card of unity of the opposites occurring in the individual.

The figure in the SEVEN OF PENTACLES is looking back toward THE FOOL. THE FOOL is looking back toward THE STAR. THE STAR is looking back toward THE MOON. And THE MOON is looking toward the KNIGHT OF SWORDS. There is a whole line of figures facing left and gazing down along the wheel. It is like a looking back along the stations of the life.

Now I see another similarity in this pattern. Going back to the figure in the TEN OF PENTACLES, we see that the young child there is looking back over the shoulder. That, I said, was a looking back toward the unconscious world. I see it now as also looking toward the card at the apex of the wheel, at the figure in the SEVEN OF PENTACLES.

So, the figure in the final card gazes back over the long life and, I would say, as shown in the last four cards, will reap the harvest that she has so well deserved as a true daughter of Persephone. That is, through the QUEEN OF PENTACLES and the rich bounty of Ceres suggested by the floral gardens in the FOUR OF RODS, she will attain the square of consciousness. This QUEEN OF PENTACLES, this daughter of Persephone, in the unconscious world finds realization in the harvest of mating with the logos principle.

Finally, putting the SEVEN OF PENTACLES and the QUEEN OF PENTACLES side by side we see an amazing similarity of faces. That's about all I can say, so now I'm going to ask you for your general reactions. To me the pattern is quite clear as to what the cards say. How far the cards are accurate in respect to reality I shall leave you to qualify.

F: It's an astonishing reading. First, it was enormously startling as the cards were laid out, and then even more so as you gave the reading. Up to the nine o'clock point, which I see as you did as the point at which I have arrived in life, these cards seem to have laid out the events of my life in sequence, both on the psychological and on the mundane plane. I am particularly impressed with the first six cards. Of course, the one face down, the Unnamed Namer, we will not know on the earthly plane. But the second and third cards, the QUEEN OF PENTACLES and DEATH, aligned as they are as the archetypal prefiguration of a life, followed by the FOUR OF RODS with its rich feminine qualities paired with the suggestion of loss or absence in the masculine THREE OF RODS, were very startling. Your interpretation of these cards as parental symbols in both the inner and the outer world is amazingly correct.

My mother was a woman who was very Cerean. She was richly endowed in her relation with the world and all living, growing things. Anything grew beneath her hands. I would say that all the symbols in the card—the garlands, the castle in the background—would represent my mother's potentials. That she did not realize them fully in the external events of her life does not deny the fact that they represent the essence of her personality. Though she was shy and not always able to express her feelings, the kinds of relationships she had with people, and certainly with me, were very deep. It was on the feeling level that people responded to her always. As I look back I realize now how great was the loss that she was unable to achieve her own fullest capacities. But they were there, as shown also in the card above her, the QUEEN OF PENTACLES.

Next to her is the THREE OF RODS. Again, it was startling that you would have read from that card the possibility of the death of the father in early life. That is exactly what happened. My father died when I was between two and three years of age. This card is directly below DEATH, the archetypal parent. The layout is enough to boggle the mind!

I must tell you that one of my earliest fantasies as a small child was to imagine that I was Persephone. I visualized my mother as Ceres and myself as Persephone being snatched away and carried to the depths of the underworld. There, of course, I reigned as the Queen of the Underworld, the Bride of Death, permitted to return to earth only after certain events had taken place. In her rage at the loss of her daughter the mother makes a wasteland of the world until she gets her daughter back. She had to make a pact with the gods to do so.

R: A pact with her opposite principle, really.

F: Yes. So you can see why it struck me as extraordinary that these four cards would turn up first, reminding me instantly of my childhood fantasy. It went to such lengths that I used to wander alone in fields, picking wildflowers, and really half expecting to be abducted, fearing yet wishing for the "longed for terror," a feeling which I believe is in every feminine psyche. Also, I think the fantasy expressed my deep longing to be assured of my mother's love for me.

Looking back, I know now that my sensitive mother must have understood a great deal more of what fantasy life meant to a small child. I remember once coming home from school and finding that my mother had placed a bowl of pomegranates in my room.

Then, when you had completed your reading and we came to the final card, the SEVEN OF PENTACLES, and you spoke of the gathering of the harvest as a daughter of Persephone, my mind reeled once more at your intuitive reading of these cards.

I think you said the sixth card represents the relationship of the individual to the world, moving around the inner circle as the essence of the individual's connection with the wheel of life. This card is THE LOVERS. I believe that I have always related to people in the way you described, but quite unconsciously. In Jungian terms I could be called an extrovert. That is, a predisposition added to conditioning led me to seek my own reality in the outer world rather than in the inner world. I felt I existed only as I was reflected back to myself by others. I was only dimly aware that I was constantly seeking something and never quite finding it. I think you are probably right that the loss of the father had a great deal to do with the shaping of this attitude. I was looking for that absent half, seeking a balance.

The first three inverted cards on the wheel led you to speak of energies that were working against me rather than for me. You also said they made you think that the first years of my life might have been unusually difficult. If the cards had been in an upright position and not inverted as they are, they could be very power-

220

ful and very rich. But as it happens, those years *were* very difficult for me. After my father's death my mother was ill for several
years, and I lived with my grandparents. I was separated from my
mother for a long time. Then she remarried. Now I am drawn
back to the card the THREE OF RODS, showing the man with
his back turned. My mother married a man who was very generous in a material way. We were not wealthy but we lived well and
I never lacked anything I wanted. It was the whole bag of good
schools, pleasant social life, and such. But my stepfather was
absolutely incapable of demonstrating affection. There was a
coldness, a hollowness, between this man and me that my mother
spent the rest of her life trying to compensate.

The TEN OF PENTACLES I see as symbolizing a rich heritage, not in worldly goods, but in the sense of family inheritance as it was given to me by my grandfather. He was a remarkable man of great wisdom, intellect and gentle wit. It seems to me
that there was combined in him an ancestral heritage of many
generations of these fine qualities. Perhaps the inversion of the
card is an indication of the loss I felt when I was separated from
him after my mother's remarriage. In any case, he was an
enormous influence in my life, opening my mind and pointing me
toward . . .

R: THE SUN?

F: Yes, THE SUN in the sense of the development of the
intellect.

The SIX and the SEVEN OF RODS I think you have also read
with amazing accuracy. The suggested potentials in the SIX OF
RODS were unrealized, and I believe this was because of the
contention that you saw in the SEVEN OF RODS. You are right
that it was a struggle on the psychological level, though I was too
young to know this at the time. I would add that it was also
difficult for me in day to day life. I simply could not adjust to
my mother's remarriage and to the replacement of my beloved
grandfather by an undemonstrative man whom I didn't understand or appreciate until many years later.

Remember, we are talking about a time that is almost fifty
years ago. I lived in a period and in a class of society in which
children were brought up in specific ways, with moral and ethical
values that gave little recognition to possible individual differ-

221

ences, particularly in the psychological sense. While my mother was a sensitive woman, warm and kind and generous in many ways, I think she was locked into the attitudes of her time and of her own up-bringing. So, I was raised to be a well-bred, good little girl. I can look back on it now and see that this emphasis was to my detriment because the effect was to cut me off for most of my life—until recent years—from the world of fantasy and fairy tales and mythology, from any avenues that might have led to individual creativity, from any recognition of or coming to terms with my own inner life. I was propelled by my circumstances toward external values, making good in the world, being liked.

R: That is what the card THE DEVIL symbolizes—bondage to the mundane plane.

F: Yes, a fulfilling of the pattern that we saw predicted. And it certainly came.

THE SUN, I would say, appears on the wheel at about mid-adolescence. That was when the delights of the intellect began to open up for me more fully, perhaps as a compensating factor. The intellect was forced to take the place of the loss of an inner life. I think the tendency was already there, but it became imbalanced, all one-sided. Incidentally, one of the first things I saw in this card was the open book upon which THE SUN seems to rest.

In all these things we have been talking about there was some good along with the bad. Intellectual growth led me into the world of literature and poetry, and to an appreciation of music and dance, pursuing my own developing tastes and preferences. It opened up the world of the arts forcefully and excitingly for me. I think this, coupled with the deep inner need that the card THE LOVERS represents, is an indication of the way in which I was compelled to go. Since I was unable to look inside myself for avenues of expression, I had to try to find a reflection of myself in the outer world. From this point on in my life I sought and have had as friends creative people—painters, writers, musicians, dancers. I have often wondered why I was accepted by these people, since I have never had the courage or the compulsion to search out any latent talents in myself and have always had the most prosaic, boring kinds of jobs. This acceptance has always puzzled me.

R: Let me speak on that. I think they recognized the creative person in yourself. Even though you haven't enacted on the mundane plane what you should have or might have, your temperament and qualities are those of a creative person. Let's go back to what I said about the two paths. Although THE LOVERS is the the card that represents your orientation to life, on another level in the medieval deck it is called The Two Paths. Interpreted thusly it suggests that point in your life when you submerged the sensitive side of your being to the common-sensical way of how one ought to act, which we see the young people today in such reaction against.

F: Yes, I agree. And there was a price to be paid for my submission. We can see it in the cards, and I can tell you that I certainly lived it. I look upon the next four cards, THE TOWER, THE DEVIL, THE FOUR OF SWORDS, and THE FIVE OF SWORDS, as symbolizing the period in my life that followed the bursting sun of intellectual delights. THE SUN never really left me, but I paid an awful price for the loss of an inner life. These cards reflect that downfall beginning in THE TOWER, which looks like something that is in terrible danger with lightning striking at it, and it is aflame. This card is followed by THE DEVIL, showing the separated lovers with their backs to each other, and this suggests exactly what happened to me in an inner sense. I got separated from one part of myself, and my life became so one-sided that I could only go on blindly, paying a deeper and deeper price. It was a long period of unhappiness, illnesses, an unsuccessful marriage, the war years, and the death of my mother. I see these cards as representing those years from adolescence up to my early thirties. They were years of constant struggle. Nothing came out right. Today, with the help of analysis, I realize that it was the division of self that caused the suffering—the inability to bring together the two parts and find a balance between an inner and an outer life.

Now, in spite of all the negativity there, I must say that THE LOVERS has nevertheless helped me. I have never been without friends, deeply warm relationships that were very sustaining during those dark years. The dark years though, culminated in a strong suicidal tendency, as you seem to have seen in the inverted FOUR OF SWORDS, even though you also saw the potential of the three loves to come.

223

Then, as you said, in the FIVE OF SWORDS we see that the armor, the outer sheath, is gone and three of the swords have been gathered up, representing some kind of positive activity. Unconscious or not, this suggests a returning strength, some determination to pull out of the darkness. Also, you pointed out the two crossed swords as possibly a choice of paths. Didn't you refer to a beach or a crossing of water?

R: Yes, I referred to the film "The Savage Eye," and the suggestion of new birth symbolized by the child on the beach, and the naming of the waves. I think at the moment I spoke of this you did a little flash on it.

F: Yes, indeed, because this card and your interpretation of it describes the period when I first sought analytic help. While it was more of a rescue operation than a new birth—I did not go into deep therapy—the wonderful man I went to helped me to get on my feet again, physically and emotionally, so that I could face life once more.

It was then that I literally stood on the beach of a new beginning and decided to cross the sea. I took a trip to Europe (staying for six months) all by myself, which, considering the timid person I had been in the past, was a courageous thing to do. But I had to do it—it was like a compulsion. I felt a strong need to cut myself off, not from friends or former pleasures, but from the dark pattern underlying the old life. I wanted to move out into the world again and to find newer, stronger ways to be.

R: Then, in the chronology of the mythic hero's journey, this is the point of return to the world from the abyss.

F: Yes, it was. Again, it was startling to see the PAGE OF CUPS turn up as the next card, especially as you had foreseen in the previous two cards the possibility of three loves to come. I felt when you were talking about them that you sensed that these would be rejuvenating factors, and you were right. As soon as I saw the PAGE OF CUPS I thought of the man I met when I made that voyage across the sea. He was a European, a man of great loveliness and vitality, sensuous and worldly. He was the first love. He made me feel as though I had come back from the dead. Through him, for the first time in my life I knew what it meant to be a woman. Though our association was a relatively short period of time, (eventually I had to return to this country and he remained in Europe, and we have seen each other only a few times in the intervening years) that relationship was so deep and so meaningful for both of us that we have remained friends to this day.

R: Do you by any chance know his astrological sign? Because of the cup I associate him with a water sign.

F: I don't know his sign, but your association is apt. He was for some time in his younger life an officer in the merchant marine of his country. How do you like that?

R: I like it! I like it!

F: He was very significant in my life because I think that he recognized, responded to, and brought out the best of me in a feminine sense. You are right that up until this point, unconsciously, there had been a very negative animus factor working against me. I can use such words now that I am in Jungian analysis, but I would not have understood the terminology earlier.

R: I would like to point out something else I see in the cards in connection with that. We have a vertical line descending from DEATH to the THREE OF RODS to the FOUR OF SWORDS. Although each card stands for a different thing, there is the same principle functioning, extended into the outer world, and into the FOUR OF SWORDS where you hit rock bottom as a result of the negative animus principle.

Now, you said that the man of the PAGE OF CUPS made you feel like a woman for the first time. Notice that a vertical line also extends from the QUEEN OF PENTACLES to the FOUR OF RODS to the PAGE OF CUPS. This is your feminine principle. This shows the feminine principle sustaining you from within the archetype, through the mother and that rich heritage, down to the enactment of it in the form of love on the mundane plane.

F: It is really amazing. When I saw the PAGE OF CUPS followed by the PAGE OF SWORDS, I thought immediately of the two men I had loved. Perhaps one of the old cliches is true: when you are ready for love, you find it.

R: The law of attraction.

F: It must be so, because the first love was followed by another deep and loving relationship with a man who was exactly as you have described him in your reading of the card. He was intelligent, witty, talented, very successful in his profession. You were right also in your interpretation of the cloudy background as a turbulence in him on the unconscious level. For a number of reasons there was never any question of marriage, but this relationship was close and deep and lasted for many years.

This man gave me a further and deepening sense of myself, especially in relation to the world. Again, it was a development of femininity. I became a little braver, a little less uncertain of myself.

R: Also more relatedness, possibly, to your own masculine principle, to your logos principle?

F: I wouldn't have thought of it in those terms at the time. But each man in his own way did contribute to a recognition on my part not only of my own femininity but of the full value of masculinity in its own right. These two men brought me to understand very deeply what the relationship between a man and a woman can be. This, not in an idealized way but in a true appreciation of each other's qualities—likenesses and differences—and to value those qualities in each other. I felt as though I was being truly recognized and valued, and this made it possible for me to recognize, instead of fear, the value, the masculine principle as it was embodied within my lovers, or within the logos, or in any other such terms and symbols.

R: As it is embodied within yourself. To no longer fear it within yourself.

F: That particular insight was yet to come. I knew nothing of such concepts at that time.

Now we come to the THREE OF PENTACLES. This card suggests to me something rather cloistered. I think it suggested somewhat the same thing to you, but I don't remember what you said. I can only give you my associations with this card. It appears on the wheel at what would be roughly my forties. I had reached that age when I think that any thinking/feeling person of some sensitivity begins to realize that the major portion of his life has been lived. We begin to slow down a bit. Some of the youthful drives and urges begin to be replaced by more reflective attitudes. In spite of the positive things that had come to me through the two loves, and though I had friends and was functioning in my work, I was still troubled. I still felt unfinished.

R: Let me refresh you on what I said about this card. I related the structure in it to the consciousness, and I said that at this point you probably wanted to do some work shoring up the psyche.

F: Exactly. I'm glad you reminded me of that, because that *was* the period in which I tried to do just that but was unable to do it alone. I knew that I wanted some help but I didn't know in what direction to look. Something led me to the work of Jung, and I spent a whole winter reading his entire work. Then I knew that this was the path that might lead me to some answers. I found it through the guidance of a friend, the doctor I am seeing now, and I think this has been one of the blessings of my life. He is, in my mind, just what the card the KNIGHT OF SWORDS shows. He is the third great love. I do not mean this in the usual banal concept of the transference to the analyst. I mean that he is the man who will, as you pointed out, help me to slay the dragon, to free myself, and to come to know the meaning of love in the spiritual sense. I feel very hopeful about the outcome of analysis. Since, in my view, the cards you have laid out for me have been so extra-ordinarily accurate as to the previous events of my life, I may hope that I will emerge into what the final cards seem to indicate for the last years of my life. Whether that will be two years or twenty really doesn't matter if the hoped-for fulfillment is found.

R: That is, the promise of individuation that is shown.

F: I hope so. The KNIGHT OF SWORDS is followed by THE MOON, which I think indicates another, perhaps a fuller, realiza-tion of the feminine principle.

R: Of course! I missed that before. That, even more than the ego or persona integration, is what THE MOON symbolizes. Diana the chaste goddess of the moon, Ceres, Persephone, they are all of the same ilk. So, absolutely, it is a re-establishment of your feminine principle.

F: This card seems very significant to me, and especially as it is followed by THE STAR, which would seem to indicate the realization of Selfhood in whatever way it may come for me. THE MOON appearing later rather than earlier in life makes me feel that the qualities it represents will be used differently, perhaps more peacefully, than might have been the case had it appeared in more youthful days.

R: Yes, perhaps more in relation to what you said about Jung

227

and the age of reflection. Jung is regarded as the philosopher of the later years and of the integration of the death consciousness into the life, which can result in the individual growing and evolving tremendously in the face of that. I always laugh at people who say because of death life means nothing. I say that life would mean nothing without death.

F: In relation to this integration—and especially in relation to the negative animus that had been working against me—let me show you some drawings I have been making. In Jungian analysis the attempt to draw dreams and visions is an important aid. I am not an artist and these are among my first attempts at drawing. Well, here, as you can see in this drawing, a beautiful and young animus figure has appeared.

R: In commenting on this for the recorder, which has ears and can hear but hath not eyes and cannot see, this drawing looks like a Cambodian dancer with a many-tiered silver headdress. The face is blue. These are exactly the colors that we see in THE MOON.

F: After his appearance in a dream, it has been as though he has released these other mandala drawings, these with the female face in the center.

R: Extraordinary. I have seen drawings like these in Frances Wickes' book *The Inner World of Man,* and I have seen some reproduced in Jung's book on the collective unconscious and the archetypes. Most of those drawings were done by artists who had gone into analysis, but you say you are not an artist. I can only say that there is artistry here in the beauty of the symmetry, and in the faces that are like open lotuses wherein lies the jewel of the Self.

F: The feminine principle evolved?

R: I think we are beyond that stage now. I am looking at this in a mythic way, and a philosophical way. When that lotus opens up, it has involved both the masculine and the feminine principle integrated to get it open, and within is the jewel of Selfhood which is sexless and eternal and divine. Looking at these faces I get the impression of looking down into a pool. Perhaps the pool is the waters of the unconscious, and the flower of the individual has opened up, and within is this face which is in repose. It looks like a Buddha in mediation, which to me means a stillness. And that, more than anything I could have said, sums up the consciousness you arrive at in the Zero card, where you get off the wheel and achieve cosmic consciousness. That can only happen after integration of the masculine and the feminine elements.

F: These were autonomous drawings, straight out of my unconscious, and done as a part of therapy. I still feel I have a long way to go. But I hope to arrive, through the quiet wisdom of THE FOOL, at a sunset harvest. Perhaps that is the attainment suggested in the final card the SEVEN OF PENTACLES.

Let me say lastly, that this reading has been a fantastic experience. I had never before seen the Tarot cards. I had heard about them but thought they were used more as a parlor game, or for fortune-telling. But this is far from a game. The cards and their symbols in the hands of an intuitive reader like yourself are a world opening. It is an extraordinary experience and I thank you very much for it.

R: I am happy to have served. I think what happens when one is reading well like this is that the conscious mind and the ego of the reader get short-circuited and something else works through him. I think the principle is exactly the same as what is enabling you to create these beautiful mandalas.

Incidentally, I think there should be mention here about what a mandala stands for. In effect, this Jungian spread is in the form of a mandala. It has the still point of the turning world; it has the four quarters: the three o'clock point, the nadir, the nine o'clock point, and the apex. The red spot which you show on the brow of the face in your mandala is akin to our card which is face down in the middle of the spread, the Unnamed, the Zero point of consciousness. Everything else revolves around this like a dream; be it a sweet dream or a nightmare, it is only a dream.

Very often the mandala is a square with the circle within, or a circle with the square within. What is symbolized in those forms is the masculine and feminine united. Also, to Jung it was important because, since it had the four quarters of the world, it represented the integration of consciousness, the fully integrated individual. Mandalas have long been subjects of meditation in the East.

May THE MOON, THE STAR, THE FOOL, and the SEVEN OF PENTACLES come to you in their time.

T he date is April 4, 1971. This is a reading for Joseph Campbell. I have laid out the first four cards. The one in the place for the masculine principle is THE EMPEROR. I know that you are interested in the mythology of the Holy Grail, and this figure strikes me as almost Arthurian. He represents a benevolent inner principle within you. The exercise of such a figure in your outer life would certainly cause no confusion about your role as a man; it would make you, I would think, empathize with the warrior caste and knightly consciousness, and the questing motif.

The NINE OF RODS figure, although it is probably intended to be a man here, I am associating with the anima. In the sense that it looks as if it is in a barricade, it's held in, and I think it may be a particularly important part of your role in life to attain an anima relatedness to aid your own creativity and to bring out

The Jungian Spread

1. Face Down Card
2. The Emperor
3. Nine of Rods
4. The Magician
5. Nine of Pentacles
6. Ten of Rods
7. King of Swords
8. Ten of Pentacles
9. Judgement (Reversed)
10. Five of Rods
11. The Star (Reversed)
12. Knight of Swords (Reversed)
13. Seven of Pentacles

14. King of Cups
15. The Sun
16. The Chariot
17. Death (Reversed)
18. The Fool
19. Queen of Swords
20. Four of Cups
21. Eight of Swords
22. The Tower

your own feeling function. However, the card does represent an inner strength, on the side of the anima function, which archetypally will always be yours to rely on for creativity and personal integration.

The father is represented by THE MAGICIAN. When I look at these cards, the interesting thing about them is that each time I see a card now I see it with different eyes in the context of the reading. This card doesn't look like an alchemist anymore; it's more a businessman, someone who is bogged down by things. The paraphernalia hanging down at the top of the card suggests to me someone who is overburdened by little particulars of business, trivialities that perhaps prevent him from enjoying life more fully. Within him there is great power—it seems to be a classic case of a life gone wrong in that the potential was not realized. The power

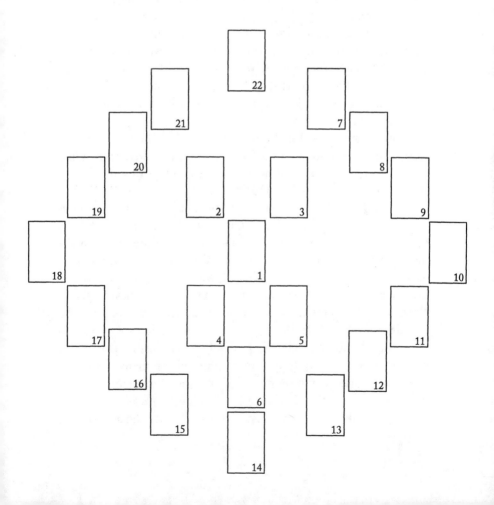

is misdirected in part by following what our culture believes a person ought to do—too much concern with the "oughts" of society rather than saying, "I will take the big leap." Maybe this is something you have recognized within your own consciousness. Very often when a child senses that the parent has not fulfilled his life potential, perhaps it is then easier for the child to take the step of striking out on his own, or entering the forest of life where there are no clearly marked paths for him to follow. How did you say it in your book *Creative Mythology?*

J: "Each thought it would be a disgrace to enter the forest in a group. Each entered at the place that he had chosen, where it was darkest and there was no way or path."

R: Well, the feeling I get about the man in THE MAGICIAN is that he is following paths and just getting weighed down with minutiae. All this doesn't suggest to me magic symbols at all—these are very prosaic things, such as a cup costing so much. The feeling I get from the card is of a trader in a small booth or stall, such as seen at a fair. Only the mundane level of the card is coming through for me. There is a sense of trading skill and business initiative associated with the man, but none of the higher levels of interpretation—such as logos consciousness—come through at all.

Now let me interpret the mother card, and then tell me how close I've come in my description of these four cards. Your father may not have known what he had on his hands with your mother as she appears in the NINE OF PENTACLES. This is another one of the cards in the deck with a bird-woman motif that reminds me of the myth of Leda and the swan, or impregnation of the female with the logos principle. The grapes on the vine and the many pentacles in the picture suggest earth relatedness and harmony between the human and lower levels of consciousness. The woman hearkens to the lesson that the bird has to teach. Normally I interpret these cards on three different levels. On the mundane level, with all these pentacles, this would mean someone who was definitely well-off, probably from birth. This man's business ventures may have been a drain on the many pentacles, which of course symbolize money on the most mundane level. He may have been inclined to take flyers in certain ways. I can't do any more with these four cards; I'll turn them around so that you

232

can see them better.

J: Well, my father was a businessman, and he started as a poor boy, the son of a gardener on a big estate in Waltham. In the early days, when he was fourteen years old, he went to work in Boston as an errand boy in a department store. He went on from there to a big company in Boston—Brown-Durrell—and he became a salesman. And then on his first sales trip he made a smash and became a very important man in the firm. When they wanted to set up a New York house, it was my father who was sent to do that, and it was in New York then that he met my mother. Her father also was a businessman. I would say that until the time of the blow in 1929 and the Depression, at which time I had gone through college and had had my training in Paris and Munich and all that, Dad was just sailing to the skies. So there was no problem at all as far as money was concerned. Then it was a terrific blow, and I would say from 1929 until the time of his death in 1949 he had a rough time. During that rough time all the savings and everything else were just eliminated. In 1939, the year after Jean and I were married, he really smashed economically and went to Honolulu—my sister was already there—and opened a little shop in Honolulu. He was in the hosiery business, and practically all the hosiery men in the East had been his boys. So he went there and opened a little retail instead of wholesale shop. They sent him all the goods, and he had about eight years of really glorious success; it was the Indian summer of his life. My mother and sister were very close to take care of him and so forth. He died realizing that he had run into trouble again, and we had a little problem picking up the pieces. That's the story of my father, and what you said there I think is in the direction of such a picture.

My mother was a very strong woman with great sympathy and understanding. Nature moved in her in an easy, lovely way. She was good all the way through.

What you have to say about my anima system is right, I think. I didn't get married until I was thirty-four, and the thing that was blocking my relationship to younger women was my ambition. I can't imagine any woman having tolerated the kind of dedications as to reading books and finding my place in the world and in my mind that seized me when I was a little kid. For years I have always been very strongly attracted to women. I find them delightful and never had any sense of negativism towards them, but they always want to get married. I would take them to Paul Whiteman's Palais Royale for a dinner and dance, and then they'd want to get married.

R: (Laughter).

J: And I found this to be revolting in a certain way, so there is this story of one person after another that I broke off with because of these demands. The emperor figure in the card for the masculine principle seems to represent ambition; however, it was more than ambition, it was a compulsion towards individuation and a drive towards Selfhood, which at the time was wholly incompatible with settling down and marrying. I think the ankh that the emperor holds symbolizes my interest in the mystery of nature and the universe and the question of where man fits into all this, which I felt I had to answer for myself. So it was the desire to answer these questions that put up the nine poles as a kind of barricade between the world and my anima. Until I came back to the United States in 1929, which was the year of my poor father's collapse with the Depression, I just hadn't had anything to do with women in a fundamentally serious, biological way, except for the kind of love-making that was popular at that time. I would not have thought myself of what you have put out there, but it comes out to be the way I recognize it. It's very good.

R: Uh-huh. You can see now, looking at the cards in restrospect, how they can be interpreted . . .

J: I would interpret these cards exactly the way you have, with this review that I have given. I think that is the setup of Joe Campbell.

R: Isn't it funny that they will look different to me each time. What I see in the father card is almost a man in a booth at a fair.

J: Well, I have watched my father display hosiery, with you presenting that image here. My father did not have a mustache—but otherwise I can see him doing that. This is O.K. And the bird rather than the money here in the mother card is the thing that best describes my mother's wonderful earth relatedness. Money didn't mean a damn thing to her. She had it up to that time—we weren't a wealthy family; it was middle middle-class. But in that period middle middle-class was 'way up. What people now call

234

poverty was wealth in those days. We were doing just fine. I saw the money there in that card, but the thing I recognize is the bird, not that she collected birds or anything, but her whole relation to nature was perfectly lovely.

R: I think that one of the most interesting stories that you told me about your interest in books and your intellectual or spiritual drive is the story about the public library in New Rochelle, its construction, and what you were doing. Can you just give us a quick little . . .

J: The thing is simply this: we lived in New York until 1913 or so, that is to say until I was nine years old. While in New York I became tremendously interested in the American Indians for two reasons. One was that Buffalo Bill used to come to New York annually with the Wild West Show. This was a great thing. The other was the American Indian collection at the Museum of Natural History. My dear father used to take my brother and me wherever we wanted to go on Sundays. We went three places; one was the aquarium down on the Battery, one was the Bronx Park, up at the other end of the island, and the third was the Museum of Natural History. Since that was in the middle we would usually end up there anyway after we went to one of the others. There they had a great room of totem poles, which is even now impressed upon my psyche as one of the most marvelous things. Then when we moved to New Rochelle in 1913, there was a vacant lot next to our house on Pintard Avenue, and pretty soon after our arrival workmen began laboring there. My little brother and I, aged eight and nine respectively, helped the workmen find bricks and things like that. So on the day that the library was opened, I was sitting on the steps already waiting to get in, and was the very first person to have a card at the library. Of course, the thing I dashed for was the American Indian section, and after about two years I had read everything they had in the children's library about the American Indian, and they admitted me to the stacks. So I would come out from the library—it was right next door—loaded with books, and my family presented me with a little library of my own. I had a lovely room and they bought the books I wanted. My father used to go down with me to the second-hand book shops where we could buy the reports of the Bureau of Ethnology, those big annual reports for a dollar each.

Boas was one of my people, and Cushing, and by the time I was twelve I was learned in the matter of the American Indian. When I hear these anthropologists now, they don't know a damn thing about it—I still know more than they do from what I knew when I was twelve years old about the Plains Indians and all that kind of thing. Of course, when I finally went to prep school in 1919, when I was fifteen years old, I had to stop studying Indians and get into these other things, and it broke off. Then I didn't get back to it until graduate school. I went to graduate school only because I had another year of athletic competition available, and I went in the easiest department of all, English. Just by chance I bumped into the Arthurian romances, and there were the same motifs that I had learned years before about the American Indians. And I caught fire and that is where I have been burning ever since.

R: These motifs you speak about—I don't make a ready association between the medieval European Arthurian legends and the myths of the American Indians.

J: Well, there are the standard mythological motifs of the quest and the magical adventure and the magical aid, and the virgin birth or something like that, the atmosphere and the sense of some kind of relevance to my own and everyone's life that I felt. I was again fascinated with the Arthurian material, and I remained there for a year and a half at Columbia working on that, and I was doing so well, according to their opinion, that they gave me a grant to go to Europe. And coming from a business family, I was, as far as I know, the only person in the family to have gone to college. This was all pioneer, and when I received the grant, all I thought of was England—you know that's where people go. But my professor, W. W. Lawrence, said, "Why go to England where they speak the same language you do? Why not go to France, where you can really become competent in another language." So I did go to France. In France I found that all the basic books in philosophy were in German, so I went to Germany. That was absolutely marvelous. I returned in 1929 to my father's calamity and that was that. But meanwhile I had become infected with this drive to know more and more about these mythical mysteries, because in Germany the whole thing opened up wide. I couldn't go back into the Columbia bottle again and I dropped the whole thing of a PhD. and went to work. I got the idea I wanted to write and started writing short stories. I put myself to school to a man named John Gallishaw, who was teaching short story writing. I learned a lot about the form of short stories, but I didn't have anything to say. I sat in front of a blank piece of paper for a year and I regret it enormously.

R: (Laughter).

J: Well, to finish this part of the story, the Depression was absolute; there wasn't a job in the world. I got a notion that if I went west there would be a job in another state. I did have a Model A Ford, and I drove west, and that lands you in California—without a job. So there was that funny year in Carmel and the Big Sur peninsula, where I met Steinbeck and Ed Ricketts, who I told you was Doc in Steinbeck's novels. It was then that I bumped into Oswald Spengler. I had been at a kind of an impasse, but this meeting opened up a whole new world for me, and nobody could stop me. I just started taking notes, notes, notes. I don't know what's going to happen when I pass away—there are thirteen standard filing cabinet's drawers filled—packed!—with notes; it amounts to something like thirty years of note taking. That was all I did until *Finnegans Wake* came along. And then Rondo Robinson said let's write an explanatory key to this book. That was in 1939, and I was already thirty-five years old before I got going. And the rest is all in the filing cabinets. That's what blocked the anima, I think.

R: O.K. When we talk about what blocked the anima, we come up with the TEN OF RODS. This card stands for your approach to life. It is placed between the four heritage cards and the outer wheel of mundane experience. This man seems to be carrying the fence that surrounded the anima figure in the Nine of Rods. He is obviously laboring in what seems to be service of the intuitive function. This may be a man who is gathering in the harvest of his intuitive perceptions into the whole spectrum of mythic lore.

J: Well, that could be those years from about 1927 to about 1937.

R: Now this isn't just those years. This is the *gestalt,* the way you relate to life *per se.* This is a labor of intuition.

J: Now, because of the relationship you pointed out to the Nine of Rods, I am associating this card with a barrier, something I am doing that blocks the anima fulfillment or relationship. And here we see a guy interested only in rods—ten rods. Before it was nine—that feminine number, nine Muses and all that—and here it is ten, and there is no woman around at all. I am just laboring on rods, and I would say that was about twenty years of my life.

R: Generally this card describes the superior function—in the Jungian sense—of the individual. And I know that you regard your intuition as the superior function. So here you have ten of the rods, as many as you can get, and they almost look as if they are sprouting out of the figure's head. I think in a reading I gave for you a year and a half ago with another deck, the card that described the way you relate to life was the Ace of Rods. So there is a nice parallel here.

O.K. The first card of the wheel of life is the KING OF SWORDS. This is your heritage at the moment of birth. It seems to me that this is what we talked about in connection with Arthurian legend and the Grail quest. He faces forward on the wheel of life, whereas we noted that the previous figure had his face hidden in the rods, and his intuitive orientation was predominantly to the inner world, towards which he faces. Now with this heroic figure of the King of Swords, you are ready to do battle with the world's dragons and to quest the spiritual Grail in your own life. Since you are the author of *The Hero with a Thousand Faces,* this is a marvelous heritage card for you.

The next card is the TEN OF PENTACLES. It suggests what we would have to call in modern terminology the happy home life.

J: Great.

R: It seems to be without strife. Very often when I see this card, I am taken by the child who is already looking outside of the magic circle. He is really looking through this threshold, perhaps to the day that he can himself enter the forest where it is darkest. There is no strife—there is a fulfillment there on the level of childhood. I don't see any of the traditional strife that we see today between the mother and father.

J: I never saw any of that. All this Freudian nonsense—I don't recognize it.

R: O.K. The next card is reversed, and it is JUDGEMENT. This is associated with a new consciousness. Now The Sun might appear here at this point in the life. I think this is about the time that you walked out of the library with all those books and there was a new consciousness born.

J: Right. O.K., we'll take it that way; that's the way it seems to work.

R: It is a resurrection out of childhood and into a new world.

J: It's a discovery, a second birth, you might say.

R: Now I have been taken by the fact that the sun seems to be rising in previous readings, and other times with the banner of St. George. Here I can almost hear the bugle sound as a clarion call to the young warrior to ride off and do battle.

J: Do his work, yes.

R: In *The Hero With a Thousand Faces* you quoted from Sophocles:

> For a God called him—called him many times
> From many sides at once: "Ho, Oedipus,
> Thou Oedipus, why are we tarrying?
> It is full long that thou are stayed for: come!"

However, we have forgotten that the card is reversed. Sometimes this is taken as misdirection of the energy of the card. Most often my interpretation is a reference not to the mundane plane but to the inner world. In other words, within the circle is the world of the personal unconscious, with the face down card at the center perhaps representative of the collective unconscious. So the direction of a reversed card may refer us back to the inner consciousness; hence this card represents a new level of inner consciousness, which agrees with what I said earlier about this new birth.

The next card, the FIVE OF RODS, suggests the lyceum, the market place for exchange of ideas, kind of in the old idealized concept of the university, where all theories and formulae were put to the test of the other students and the professors.

Now, here we get the beginning of the descent down towards the "belly of the whale," in your terminology, or the nadir of the life. THE STAR, reversed, is again a symbol for this new birth of consciousness, the individuation process, the following of your own star. This occurs very often in the dreams of patients in Jungian analysis, and generally speaking it is a symbol for all that is of value and meaning in the life of the individual. As a light

239

shining in darkness, it may also be interpreted as a symbol of spiritual value. Now I've been monopolizing the stage here; do you have any insights yourself into these cards?

J: JUDGEMENT, FIVE OF RODS, and THE STAR, I would understand as follows: this clarion call, the resurrection, and the reversed star thing, this field of interest was not recognized in the schools that I went to.

R: How so?

J: Well, it just wasn't taught. Now everybody studies anthropology; nobody ever heard of it back then. Even when I went to Columbia, I was unable to study along my lines of interest. Boas was teaching at Columbia University, but he was teaching at Barnard. And when I went to enroll to study with Boas, whom I had known since I was nine years old, I was told that he was over at Barnard. So I never could study the thing that I was interested in. I did study other things that were very important to me since then, but my own clarion call and star were really reversed, and the contentions of successes and achievements were in the field of the academic, and also in my mind in athletics. So my star remained upside down and hidden until I went to graduate school, because I had a year of athletic eligibility left to me which I thought I should take advantage of because I was captain of the track team. Then I rediscovered my star and it was reintegrated into my field. That accounts for this curious delay, I think, in my whole intellectual and scholarly development. So the FIVE OF RODS, to my mind at least, does not describe the ideal academic environment that you mentioned in connection with the lyceum as much as it is a picture of the contention and strife which I encountered in trying to follow my star. Had there been courses offered in anthropology, or had I been able to study with Boas, then perhaps a more harmonious card would have appeared for this point in my life.

R: Incidentally, the FIVE OF RODS is more often interpreted as contentiousness, so you hit the card right on the head there, and I missed that.

J: This is very amusing, the way this thing is panning out.

R: Since we have talked about aerobics, and I have been trying to follow in your steps in that program, you mentioned one time that you had run the mile in . . .

240

J: That was a half-mile in 1:53, which at that time was within two fifths of a second of the world's record. Now it's another story.

R: Well, now it's only about 1:45.

J: Yes, that's a hell of a lot faster.

R: When I was in college they were winning it usually if they came in in two minutes.

J: Oh, I know. Those were college dual meets. But in the inter-collegiates and in the AAU running it is fast—it's always been fast. And at the time I was running, the half-mile was the one where everything was going on. There were about six fellows who were neck-and-neck, and it just depended upon how well you ran your race as to who won.

R: Do you ever hear anything from these guys or know what happened to them?

J: Well, I know what happened to only one, because he still is functioning at the New York Athletic Club, of which I am a member. That is where I swim. He's one of the officers in the "spiked shoe" branch. He's the chap against whom I ran my 1:53 near-record race. I won it by about a nose. His name is Eddy Swinburne. That was 1926.

R: This is a further point, and I think this is where both of us depart from the attitudes of the young today, who are lethargic and underplay the importance of the body terrifically. Your heritage card, the KING OF SWORDS, suggests a man who has as much physical prowess as he does intellectual brilliance. I don't see that there should be a separation of these things; you know they really go together and are self-supportive.

J: I said to a friend of mine only the other day in regard to all these lectures that I had to do, I regard a lecture as I used to regard a track meet. You go to sleep before it, you think of nothing else for about a day, and when the time comes you are hot and ready and you give your lecture. It's the same spirit I carry into this thing.

R: Absolutely. That is a good card then.

O.K. Now we have a duplication of the man I have just spoken about, only this time he is not the King, but the KNIGHT OF SWORDS.

J: Well, where are we now in my life? I have come back from

241

Europe to the Depression; I am upside down because the card is reversed.

R: Yeh, you are going off to California in that Model A.

J: This is that awful period.

R: In what sense?

J: Well, awful in the fact that there wasn't a job in the world, and I was interested in things that nobody else was interested in. Was I going to write, was I going to teach, what could I teach? If I was going to write, I wouldn't try to get my PhD; if I was going to teach, did I have to get a PhD. It was just a fantastic mess with a range of interests and possibilities that I really had to study. I have the notes at home, the diaries and journals that I kept at that time. What was it that I was pointed towards?

R: It's nice to know that the author of *The Hero With a Thousand Faces* was once at a loss in life just like everybody else.

J: I was an upside-down knight if there ever was one.

R: This is the card that I talked about—I said I always think of Leda and the swan when I see it.

J: SEVEN OF PENTACLES, reversed, huh?

R: Did you encounter in California some girl that you thought of marrying?

J: O.K.! (Laughter). That's what I'm not going to tell you about. (General laughter).

R: Anyway, she seems to have had kind of a Leda presence about her, a sort of charismatic quality and a great relatedness to her own logos principle. Now here we get into the relation between this card and the mother card, the Ten of Pentacles.

J: I noticed that.

R: It would seem to me that having had a mother like that and having been brought up in an atmosphere that was free of contention, in which the woman was very much a woman, that in your own outward quest here you encountered women that were but poor shadows of the ideal damsel that you were seeking. On his journeys a knight encounters many damsels in distress, and he recognizes that by marrying them he can alleviate their distress, but this will not help to attain his goal. As a matter of fact, it may impede him in his progress.

J: All right.

R: Do you want to say anything about that?

242

J: Well, there was such an occasion, and it was upside down.

R: Now here you are in the "belly of the whale," and I find this very interesting, because the belly of the whale, a concept that you discuss in *The Hero With a Thousand Faces,* is on the mundane plane social disgrace or psychic depression, and on the spiritual level may be the dark night of the soul. But in effect the resurrection from it into resolution of the problem has been by your going within. The recognition is that the whale that encompasses you is the personal unconscious. You have been swallowed by your *yin.* And so what this KING OF CUPS is doing is relating to his own unconscious, and when I see a cup I always think of the unconscious and the individual's relatedness to it. He is becoming a master of his own unconscious, which sets things upright again in the world.

J: Well, that is right, my friend. Immediately following this business I returned to the East and had a job at a prep school, which I resigned from after one year—the prep school where I had been a student. Then I went back into the woods for a couple of years, up in Woodstock, and it was in those years that I pulled things together, and that was followed by getting the job at Sarah Lawrence, which carried me out of that distress. If you read it that way, it fits those years just before I got into Sarah Lawrence College when I was thirty years old. So this is bringing us up to when I was about thirty, and it is astonishingly appropriate.

R: At this point the Knight of Swords has found the King of the Grail whom he was seeking.

J: He has found himself.

R: He has found the spiritual meaning of the Grail within.

J: Right.

R: Forget the other six cards—after one has done that in the "belly of the whale," one has nothing to fear. You said that earlier today in relation to what piece of knowledge?

J: It was the pulling together of what I discovered when I was at Carmel, namely Spengler, then Joyce, Mann, Leo Frobenius, and the relation of all their ideas to my mythological thinking and to Jung and Freud. All that happened in this period here, and finally I knew what my thought was, and then came the job at Sarah Lawrence. So if we take this as the first half of life, representing that period of questing and agony, and getting down to the six

243

o'clock point over here, this is just quite a remarkable production you have laid out in front of me here.

R: The next card does come upright, and it is THE SUN. Now you have had THE STAR, THE SUN, and JUDGEMENT.

J: THE SUN is the fulfilled personality and so forth. It's discovering Jean,* you might say.

R: The very next card is THE CHARIOT, and here the figure has at his shoulders the symbols of the half-moon, which suggests a unity finally with the feminine principle, which heretofore the life had been barricaded against.

J: That's right.

R: I think you should talk about Jean because she is such a consummate artist in her own right, and she has appeared as the goddess, really, in "The Coach with the Six Insides".

J: Well, these two cards which you just laid out, THE SUN and THE CHARIOT, seem very appropriate at this time. I think of that Sun as fulfillment of the personality quest. Here the King of Cups found his mystery and now he comes to manifestation, the sun has risen.

R: I think of the sun as coming up out of the cup; thus a fulfilled personality arises out of the unconscious waters.

J: And THE CHARIOT, the way I think of these cards, is the mate to The Empress. That would be the role, Jean being my empress, and she certainly is—I don't doubt it for a minute. Through her I came to whatever kind of psychological maturity I have achieved. This kind of things isn't psychological maturity, this is inward quest and all that, but functioning in the world as a valid human being requires something more; and I think this comes along in this quarter here. I am glad to see the sword is still present in THE CHARIOT.

R: That is true; the quest has not been forsaken. This is an important insight, I think, that one of the reasons for the anima fear—and now here we get into Freud and have nine million levels functioning at the same time—is that the hero or the quester had a fear that in giving up the quest by marriage to his opposite he would have to sheath his sword, which I take to be symbolic of

* Mr. Campbell's wife, the dancer Jean Erdman, who is perhaps best known for creating a brilliant dance version of *Finnegans Wake*, "The Coach with the Six Insides".

244

your knightly intellectual and spiritual quest.

J: O.K.

R: But here it is still present, and a Freudian level is symbolized also. (Laughter).

J: Yes, that's right.

R: Your Star has not been forgotten, either. It is present in the middle of the forehead of the charioteer. Well, let's put it this way: the knight or king finds the right sheath for his sword, and in that way the quest does not have to be abandoned, but it is facilitated.

J: Yes, that is very good. Now, let's see what happened to me. This is the most thrilling adventure story! (Laughter).

R: This is another card that is turned inward, DEATH, reversed, and it suggests to me inner transformation. After meeting with this goddess figure, the result is the death of the old self.

J: No doubt about it.

R: It's really awfully impressive to have the card Judgement, in the sense of resurrection, and The Star, The Sun, The Chariot, and Death, all in the same spread, because they are all on the same theme. Really what you did was to evolve out of adolescence with the new birth that we see in creative and artistic people, a new consciousness about the world, the artistic or intellectual birth here (Judgement). Down here there is a birth onto the psychological level of individuation (The Star). And then down here (The Sun), the meeting with the goddess, there is a completely new transformation; it's almost four quantum jumps in the life and consciousness.

J: Very interesting.

R: (Turning over the next card) You must have stacked these cards! Here's the fourth quantum jump now.

J: No—what do you have now?

R: Well, what would be the only other card in the deck that could top all those I have just spoken of?

J: I suppose The World.

R: What's adjacent to The World?

J: Well, Judgement. We already have that.

R: Well it's adjacent on the mundane side.

J: Oh, THE FOOL. (Laughter). That's Joe Campbell, Author. Finally wrote a book.

R: This is the card of cosmic consciousness, if the other cards in the reading point in that direction, and we have shown through the many cards of transformation that that has been the case. Maybe this is the next quantum jump to the highest plane of consciousness.

Now the next card is the QUEEN OF SWORDS.

J: QUEEN OF SWORDS, all right, well, what can you tell me now about this one? (Laughter).

R: I see this as a figure that you may have encountered after your marriage to Jean, who may have been a threat to the marriage. This particular figure has been described in some of the other readings as a female who you might say is a Women's Libber today, but in the context of your life I see her as a threat to the marriage, perhaps. She probably didn't have very much sympathy for Jean at all; she wanted you on her terms. But her approach was almost the approach of the King of Swords, almost a warrior approach to getting what she wanted out of life. Can you talk about that card without getting in trouble at home? (Laughter).

J: Well, actually the figure there is a very important person in my life, and while for a season there was a sense of a possible threat, it was not an actual threat, and it hasn't been, and her relationship to Jean is very good. She represents a kind of intellectual lucidity and a very keen feminine mind, which has done me a lot of good in helping me to relate to the practical side of my theoretics rather than the mythological, mystical side. By a very curious coincidence, her astrological sign is Sagittarius, which the position of that sword there almost represents. This is a very important figure for me, and she comes right at that point in my life. You know, when a thing like this hits, it looks like a disruptive episode, but it has not been.

R: Well, I can see right away how this figure's appearance in the context of an average life would be disruptive. But if we look down the pattern of these highly-charged cards of self-development which have appeared previously, we realize that a stability and clarity of life purpose have already been formed in the individual so that an ordinarily disruptive force is ineffectual, or transformed itself into a positive influence.

J: Yes, and you don't get a wreck; you get an addition to the life.

246

R: So ultimately all problems can be encountered, suffered through, survived, and a new being is the result. I associate the Swords suit with the Fire signs astrologically, so I would have to say if this woman were not Leo or Aries she would have to be Sagittarius.

J: That's what she was.

R: Your next card is the FOUR OF CUPS. Probably after this relationship, a new harmony between you and Jean was a result. Perhaps she responded to the goddess within and made a quantum jump herself.

I take it to be her hand that is offering the cup out of the cloud, and perhaps this means that the feeling function has been added to you so that at this point in your life you stand fully individuated with all four functions working together.

J: Jean is very strong. There's no question about it. This is fascinating, the way the card sequence has shown that.

R: Now the only problem brought over from the archetypal world was the situation of the caged or locked-up anima figure, symbolized by the reversed Nine of Rods. Of course, the best expression of anima relatedness in the life is through the feeling function. Creative sensitivity is heightened at the same time through relatedness to the female within. So through that marriage with the goddess that Jean represented, the gift to you out of the cloud is the gift of completedness on the side of the four functions. The feeling function is being given to you.

J: Good; that sounds right.

R: I suppose you have talked about this with Jean before. Did you feel that the feeling function was your inferior function?

J: Yes. Feeling and perhaps sensation. These are the inferior functions, I am sure. Thinking and intuition are my major functions.

R: I find that hard to believe about sensation for anyone who has a track record that is two fifths of a second off the world's record. I think here the readers of this book will find it interesting to hear about the fantastic pace you are setting at age sixty-seven in the aerobics exercise program. What is your time now for a thousand yards in swimming?

J: Well, ordinarily twenty-two minutes, but occasionally I come in at twenty minutes.

247

R: Last summer when I found a pool long enough for me to attempt this, I decided to try it. I regard myself as the world's greatest bodysurfer, and I often go out in the Pacific Ocean in the storm surf all by myself. They say to use the buddy system, but I can never find anyone foolish enough to come along. But when I hit about five hundred yards in that pool, I found I could barely raise my arms any more.

J: Oh, I can't believe that. (Laughter).

R: Oh, absolutely. So there you are at age sixty-seven, and you are doing this. It is incredible. This matches the King of Swords and Knight of Swords.

J: This is the will to conquer.

R: Right. Also you conquered the whole field of mythology for your generation, as far as I am concerned; you started with the American Indians at the age of twelve. (Laughter).

J: Where are we now in the card chronology? About where I am now, I guess.

R: O.K., the card is the EIGHT OF SWORDS.

J: Well, I retire next year, so perhaps that is me, not knowing what the hell to do. If Jean wants to go on dancing, composing, my decisions about the future and my residence will be determined by her decision. That is a blindfolded figure, isn't it?

R: Yes.

J: So perhaps the cards are saying, "We have told you all that you have done, and now you do not know what's ahead." Which is true. There are many possibilities for different jobs, but at present I am decidedly in the dark about what I will be doing. There is no anxiety on my part about the future, however.

R: I feel I must tell you, since this is a card of future possibilities, that it can represent a situation of crisis that may be full of unhappiness.

J: I can see that too.

R: There is that potential there, but there is no point in being a doom-sayer because it is a future thing. With the realization of this life consciousness, undoubtedly you already know that problems are the proving ground of the soul anyway.

J: No problem then. Now let's see what happens after that. THE TOWER. Something is going to happen. No doubt about it. (Laughter). O.K., we have something coming.

248

R: Yes, we spoke of this card earlier as one in which the crystall-izations of the mundane plane and the whole weal of the previous life are broken down. It is a preface to a new birth. You have had so many new births already on this wheel of life that this may mean a preface to stepping off the wheel, since it is at the apex.

J: That is a pretty good story. Quite astonishing to me. As I look at it, it fits all right, and the high points are the ones that came up.

R: Every once in a while when I feel that the life is ready for it, I like to turn over the Unnamed Namer, the face-down card. We talked about the nature of your wife, who is a goddess figure, and I recall that you paired her with The Chariot and actually called her the empress. Now here she is at the very center of the wheel of your life.

J: THE EMPRESS. (Laughter). All right, she wins.

R: She is almost the *modus operandi* of the life here because, although you were unrivalled in the athletic and intellectual world, the archetypal heritage showed that you had one Achilles' heel, the lack of relatedness to the opposite principle within. She made that all happen, so she is at the center of wheel.

J: I am really not surprised. She makes it all happen, keeps the wheel turning. O.K., you have a reading there!

The Grand Experiment

1. King of Cups
2. Six of Pentacles
3. Four of Rods
4. Eight of Cups
5. Six of Cups
6. Eight of Pentacles
7. Knight of Swords
8. Four of Cups
9. Page of Swords
10. King of Pentacles
11. The Lovers
12. The Devil
13. Ace of Pentacles
14. Three of Rods
15. Ten of Swords
16. Three of Cups
17. Five of Swords
18. Three of Pentacles
19. The Star
20. The Empress
21. Three of Swords
22. Ten of Pentacles
23. Two of Rods
24. Two of Pentacles
25. Nine of Swords
26. Two of Swords

9 NINTH HOUSE						62 URANUS
10 TENTH HOUSE						64 PLUTO	55 SATURN	8 EIGHTH HOUSE
11 ELEVENTH HOUSE						63 NEPTUNE		48 JUPITER
12 TWELFTH HOUSE							

56 57 58 59 60 61
49 50 51 52 53 54

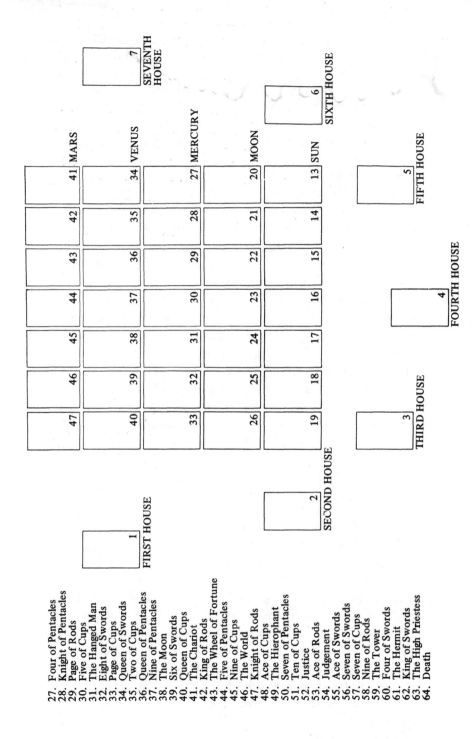

27. Four of Pentacles
28. Knight of Pentacles
29. Page of Rods
30. Five of Cups
31. The Hanged Man
32. Eight of Swords
33. Page of Cups
34. Queen of Swords
35. Two of Cups
36. Queen of Pentacles
37. Nine of Pentacles
38. The Moon
39. Six of Swords
40. Queen of Cups
41. The Chariot
42. King of Rods
43. The Wheel of Fortune
44. Five of Pentacles
45. Nine of Cups
46. The World
47. Knight of Rods
48. Ace of Cups
49. The Hierophant
50. Seven of Pentacles
51. Ten of Cups
52. Justice
53. Ace of Rods
54. Judgement
55. Ace of Swords
56. Seven of Swords
57. Seven of Cups
58. Nine of Rods
59. The Tower
60. Four of Swords
61. The Hermit
62. King of Swords
63. The High Priestess
64. Death

he date is April 10, 1971, and this is a reading by the spread that I have designated the Grand Experiment Spread because it is the first time I have attempted it. It utilizes a twelve house horoscope spread and an astrological spread in which seven cards are placed down for each of the seven planets nearest the earth. The planets not used are Pluto, Neptune, and Uranus. However, in this particular spread I am going to use one card each for those three most distant planets. The purpose of this is to attempt to see if there is a correlation between various methods of divination. The chart of the person for whom the reading is given, Miss Coco Cutler, is well known to me, and I have pretty much memorized the chart during the last week so that I will be able to find whatever correlations there are. I shall also be referring to the *Ephemeris*, the book that charts the positions of the planets from day to day. We will be dealing particularly with her progressed planets. I have the natal chart, and each year of the life can be figured in a progressed chart by looking at the next day after the individual was born, which would give the positions of the planets for one year later in the life. For example, if one wanted to calculate the present positions for the progressed planets, he would count off the number of years that have elapsed since the birth. Then figuring one day for each year, he could find the positions of the progressed planets. Now, since fifty-six years have passed since your birth, we count fifty-six days since the birth and we arrive at the positions of your progressed planets.

Now I am going to start with twelve cards for the twelve houses of the individual, and I will turn up the card that will represent the First House, or that degree on the horizon that was rising when this person was born. The first card is the KING OF CUPS, and the feeling I get about him is one of royalty and of a regal personality, naturally because he is a king. I think he doesn't seem to be harshly authoritarian or tyrannical. He seems to have nice harmony with his own feelings. Now as I look at the chart, I notice that the rising sign is Cancer, 29° of Cancer rising at the moment of birth. It has been my association so far in reading Tarot to make a correlation between the Cups suit and the Water signs of the zodiac. This seems a natural association because cups do hold water. I associate the Fire signs of the zodiac with the Swords suit, and I associate the Earth signs with the suit

Pentacles, and the Air signs with the suit Rods, or Wands, as they are sometimes called. In this first card we do have the Cups suit, which suggests a Water sign rising. That is the case here, and the interesting thing is that the Ascendant is close to being Leo rising, so probably in your Ascendant you are a mixture of Leo and Cancer. You take on some of the qualities of Leo, even though you do have a Cancer rising sign, and I think the card conveys a feeling of great power and a leonine kind of personality. I detect a sense of pride in him, but there is great feeling flowing through him. So as a description of your First House, and as a description of that rising sign, the card works quite well.

Now the card that represents the Second House is the SIX OF PENTACLES. I associate it with Earth signs, and your Second House is occupied by an Earth sign, mostly Virgo, a little bit of Leo, and the interesting thing about the Second House is that it governs the possessions of the individual, the finances and monetary gain. The woman in the card is obviously very concerned with frugality. I call that card the "counting the pennies card," and she is keeping the budget balanced and is quite preoccupied with the pentacles.

Now the Third House is the house of communication and the so-called lower mind, and here we have the Rods suit. The FOUR OF RODS is the card. You have Libra occupying your Third House, an Air sign, and Rods are equivalent to Air signs in my way of thinking. They say Libra is the sign of harmony in the zodiac. The scales of course represent Libra. The FOUR OF RODS is a picture really of harmony. The floral gate that leads to the castle suggests an ideal home. I think that for you, more than anything else, the question of harmony and balance within the home is kind of the ideal that you hold and hope for.

Now the next card is the EIGHT OF CUPS, and I am impressed by the fact that the Fourth House in your zodiac is occupied by Scorpio, and Scorpio is the natural Eighth House sign. The Eighth House is called the house of death, and one of the things that the Fourth House is associated with is the home and the father. There is a relation of course between Cups and the Water signs, but the quality of the EIGHT OF CUPS suggests abandonment. The figure has his back to the cups, and there seems to be some kind of loss, unhappiness, turning away. Perhaps this is a

253

picture of the father leaving the home early in your life; it suggests absence from the home. You don't have any planets there, but if you could talk briefly on the relation with the father there it would be of value.

C: My father died when I was between two and three years old.

R: Well, in that sense it could be said to be abandonment.

C: Yes.

R: Now, the card occupying the Fifth House is the SIX OF CUPS, and your Fifth House is occupied by a Fire sign so there isn't a correlation there between the suits, but the thing that comes to mind is that Sagittarius, which occupies your Fifth House, is the natural sign of the Ninth House, which is the house of the higher mind, religion, and philosophy. The presence of Sagittarius in the Fifth House tells us this: the Fifth House is, among other things, the house of love affairs. So you have the natural sign of the house of the higher mind occupying the place of your house of love affairs, which suggests very idealized concepts about love. The Moon also occupies your Fifth House, and is associated most often with the personality or the role in life of the individual. So we can say here that your role in life or your main concern is connected with love and the emotional fulfillment that is the result of that. The card, the SIX OF CUPS, seems to describe that very well. There are two children involved, which tells me in part that maybe the kind of idealistic love concept you have is only possible in childhood, that is in the enactment of it.

I will just put down the Sixth House card, and then I will let you comment on that last card. The EIGHT OF PENTACLES is the Sixth House card. The Sixth House is occupied by Capricorn, and Pentacles is associated with Earth signs. Now the Sixth House is called the house of health or service, or work. It is often associated with the job that one holds in life, and you have Capricorn qualities associated with the jobs that you hold. You have a great deal of persistence on the job, you get things done; you plug along and see that whatever has to be done is finished. This man here in the EIGHT OF PENTACLES is a craftsman, and he seems intent upon hammering up the pentacles, or proceeding in a laborious way to get the work done. Probably you don't like work because of the particular qualities of Capricorn and its appearance there in the Sixth House. For example, if you had

254

Sagittarius there instead of Capricorn, then the work situation would be more ideal—it would become fulfillment of your highest nature because Sagittarius is the natural sign of the Ninth House, the house of the spiritual mind. So this is a sign of plodding along and hard work, and probably not too much remuneration for the work. It is kind of menial things; I don't mean to say that you have been a domestic, but I would assume it would have been office work and pretty monotonous really.

All right now, that takes us through half of the houses, and if you can comment at all upon anything I said that might be anecdotal in nature, and throw a little more light on what I have said, please do.

C: My first associations are pretty much in startled agreement with the way the cards seem to coincide with your interpretation of the signs. I associate the first three cards with father, mother, and home, followed by the fourth card, which indicated some form of abandonment, which would have been my father's early death during my very early childhood. The fifth card, the SIX OF CUPS, is such a lovely card, with the two children and the six lovely vases of flowers and beautiful colors. I would agree with you that probably at a very early age a kind of idealistic approach to all things earthly, that is flowers and associations with the beauty of the earth, began to develop. I lived with my grandparents, who were an influence in this direction during those early years. Now whether or not I have carried this idealism along with me throughout my life I am not quite sure, that is, totally in the form of idealized love. However, I have been an idealistic person. It has always been a struggle to bring those ideals into relation with the realities of life without bitterness or loss of hope. But I am an idealistic person in that sense.

The next card, the EIGHT OF PENTACLES, is an exact description of what my adult working life has been—the most prosaic, mundane kinds of jobs, approached in the spirit that you described. But I am tenacious and . . .

R: Resilient?

C: Well, I was when I was younger—dependable, all those solid qualities that get the job done were very much there. I didn't like them, was never highly paid except on rare occasions, but in general it was a run-of-the-mill existence. I was simply earning my living. The only thing I can say about that other thing there is that the card suggests not a total blackness, but there is a lovely blue sky in the background, and I would say I associate that with my earlier years when it was still possible to see up and out and high, and get beyond the routine of daily life.

R: Incidentally, I think this is a point of interest—one way in which you determine the health of the individual is to look at the sign that occupies that Sixth House of health, but you also then look at the ruler of that sign and where it appears in the chart and what kind of aspects it has to other planets. Through this there is a way of being able to describe what physical ailments will come to the individual because each particular sign of the zodiac rules certain areas of the body. Of course, each sign has a particular ruler, and if it is in harmonious relation, then the health is generally good; but where it is not in harmonious aspect, the health may be bad. Now the ruler for Capricorn is Saturn, and it is up there on the cusp of the Twelfth House. It sits there like the guardian of the gate, and the Twelfth House is concerned with hospitals and confinement. Now Saturn is in Gemini, which suggests the nerves, as well as the hands of the individual. It is negatively aspected by some other planets, so one would have to say you have had an affliction of the nervous system and of the hands.

Now I will take this another way: Mars governs Aries, and Mars is in a negative aspect to Saturn that becomes quite precise around the age of twenty-eight, but it begins to be felt in your early twenties. Aries rules the head, as the first sign of the zodiac. Since Mars is its ruler and it is positioned in Aries in your chart, we could say that the negative aspect to Saturn might give you some problems with the head aching at that period that I mentioned, the early twenties. I would think it would become most intense around the age of twenty-eight. Now can you talk briefly about your nervous system *per se,* your hands, and any headaches?

C: Well, my nervous system seems to have been rather a delicate one from a very early age, with a nervous affliction of the stomach. I was highly emotional always, and this was accurately recorded by the rebellion of the stomach. By the time I was twenty this had evolved into very, very severe migraine headaches, so severe that I would be hospitalized for many weeks at a time, with all kinds of treatments up to the age of twenty-eight. Over the years I had had every known treatment for migraine, including surgery—incidentally, I have had surgery thirteen times in my life. I had begun to look for other avenues, and began studying medical journals and particularly psychiatric journals. I came across for the first time the association of migraine with neurotic illness, and I sought help then for the first time through a psychiatrist, whose field had been neurology. The migraine headaches finally went away in the course of therapy. The trouble with the hands didn't turn up until late in life, about ten or twelve years ago, when the first symptoms of a neurological disorder began in the hands. Eventually I had to have surgery on my right hand three times to correct this disorder.

R: Now we will be talking about the Seventh House, which is called the house of partners of the individual. The card is the KNIGHT OF SWORDS, and I am taken by the cloud patterns in the background of this card, but I also get a feeling of one-dimensionality associated with this figure. It is a Swords card, so there should be a Fire sign in your Seventh House, but that is not the case; there is an Air sign there, Aquarius. Aquarius is the sign of altruism and humanitarianism, and we are supposedly about to enter the Aquarian Age, and a knight, therefore, is a good figure for this ideal approach which is associated with Aquarius. The interesting thing about the chart is that the planet that I associate with the animus figure in a woman's chart occupies your Seventh House, so that is your partner, and in effect this explains some of the idealism associated with your concepts of love. In other words, you are looking without for the idealistic archetype within. It is very difficult for anyone of flesh and blood to fulfill this expectation or to attain the ideal that the animus represents. Of course, in some the animus is not ideally constituted, but I think it is in your nature from what I have seen of you, and there is a problem of getting this archetype down to earth so that relationships can be longer lasting with the male animal on the earth plane. Do you want to make a comment about it—if you could mention something from therapy, an insight that had been given to you by an analyst, or that you have attained yourself recently . . .

257

C: Yes. I associated that card exactly as you did from the moment you turned it over. My association went swiftly to the thought of the idealism that was my own, but which I sought through someone else. I married a man who in my opinion would have fulfilled those humanitarian ideals and purposes in life, and he did attempt to do so because it was in his nature as well. My mistake was in unconsciously placing the whole burden upon him, and it was only many years later, in the process of therapy, that any knowledge of an inner archetypal direction was pointed out to me. I am only beginning to understand now, and I think, now that I am an older woman, that what you say is quite true about worldly associations with men. What you say would have been truer when I was younger, but at my stage of life it is far more important for me to come to terms with my own archetypal animus figure and proceed from there. When and if I do this with some success, then the relationships with men, which have not been unpleasant throughout my life by any means, could have a deeper, fuller meaning than they have had before. I am only recently beginning to be aware of that.

R: Incidentally, I think it is interesting to know that you have begun automatic drawings of what you regard as your animus figure, and he does come over as a god in the drawings. In some of the early ones which you showed me, he is a little bit threatening and malefic.

C: Yes. When those automatic drawings began a few months ago, I began doing them after having had a dream of a god-like figure that very much impressed me, and I tried to draw him. The feeling was very strong to try to draw this very beautiful figure. But what surprised me was that drawing after drawing—there must have been a dozen of them—came, and I could not draw him. Each drawing was a frightening mask of fear, anger, all the negative aspects of the animus, and they startled me, frightened me, made me angry. I couldn't understand what was happening until after they had all presented themselves and I had suddenly to accept the fact that they were coming out of me. Then one day I sat down to draw—and I never knew what would happen when I sat down to draw—and I drew the beautiful young god. It was a real turning point in the whole business.

R: This is a very good point in fact of the awareness that the animus figure can be transformed. The more we know about these archetypes within, the easier it is to do this. The more highly conscious the figure becomes—well, I suppose it never becomes conscious, but the more conscious we are of the archetype within—the less it is able to interfere with our conscious relationship. It is then not projected with such great intensity and frequency onto the other persons that we deal with in our lives.

C: Yes, and in relation to those negative animus drawings, when I had recognized them and accepted them as part of myself and knew what they were and where they were coming from, they ceased to have the same effect, the same power that they had had before. I can look at those drawings now and they are not nearly as frightening as they were before.

R: Incidentally, in looking at your Seventh House there, one could say that probably the level of your animus is the third, what is described in *Man and His Symbols* as the figure who is the "bearer of the word." He speaks for the whole society. He would be kind of a political figure of a very humanitarian bent.

Now this card leads us right into the Eighth House, which is associated with death and legacies and everything connected with the dead. This card is the FOUR OF CUPS, and your Eighth House is occupied by a Water sign, Pisces. First thing, on the mundane plane, because your Jupiter is in Pisces in the Eighth House, one would have to say that you probably have had a very substantial legacy at some point in your life. No? Well, . . .

C: I have come into a very small legacy, and I have certainly benefitted by an enormous amount of generosity here and there, but not substantial, no.

R: All right, then, I will get off the mundane plane interpretation of that. Jupiter and Pisces, connected with the things of the dead of the Eighth House, would suggest interest in the occult and psychic abilities, astral, intuitive experiences. I notice that across the zodiac is Neptune in Cancer, right on your Ascendant, and to me this is the mark of the mystic. I have a very gifted friend in the psychic field who has Neptune on the Ascendant. Your Neptune makes a beautiful trine to your Jupiter in Pisces in the Eighth House. One would have to say that your interest in politics and political activity was really the round peg in the square hole. You probably only now are becoming interested in mysticism, because there has been a change in the orientation in the society, where the young now are not too interested in political solutions, so it would seem that this is the feeling that you have the greatest potential for, or the greatest means to, self discovery along these lines. Pisces is a very psychic sign, and to have Jupiter there, which is a benefic planet, leads to expansion of the Piscean qualities. This would suggest that you would be quite interested in the mysteries connected with death, the question of survival, reincarnation. If you are only coming to it now it is a shame, but you are really a person who is deeply interested in Jungian analysis, and I do say that Jung is the analyst for the last part of life, when you are ready to face death. I have found this a source of interest to me ever since I was born. I realize that the moment one is born he begins dying, so life is a preparation. Would you like to talk about that card briefly?

C: Yes. I would say that in the last few years I have been aware of the fact that there has been a latent interest in things psychic. Due to Jungian analysis and, as you say, the temper of the times, I have been led to something I think I have really in a sense been avoiding; but it was there all along and was behind this great humanitarian interest and this great desire to communicate with other people, and to write things and make everybody feel better and understand one another. There is in my family background some tendency in this direction. I think that my mother had definite psychic potential, but it was suppressed because she feared it. And her older brother very definitely had extraordinary powers of ESP. I just think it has been lying there waiting.

R: I just noticed something—when you said *write,* my eye went immediately to the hand bearing the cup in the Four of Cups. This card in standard interpretation is often called a gift because a cup is being proffered to the individual under the tree. Jupiter is the gift-bearing planet in the zodiac. It brings all the good things to one in the lifetime, and as I said before, Jupiter in Pisces would bring you gifts on the side of psychic potential and of an Eighth House nature, that is, some kind of gift from the dead. Very often they say that automatic writing and automatic drawing are the result of a spirit or departed person taking over the hand or even the personality. It seems to me that the automatic writing that is coming through now may be this kind of gift that we see.

The hand is the gift. It is coming down from the astral plane; it is the gift out of the cloud, coming to the individual from another dimension. Very interesting way to look at that card.

C: For me, with my interest in the Jungian interpretation of these things, I look at it not so much as a gift coming from clouds or from above, but my interpretation is "projection," that actually any gifts that do emerge are from the archetype, from the collective unconscious, which in a certain sense is the same thing.

R: Well, this is what the symbol on the back of this deck means, the snake with his tail in his mouth. When you go all the way in to the collective unconscious, when you get all the way into yourself, you are also all the way up and all the way out to God. Or if you try to get all the way up to God, you will find that you have gone all the way into yourself. I feel that the biggest source of atheism today is the misconception that we have that there is an extraneous force or consciousness that is God. Hence, we look for signs or messages or a presence that can be seen and touched, and when we can't find it with our five senses we conclude that God doesn't exist. Of course, God is the idea of going all the way in, and it's all the way up at the same time.

Now the Ninth House is a very highly charged house for you because it is the house of the higher mind, which is philosophical and reflective in nature. It certainly is the house of intuition, and the interesting thing about your Ninth House is that you have a conjunction of Mars and Venus. Now any astrologer looking at this would say that it makes you very amorous, susceptible to all that inflames the heart. Mars is the god of fire, martial passion, and is giving you a very passionate heart. Again this is in a house that is ideally constituted, this house of the higher mind. So the card is the PAGE OF SWORDS, and I think we have our friend again, the sword-bearer, this inner animus principle being sought in the world. This is the ideal man who can resolve the problems of the life and with whom there will be harmony. There is a nice trine between this conjunction of Mars and Venus, conjunction meaning within 9° on the zodiac. And also your Venus is in Aries, which would normally make you amorous anyhow because it is a Fire sign. Mars is in the place it likes to be most, in Aries, which it rules, so you are getting, not double, but about nine times power on the side of idealistic love. Your heart is just being consumed by the fires of idealistic love, really. The conjunction of Venus and Mars is perhaps suggested by this card. The sword suggests the very masculine nature of Mars. And then, although he is called a page, in plays women often played pages, so this figure could be interpreted as a woman, and I see it as the amorous side of yourself together with the Mars principle, the energizer of the heart as it appears in your conjunction.

The next card is the KING OF PENTACLES. This is the position of the Tenth House. I have had this card come up before, and I have asked people if there was a certain person of Taurean nature in their life, and very often it has been true. The king has peering over his shoulder a bull, which is the symbol for Taurus. Where the Sun appears in the zodiac determines what sign the individual is. Of course, your Sun is in 10° of Taurus, so you are a Taurean. Again we have the pentacles associated with Earth signs, which Taurus is. There is a conjunction of Mercury and your Sun, and here if we take the Sun to be represented by the bull, then the man is the Mercury side of yourself, which is the mind of the individual in the chart. So they are together there in the same place. This particular conjunction normally in my experience means a very nimble intellectual mind, and some astrologers disagree on that, but I have found it to be true in my own experience.

C: You would never know it from my inability to speak tonight, would you, Dick? (Laughter).

R: Now we get to that Eleventh House I was talking about before, the house of ideals. This is the house of hopes and wishes, and the sign that occupies it is Gemini, The Twins, and the card that is turned up is THE LOVERS. It suggests the idea of The Twins in the sense of not both masculine twins, but an individual desiring union with his opposite, which would be the animus in the case of the woman and anima in the case of the man. So what you hope for most of all is qualified by the card THE LOVERS, and it is this ideal love relationship again, in the card depicted very beautifully.

And then we are going to the Twelfth House, and this is the bugaboo of your houses . . .

C: Of all houses? For everyone?

R: Yes, of everyone, but in some charts it doesn't have as much

262

significance when there are no planets there. The malefic of the zodiac is Saturn. Saturn in that particular house gives the house added strength and gives Saturn more powers in a negative way if it is negatively aspected in the chart. I will turn over the card . . . (Laughter). That old devil power! Actually Saturn rules Capricorn, which is of course a goat, and THE DEVIL is often depicted as goat with his small horns, and this is how he looks here. The very entrance to the Twelfth House, or in some ways the underworld, is guarded by Saturn in your chart, and then there is a conjunction of Pluto. Pluto is the god of the under-world. This is a very close conjunction, and it means that this particular configuration has again added power. There is a pull between the desire for happiness, idealized love, and this kind of double destruction power in the life. Of course, I don't have to tell you that this may have been the theme of your life, almost like a French movie, the separation of the lovers, and the card bears this out very specifically, very accurately. The qualities of Pluto are influenced by its appearance in Cancer in your chart, which can make for depression. Cancer is an emotional sign; the Moon rules it, so it can make for great dejection of the emotions. You can imagine the emotional level descending down to hell, a personal hell where Pluto rules. Pluto is also, on a higher level, the collective unconscious and the paraconscious mind of the indi-vidual. It is something that you haven't been aware of before in an astrological way, but it is something that I will be discussing in the future with you as to what planets will be conjunct this negative influence in your chart, and how you can master your stars by insuring that you have around you friends who will give you a mental boost during these times. And this is the way that you dominate your stars. The zodiac is a way to self knowledge, and the more you get introspective with it, the more you can see how it does work, and knowing your tendencies can help you control them and set up either buffer zones or opposite reactions.

Can you give me your reactions to the last two cards? THE LOVERS occupies the house of your hopes and wishes, and THE DEVIL, or the Saturn power, is in the place of the Twelfth House. It can lead to excessive dejection in the life.

C: Yes. Well, I think I can't add much to what you have already said, except to say that again THE LOVERS is an ideal that I still

263

have, but that ideal has been transferred from the outer to the inner world. While what the card THE DEVIL and the Twelfth House represent is holding sway at the moment, my hope is that I can come to terms with this so that the realization of THE LOVERS can come about.

R: Now what we are going to do is go through all the planets and set out seven cards each for the first seven closest planets, and then I will put out one card each for Uranus, Neptune, and Pluto. There will be 52 cards added to the twelve already laid out, which will give us 64 cards.

All right, I am going to deal first with the Sun. I will deal out seven cards that will progress from the natal position, or the moment of birth, up to the future. The first card is the ACE OF PENTACLES. Now Pentacles is associated with Earth signs in my mind, and so that becomes a good description of your natal Sun. Also, that giant pentacle there suggests to me the Sun in Taurus.

The next card is the THREE OF RODS. Taureans of course are known for stability, and this gives a certain inner rudder in your life, a quality of being down-to-earth. But then when you got to be around twenty years old, your Sun progressed out of Taurus into Gemini, and the card we have secondly is the THREE OF RODS, which shows a man looking at a blank sky. To me there is a feeling of disillusionment coming from the card, dejection, a feeling of being let down by life. Really he is looking out on the vista of life. And when your Sun went into Gemini, it of course then took on Gemini qualities, one of which is the swing of emotions that is often seen in a Gemini person. They are often described as being two people, or schizophrenic. This latter is of course only true in the least evolved Gemini types. Gemini is in the Eleventh House, so it would suggest disappointments of the ideals at that time, or great swings between the heights and depths in the life, beginning around the age of twenty.

The next card is the TEN OF SWORDS, and this is the card in which a man is pictured being hammered into the ground by ten swords. What this represents is, I believe, the conjunction of your Sun with the power of Saturn at the threshold of the Twelfth House there. In other words, a great depression and dejection would be felt at this time in the life. All of the qualities that I mentioned earlier connected with Saturn are there, and they work this effect on the individual. This occurred in your life at about the age of forty-nine, and if you can talk about that briefly it would be of interest. In other words, in forty-nine years the Sun moved out of Taurus, through Gemini, up into the Twelfth House where it is conjunct Saturn about the age of forty-nine.

C: I think it was in that year, or the one just preceding it, that life really had pinned me down. I went into therapy in an effort to come out from under this depression. Really a killer. So that sets it; it's quite accurate, both the cards and the chart. It was a period of depression.

R: Uh-huh. You see, if you think of the planets as moving counter-clockwise around the zodiac, you can see that those over here will be moving up towards this configuration at different times in your life, and this is the tip-off as to what happens. We can describe pretty accurately your state of mind all through your life because of this conjunction of Saturn and Pluto in the Twelfth House.

Now the next thing that happens is that the Sun moves very soon thereafter to a conjunction with Pluto, because Pluto is right there in the Twelfth House. That would be at age fifty-three, roughly. Now this conjunction would give you an interest in exploring these archetypes, which you are doing now, and it may have been at this time—I believe I said it was three years ago—that you got a real impetus to go in and investigate the archetypal family. Because Pluto is the collective unconscious and personal unconscious, and also paraconscious mind, it depends upon which particular level you want to approach him. He is also death in the sense of being the common denominator, the no-thing, and he could be interpreted as the Zero card in my Jungian Spread. Here you have the THREE OF CUPS, and it seems to me that this is you, your animus figure whose face we cannot see—he has long hair . . .

C: Sign of the times.

R: Yes, and your shadow or perhaps feminine principle. These are all figures that come to mind. Now out of an investigation of these areas arises the one flower of Selfhood, that dominates the scene behind them. This is what comes of our contacts with Pluto. Because it is in the Twelfth House, it has tended so far to drag you down, but when you get all the way down, as they say, there is no place to go but up. When you have gone all the way in, you have gone all the way out to God. So in what way did your life change between the ages of forty-nine and fifty-three?

C: Well, at forty-eight or forty-nine, when I went into therapy, I think I was frightened and desperate and wanted a hand up to pull me out of it. I don't know what went wrong, but I left therapy in about eighteen months, and then there was a period of several years where I just struggled along. I just went down into a period of great crisis and went back into therapy with the same therapist. This time there was a far more cooperative attitude. The previous time there had been a sense of failure, and it took a few years and another crisis, an inner crisis, to make me realize that I hadn't really been there. I had asked for help but I wasn't really helping myself, and it was at the age of fifty-three that I went back with a new attitude and determination. And though it is certainly having its period where I am discouraged with myself, its ups and downs, it has been the first encounter, as you know through the automatic drawings, with the collective unconscious and the archetypes.

R: When you left therapy originally, was it with an attitude of feeling better, or was it what the card would seem to indicate, utter dejection?

C: Oh, it was despair. A suicidal despair.

R: At that point, nothing, not even a really good analyst, can help you.

C: No, no one can reach you when you're that far gone.

R: But even if you're an astrologer, aware that Saturn is conjunct your Sun, I think the only thing you can do at that point is to approach it with the attitude that time does heal all things and that sooner or later the depression is going to be attenuated by one day's leading into another. This is what comes of having a knowledge of the chart. And now that I have done your chart, and will be in touch with you always about whatever is going on, I want also to extend to you the opportunity to call me at any time of the day or night. Just say, "What the hell is happening," and perhaps I then can tie in something in the zodiac and tell you when the light is going to turn on again.

C: Thank you, Dick.

R: I will always be your personal astrologer because the relations of your chart and my own are quite unusual. I know what you're up against, and I know what it can lead to for you.

Now the next thing that happens is the FIVE OF SWORDS, which suggests a battlefield, which has negative connotations. In this case I don't see the idealized clouds any more, I see a sky that reflects all the blood on the plain of the battle. The man is faced with two paths to take, crossed swords in the foreground. I think this card refers to 1970 or pretty much the present. Let me explain to you what has gone on in your chart. As you know, we placed your Sun up in the Twelfth House conjunct Pluto just three years ago. Now what the Sun has done is to move beyond the conjunction with where Saturn was when you were born, which gave you all the utter despair of the Ten of Swords, and it has now moved to the point that Saturn has moved to during the lifetime. In other words, Saturn doesn't sit still either, and it has moved just a little way into the Twelfth House and is in about 5° of Cancer. So your Sun now has moved up to that point, and the other thing that has happened is that Mercury has gone all the way around with the Sun and moved further into Cancer, and then it began to go backwards, so now it has come back to that same point to which Saturn has progressed. So now you are lined up there, or you were during the past year, where your Sun and your Mercury, your mind and your soul, were under the Saturn depressive influence in the Twelfth House.

C: They sure were, and they aren't out of it yet!

R: They are fairly slow moving. Now this FIVE OF SWORDS suggests a couple of possibilities for you. It is quite a burden to bear at this point, and it could make you go up or down. It could tend to utterly destroy you, make you feel suicidal, or, doing the kind of things you are with the automatic writing and all, you can just claw yourself up this cliff of life by your fingernails, with one ledge up and then slipping back two, but then one ledge up again. This is what was happening during the last year. I remember that you had said to me that the last year was the worst one of all. Well, that's why. Now the Sun will continue on through the Twelfth House, and what is needed is work on the consciousness, and I think we talked about this just the other night. I said that when a building appears in a dream it is a depiction of the level of consciousness of the individual. One girl told me about a dream

267

she has in which she is always in the same building. Well, her unconscious is seemingly kicking around in the egg or womb, and it wants to progress to a new building; it wants to attain a new level of consciousness. So what you will be doing in the THREE OF PENTACLES in the coming years is shoring up the positive qualities of your psychic makeup, and it will be hard work but interesting work too. It will jibe with the idealism—this looks like an arch of a church. It will be saving labor for you.

Now the final card is THE STAR, and I think what this indicates for you is the individuation process and mysticism. The peacock with all those third eyes all over it suggests a very mystical bird. Now you will notice that the next planet your Sun will be encountering as it moves along is Neptune. This conjunction of your Sun and Neptune I think will lead to a real psychic opening up of yourself, and the ability to look back on the old terrors of life and see that they happened for the purpose of your evolving to the point that you will reach when this conjunction comes along. Now you have to keep yourself in good condition because this doesn't occur until you are eighty years old. All the time your Sun will be moving through Cancer, and this will enable you to really get down to the watery elements of the Crab, the ocean of the collective unconscious. The Bull may not be wholly at home in this, but he will be swimming.

C: Well, he carried Europa through the seas.

R: That's a very good point. He's carrying you to the Neptune there.

Do you want to talk about 1970 just a little? Has it been the worst year of all?

C: I think it has been the nadir of my life. Now that we are into 1971, I look back on 1970 and I compare it with all the other times that I thought I couldn't live through. They weren't good but they just didn't know what was coming—it took 1970 to show them what was really bad.

R: Yes, well, the reason for that was that those other bad years are conjunctions of singular planets, in most cases your Moon coming around and being under the negative power of Saturn. In this case Mercury, which represents the mental state, had gone through this at some earlier time in the life and was moving well along in Cancer. Then all of a sudden it stopped and began going retrograde, and almost as if under the pull of a magnet came back to Saturn just at the moment that your Sun had arrived there from a different direction. So this was like a double blow, probably twice as bad as anything you had felt before. Incidentally, we will be talking, when we come to the Saturn cards, about how it influences your Venus or heart, and how it has intercepted the happy resolution of your love relations in life. This is because it's in a square to your Venus, which isn't an harmonious aspect at all. It's almost as bad as having the Saturn right there in the same place where the Venus is.

The next planet I shall be dealing with is the Moon. The Moon represents the personality of the individual, the persona in the Jungian sense. When people read their astrological Sun sign description and realize they are not like it at all, it's very often true because they are more like their Moon than their Sun. An astrologer always looks at the Moon and the Ascendent of the individual before launching into a description of the person. Now the first card that comes up for you is THE EMPRESS. This is one of the Major Arcana, and I don't think we've had any of those yet. The Moon in your chart appears in the Fifth House, and we have said that the Fifth House is, among other things, the house of love affairs. Now the woman in this card has on her shield the symbol for the goddess of love, Venus. And she bears the scepter of rulership on the earth plane. It suggests that at the level of human consciousness love really is the ruler. And I think this is true, and if not true, perhaps we can effect it in the so-called Aquarian Age on a more humanitarian level.

The next card, the THREE OF SWORDS, describes the heart being pierced, and this suggests great unhappiness. I am going to take a look at the *Ephemeris* to follow through with the progressed planets from birth and see what this card represents. Well, the Moon is so rapidly moving that it makes a complete transit of the zodiac in about twenty-seven and a half years. So when you were fifteen years old, your Moon went into the Twelfth House, and we already talked about what this does for you, what power it has because of the conjunction there of Saturn and Pluto. So I'll ask you to describe what looks like great emotional tribulations and really a rending of the heart. It would seem as if the ideals that you hold so strongly are completely torn asunder and you are pressed down to the center of your being by the hard karma of this progression. Can you talk about age fifteen?

C: Yes. I can tell you that it was exactly at that time that my self-esteem was almost thoroughly destroyed, and it has never wholly recovered. There is a chance for it now forty years later, but the damage has been there throughout my life. It was a wound to my self-esteem, and it was in psychological parlance a trauma of major proportion.

R: Uh-huh. What caused it?

C: It was within the family structure, and I thought that I was pursuing my way of being, my studies, in the way which would please my family most. All the pressures had been toward intellectual goals and so forth—and it sounds so silly to talk about it. I'm not sure I want this in here . . . Well, I think that I had been going in the direction that my family wanted me to go in, and there must have been some inclination toward the delights of the mind because I did enjoy pursuing them, but there was always a sense of conflict, of separation, of division that I couldn't understand in myself. I took great pleasure in the fact that I was able to announce to my parents that I had received acclamation and honors at school, in a personal way as well as an academic way. And when I brought this news home, expecting it to be received joyously, I was instead made to feel as though I were an empty boaster and this was not a proper way to behave. I will never forget it; it was a crushing blow, absolutely crushing. To have achieved what was far beyond anybody else's actual expectation, and then to have it minimized practically out of existence, allowed to have no pride because it would be immodest, really threw me. It caused a lifelong distortion in my expectations of myself and attitudes toward life. I don't know how else to describe it.

R: Now the next card is the TEN OF PENTACLES. I have a feeling here of the ideal home. The man and the woman are looking through the archway to the idealized castle in the distance, and this suggests really the ideal homelife. I am going to check and see when your Moon went into this Fourth House, which begins with Libra and ends with Scorpio. From age fifteen to twenty-four it moves down here and goes into the Fourth House or house of home. What happened at age twenty-four?

270

C: I married.

R: You got married for the first time?

C: Yes.

R: And was it kind of ideal for a while?

C: No, it really wasn't, but I idealized it.

R: Uh-huh. All right. That's good enough. Let's see what happens next. This man in the TWO OF RODS holds the globe—I always think of it as a crystal ball. Of course, with crystal gazing or any divination, you are really only looking into yourself. I tell you as much about myself during one of these readings as you do about yourself. The two rods suggest a gateway or threshold of initiation. And what is going through the life with this idealized youth is a kind of exalted attitude, not only towards the world, but borne as a kind of archetype within. I am getting this from the rose and the lily as a kind of insignia that he carries with him in life. It qualifies this youth. These are very idealized flowers as such. Now what is the relation to your chart here and to the Moon? Well, the next place that your Moon would go after going into the house of home, the Fourth House, is the Fifth House, and it gets back to the same place that it was when you were born. Generally around age twenty-seven or twenty-eight one comes face-to-face with the question, "Who am I? Where am I going in life? Why has what has happened to me happened?" So this is what I get out of his gazing into this crystal, his looking for answers as to who and why. Now what happened to you around age twenty-seven or twenty-eight?

C: Exactly what turned up in the previous cards. That was the first experience with therapy. I went into therapy that first time at age twenty-eight, twenty-nine, because of the migraine, but also because for a number of years before that, let's say from the time I was about twenty, I had wanted to go into therapy. I was very interested in it, and I had read a great deal about it.

R: About Jung, or Freud?

C: Mostly Freud. It was that time and that many years ago, but I never liked orthodox attitudes and so was looking for someone who was not an orthodox analyst, or an orthodox Freudian, or a dogmatist of any kind. And I found one, just as again many years later I went into Jungian analysis with the same attitude. But it was a period of needing to know who I was and where I was going. And I had to do this against all kinds of opposition from husband and family. There was a need, and I did it.

R: Well, the next thing that happens is that the Moon moves up and it forms a conjunction with your natal Jupiter, which brings good things in life. It is in this year that my progressed Moon has moved up to a conjunction with Jupiter, and this is the year of the publication of this book.

In your chart, this is when the Moon moves into Pisces; well, this happened when you were thirty-five. I get the impression here of two worlds in the TWO PENTACLES, and it suggests maybe a journey. What happens when one's Moon goes into the Ninth House, which is also the house of long journeys as well as the higher mind, is that very often one takes the trip of a lifetime. I am getting the feeling here of a man, and he seems to be very compassionate and understanding. He is probably the first one to acknowledge you as you are and as you know yourself to be, and the others before hadn't really understood. Anyhow, the parents didn't understand earlier what they had on their hands, and your sense of self-esteem and your sensitivity are so high that loyalty—and love is a manifestation of loyalty—is very important, whether among friends or even on the job. You do a little something for somebody, and if they don't respond you are hurt ten times as much as the ordinary person would be hurt by it. So let's talk about the age of thirty-five, when the Moon began a conjunction with the beautiful, beneficent bringer of good things, Jupiter, in Pisces. Also, an opening up of your own feelings occurred at this point—Pisces is the sign of feelings.

C: Yes. Well, I had been divorced for some years, and I did travel during that year, and I did meet a man such as you described him. And there was a period of opening up for me under the affection and interest of this man, and while we didn't stay together we corresponded over many years. For me it was a real opening up through the correspondence because I wrote what I had never written before. I am not referring to anything like classic love letters, but an opening up of personality in response to this man. And incidentally, it may interest you to know that twenty years later he told me he had saved all my letters and had them bound, that they meant a great deal to him too. So it was really quite a flowering in one sense.

272

R: I just realized something about you and creativity because this is a chart for a creative person. I have read a beautiful fairy tale you have written, and I have seen the automatic drawings, but outside of that I don't know of you ever taking a flyer at writing. Did you?

C: No . . .

R: Or painting?

C: Tried a few times, but . . .

R: Let me tell you why you always stopped. And this ought to prove astrology a winner here. Let's go back to the Fifth House where your Moon is. The Fifth House is not only love affairs but also all that you create. You have your Moon there, and that means that this is your role in life. You not only create a love affair, but you create a painting or a dance, or a musical composition. But you have Sagittarius there, which again is the natural sign for the house of philosophy. Now I think this means that you have very rarified, exalted ideas in regard to what you should achieve and that you have been stopped heretofore by the discrepancies between what you want as a goal, as a finished product, and what you feel you can attain. In other words, there is a desire to create only things that are perfect, whether you recognize it or not, and this stops you from even starting at all.

C: You are absolutely right! You must be reading my mind as well as my chart. It just makes it impossible for me to achieve anything in relation to what I most respect and admire. I wrote a lot in my younger days, that is, my school days, but during the period of great anguish that turned up in the cards, and in life, and in the chart, at age twenty, I destroyed everything I had done. I have done this two or three times throughout my life. I have never tried to publish or anything like that, but I have written poems and journals and so forth, and the only writing of mine that is still extant is in the form of a collection of letters saved by my friend. I have kept myself from destroying the few things, poems, that I have done in the last ten years. But you are absolutely right.

R: You know my poems and my book of poetry—I look upon these as my children. There is something I haven't said that also describes the Fifth House—children, all that the native creates in the lifetime. When I look through my book of poems I realize

273

that some are certainly superior to others, and some of these others have odd little quirks, and you know they are endearing in their own way. I could no more think of destroying some of them because they haven't attained perfection than I could think—if I were a father—of killing my son with a club foot or my daughter with a bad lisp. I have never been able to understand this aspect of certain artists such as Rouault, who just threw masses of paintings into the oven. I think that anything the human is capable of creating is worthwhile, and I look with love and tenderness upon all of these products of the human soul. Because the animal does not create, this is probably the area in which the human dares to be more than animal and to take the step towards God. Of course, God is the great creator of it all, so in this way we become godlike. So more power to you in whatever you create in the next few years.

C: You are far more generous than I was in my earlier years. I was more critical of myself than of anyone else, but still I could separate achievement, what I considered achievement, from that which could not meet those standards of perfection. While I could appreciate on many levels, when it came to my own work the critical faculty was just absolutely ruthless, whereas it isn't with the work of others. I feel very tender about the work of others, and the older I get the more appreciative I am of it in the terms you just described. But that took a long time coming; I was very critical.

R: This is interesting, because although I wrote short stories with great facility from the time I was in my teens, poetry presented a barrier that my mind could not make the great leap across. However, one night I got rather intoxicated in college and was listening to one of those shows that they had then, in late Cretaceous times, of poetry readings to music. You just don't hear those at all now. The particular thing that was being played made a poem leap into my mind, which I wrote down—it was completely free verse. The next morning, my roommate, who wrote Miltonic verse and spent hours scanning Milton, looked at the thing and thought it was rather good. However, his attitude toward the creative process was the opposite of mine. I submitted this to the *Atlantic* magazine, in their poetry contest of that year, and I got an award for the very first poem that I created. So this is how

274

the blocks are broken down.

Well, this is a familiar scene by now, and when the hard karma of the old NINE OF SWORDS comes up, I realize that what has happened is that the Moon has gone to that same place where it was when you were fifteen years old. It has entered the Twelfth House and is under the influences of Saturn and Pluto. This age would be forty-three. Do you think of that as being a time as tough as when you were fifteen?

C: Forty-three. What year would that be? . . .

R: That would have been 1958.

C: Yes. I think that was a period when my life swung around again after a relatively calm period and job that looked as though it would be at last . . .

R: Intellectually satisfying?

C: No, I have never had a job that was totally intellectually satis-fying, no. But it had been a period of rather pleasant associations at work. And then that came crashing down.

R: Incidentally, I am taken by what looks like a robe—one of the ways that one is reduced to a cipher in a hospital is through the shapeless, colorless smock one is encased in on admission. Did you go into the hospital then for an extended period of time?

C: I had major surgery at that time. I went into it not knowing whether I would come out of it; it really was serious surgery. And so it was surgery, job, ill health, a bad, bad period again. And the self-esteem always suffers in a period like that. It was a down period.

R: Another thing—these swords represent all this antagonism from the cosmic plane to you . . .

C: Well, it was manifesting itself on the mundane plane.

R: Well, these swords you see are a blocking out of the fantasy, idealized level behind you. In other words, your never-never land is being shown to be a world of just abject suffering and pain. What happened with me was that my progressed Moon went into the Twelfth House when I was still less than five years old, and then for operations they had ether, and they held you down, and a little kid has no ego yet to buffer himself or understand why this happens. So my vision of the world was either happy home or hospital. If you started to get something it was off to the hospital, and that was a torture.

C: Does that type of thing show in my chart, because a similar type of thing happened to me when I was about seven or eight years old. I had a very bad case of scarlet fever, and in those days no one knew how to treat it except by isolation. And I was taken from my home in a black ambulance to an isolation ward, where I was isolated for six weeks, all the time waiting to die, because somewhere I had fixed it in my mind that when you were taken away in a black car you were going to die. And it was years before I was even able to tell anyone what fear and agony I had suffered during those weeks, and I just thought that my parents wouldn't tell me. And they were not allowed to come and see me. So I know what you went through.

R: It's almost like a death camp. The question was, does that show up in the chart. Yes, you see, you were born with your Moon in the Fifth House, and at the age you mentioned it had progressed up to the Eighth House, the house of death.

Now let's get back to what happened at age forty-three. Your Moon was in the Twelfth house for about a year and a half; I don't know if you were in and out of the hospital during that period, but it was associated certainly after the surgery with a mental depression too. It didn't exist strictly on the physcial plane at all, but was mental anguish as well as physical.

Now we come to the last card, and this is the TWO OF SWORDS. Here the crossed swords suggest to me opposition. Opposition in astrological terms means one planet's being positioned directly across the zodiac from another one. Now let's see how that works. Your Moon got out of the Twelfth House when you were approximately forty-five, and if we go halfway around the zodiac, we come up to right about now, and your Moon is going through the house of health, so there are questions connected with health. But what makes the TWO OF SWORDS kind of a difficult card is the opposition between our friends Pluto and Saturn up there in the Twelfth House and where your Moon is right now. The opposition is almost like a conjunction; the forces of the planets across the zodiac are definitely felt. This suggests the same two paths I talked about in connection with the Five of Swords, that this can pull you down or you can evolve out of whatever negativism it represents.

Incidentally, your prognostication for the next place your

and you find out that this sneaky thing has taken hold, some unrecognized inner demon. (Laughter). And you are trapped in it, and all you can do is live through it.

R: It just occurred to me—I wonder why people have such trouble accepting astrology when we realize there are such biological, chemical influences on the human body. We like to say there are no influences on us whatsoever, and that is why we tend to reject astrology, but we are overlooking how many myriad influences there are on us, many that we don't know about.

C: Including sunspots.

R: O.K. The next card is the SIX OF SWORDS. When Swords come up I always thing of our friend Saturn sitting up there in the Twelfth House ready to grab anything that comes through his threshold.

C: Skewer, you mean, with all those swords! (Laughter).

R: The period in life when Venus comes into conjunction with Saturn is the year 1984. In other words, what is happening now is that Venus is still in Gemini, with its Mercurial properties. But there is a journey being made through the house of ideals. The Venus, which originated in the Ninth House, is being moved up through the house of ideals, and the ideals are being elevated to a cosmic plane. Here is the strange sky in the background, again representing fantasy and astral influences. The many swords that skewered the heart during the life are all gathered into the boat. It is almost as if they are trophies of the suffering which the individual doesn't want to forget about but has learned from. It reminds me of what Anna Magnani said to a makeup man when he attempted to cover over the lines in her face—she was proud of them and they represented sort of milestones along the way of development. So you will be pulling your way along towards the new shore. The new shore at the end of the house of ideals, of course, is the Twelfth House, which will lead you into a karmic refining of the heart. It will be a Cancerian experience; perhaps that is what the water in the card represents.

The last card for your Venus is the QUEEN OF CUPS. Your Venus will then move through Cancer, and the insights of intuition and feeling which are characteristic of Cancer will be available to you. There will be rapport between the unconscious and conscious levels, the cup and the mind here. The lightning bolts

283

coming down from the area of the crown suggest perhaps a refining from above, such as may be true when your Venus comes in contact with Pluto and the collective unconscious there in the future.

The next planet will be Mars.

C: (Laughter). Is this reading staggering you as much as it is me—it must be more for you?

R: Well, I have had six months of the cards boggling my mind anyhow, so nothing surprises me anymore. Anyhow, the card for the planet Mars contains a very martial looking man in THE CHARIOT. The ruler of Aries is Mars, and your Mars is positioned in Aries. It is in trine, or harmonious aspect, with the Moon, your feminine principle, and it is conjunct your Venus. Now this man has on his shoulders two aspects of the Moon, and they look like the personae of the stage, the masks for comedy and tragedy. Mars' sword is present; on the forehead is the star of idealism, which is certainly suggested by his presence in the Ninth House—the higher mind, philosophy.

Now the next card is the KING OF RODS, and I think what this means is that early in the life the natal Mars progresses up to the point of the progressed Venus, so that they form a conjunction. We talked about this in connection with Venus, where Venus moved up to the point where Mars was natally, and now Mars will move up to the point to where Venus has progressed. I think that rather than this being a description of you, or your planet at this time, it is more a description of a figure that was associated with that period of about four and a half years old, because I think this describes the conjunction of Venus with Mars. The figure as he appears in the card suggests to me someone who has a great knowledge of many, many facets of the world. There is a rapport with nature also, in the sense that is unusual for men, but is more associated with women. I see that in the bird in his hat, and the many-faceted headgear suggests to me a many-faceted personality. This conjunction of your Venus with Mars was at about age four and a half.

C: That would coicide with the influence of my grandfather. He was a man much as you described from the card. His intellectuality was more than enhanced—it was made alive and warm by his rapport with the world he lived in, animals, birds, flowers, trees.

It was what you described as a structure of a man. He was very much an influence in my life.

R: Was he at this age, since you were so young, kind of an influence on the formation of your animus in later life?

C: Yes, I think this is the kind of inner rapport that I am looking for now. It sort of got lost for awhile but it was always there in the background.

R: O.K. The next card is the WHEEL OF FORTUNE, and let's see what this represents. Oh, yeh. That is what I began to talk about in the previous card—your Venus moves up to a point that Mars catches up to at the age of thirteen, and this brings the natal configuration exactly together again and fuels the fires again. I don't know if you can call it a love at age thirteen, but that would have been the time of it. I think the WHEEL OF FORTUNE here is trying to tell you really about the zodiac and the way that we are kind of moved on the wheel, in some ways broken on the wheel. We are exalted through love, or we are sent spinning down into depression. This is a microcosm of the macrocosm of the astrological wheel. This would have been a time in your life that the heart was subject to the influences of all the fire that is there in Mars. If you come up with the name of a kid within the week, we will be able to get it into the book . . .

C: . . . Well, all I can think of is that at that particular age, puberty, especially for a girl, is normally the beginning of this outgoing feeling for the opposite sex.

R: There again I have completely forgotten about something I was just preaching a moment ago, the fact that there is a biological and chemical influence on the individual. We had been talking about the end of the sexual influence, but I guess we couldn't have a better depiction of puberty than a conjunction of Venus and Mars.

The next card is the FIVE OF PENTACLES, and I am going to intuit about it before I look at the *Ephemeris* to see where Mars goes next. I always think of Joseph and Mary and those Christmas pageants that we always see when we are kids, and this suggests a manger, or the desire to find a home for the little Christ child. This can be an integration of the Christ principle within. Let's see what happens here. The next place your Mars goes is into Taurus, and the ruler of Taurus is Venus, so we can think of this as an event that involved your heart or your emotions, and this occurred at the age of twenty-four. I remember you telling me that you got married at twenty-four—that was when your Moon went into the house of home, but also your Mars went into Taurus, which is ruled by Venus. So there we have a double relation within the chart itself.

Well, this looks like love or happiness or some kind of fulfillment, the NINE OF CUPS, and the next little town on the zodiac as one moves through Taurus is of course that place where you have your Sun and Mercury, 10° of Taurus. You were given a big boost to your soul, mind, all aspects of yourself, about the age of thirty-eight or nine. This is when Mars got up there. What happened at this age?

C: That was when I met my second love and enjoyed for the next few years, though in different aspects of the joining of two personalities, a similar summing of love and appreciation that occurred with the first love. Though these two men were quite different, each one gave me a great deal, each was a great gift of life for me.

R: Well, THE WORLD suggests another kind of fulfillment. We have had two fulfillments back-to-back through the help of Mars. Let's see what this could be. Oh, wait a minute. Now if I say to you that this experience you just described occurred at age thirty-eight or nine, and if we say that THE WORLD describes that, then this particular experience of the NINE OF CUPS would have occurred when the Moon had progressed around the zodiac to a conjunction of your Mars and Venus. In other words, a love experience would be the result when the Moon got there, and it would occur a few years before the experience that I talked about at thirty-eight and nine. Yes, this would be age thirty-five. This involved the figure that I think I talked about in connection with the two worlds and the water, or the ocean.

C: Let's see, age thirty-five. That was the first man.

R: O.K. Then this explains that Mars' natal position is activated by the Moon coming there, and this brings that ideal love at that time. Of course, all the years since the birth, Mars has been moving upward, but then it reaches what I take to be a better description of age thirty-eight and nine, THE WORLD, because it is the apex of the Tarot in the Major Arcana, card XXI, and your

Sun sits up there at the very mid-heaven. So this would be two joys in a row represented by this card.

Now I will just quickly throw out the last card for Mars. There we have the KNIGHT OF RODS, which suggests the movement of Mars into Gemini in 1980. This will activate all of your interests in the intellect, the mind, logos relatedness. It will be a real push. Don't get to feeling that there is going to be a deterioration of mental qualities as you get older, because this indicates that there will be a boost to them by the progression of Mars out of Taurus and into Gemini. It will also be in the Eleventh House, which is your house of ideals. Actually your Mars will enter the house of ideals in 1973. In a very few years after that it will enter Gemini, so there will be really idealistic intellectual functioning going on. There will be great energies along the lines of investigation into those things that you associate with your ideals and which Gemini governs. Briefly, what is the difference between the two men of age thirty-five and thirty-eight?

C: The first one was more idealistic, more aesthetically directed. The second was and is a very talented man, a far more worldly man. Very sophisticated personality.

R: The card is THE WORLD.

C: Very sophisticated, not without sensitivity at all, not a hard-headed businessman, but really a combination of sensitivity and intellect. Sophistication is the best word I can think of to describe him hastily and generally.

R: O.K. I think we will wind up our discussion of Mars. We have only seventeen cards to go for the rest of the reading.

Now we are going to go to the planet Jupiter, the beneficent planet of the zodiac, to see what happens there—the ACE OF CUPS! Your Jupiter is in Pisces, a Water sign, and Pisces most highly evolved is the sign of Christ consciousness. The Piscean Age began with the birth of Christ. Here we have the Sun of Selfhood or Christ consciousness evolving out of the chalice or grail, which rests upon the waters of the unconscious and also the waters of the cosmos. This suggests the position of your Jupiter as a fence-straddler in your chart. It sits on the cusp of the Ninth House. This puts it right between the Eighth House, the house of death and mystery, and the Ninth House, the house of the higher mind. So the ACE OF CUPS, in sitting on the waters of the unconscious and the waters of non-being, undifferentiated consciousness, awaits the evolution of the spiritual development which is to be attained in the Ninth House.

The next card is THE HIEROPHANT, and this always makes me think of a middleman, the intermediary between two worlds. You see he has the keys to the two kingdoms there. He points upward to remind us of the cosmic realm, and he is a kind of fence-straddler too in the same way that your Jupiter is. He is not in this world, or he shouldn't be too much of this world, if he is the priest or shamanistic figure. Now I am going to look back and check the *Ephemeris.* The only planet that makes a conjunction with your Jupiter is the Moon because it is going to go around the zodiac several times, and all the other planets that are progressing in the direction of Jupiter are too far behind to catch up in your lifetime. The first time that the Moon gets there to make a conjunction with Jupiter is at the age of seven, and again at the age of thirty-four. Now what this means is that the Moon has traveled through the Eighth House, the house of death, and it makes you concerned with questions associated with the next world, with the dead and possibly communication with the dead, which THE HIEROPHANT represents. So I wonder at the age of seven or thirty-four if there were thoughts about death and the next world which would have been brought out and amplified by the Moon going through the house of death and then arriving at Jupiter. Of course, the Piscean qualities would also lend a certain interest in psychic phenomena and the occult.

C: At the age of about thirty-four, did you say?

R: Yes.

C: That would be the year after my mother had died after several harrowing years of her illness, and if so it would have been on an unconscious level. I was quite shaken by my mother's death, but consciously was trying to take it in as reasonable and calm a fashion as I could. I had no conscious thoughts of communicating with her. In fact, I have always shied away from the idea of communicating with the dead, and it is only in this last year, through a greater understanding of my dreams, that there has been an indication that this interest lies there. But for me it still lies in the realm of the dead as the collective unconscious. That realm is so huge that we can barely tap it, and it is in that aspect of the dead, the heritage from the dead, that once we have reached it we know it is there, rather than, say, an individual experience or encounter with the spirit world or spirit voice. The manifestation of the spirit seems to me to come from this age-long contribution that the collective unconscious makes to every individual life, could the individual but encounter it.

R: O.K. Let's go on to the next card. It is the SEVEN OF PENTACLES. I think this card stands for the relation between Jupiter and your feminine principle within, and I would like to take a look at the next card also in order to see if that same theme is continued. The next card is the TEN OF CUPS, which has a very harmonious empathetic vibration connected with the picture of the cups, the lovers, and the heavenly rainbow. I see that the trine from Jupiter to Neptune makes for a very easy aspect of creativity, psychic potential, and harmony with the inner feminine principle. This is something that will be coming along for you. What is happening is this—I can see it quite clearly now—the progressed Jupiter is now at 27°—it has moved there from 19°54′—and we notice across the way that Neptune is at 27°47′. So this harmonious aspect represented by the trine will increase over the next few years so that it is exact to the minute, and it seems to me that this will make for really a blossoming of your psychic abilities. This automatic drawing, which you regard now as kind of a fluke, in that you don't know when it's going to come and when it's not, will happen more and more so that you will be reassured by it, and it will help you in your own life and in the development of your higher mind. The TEN OF CUPS to me represents this kind of marriage of Jupiter and Neptune joined by the trine, and then we have all the beautiful cups and the rainbow suggesting a drawing out of the unconscious elements, the whole spectrum of your personality which is latent in you, and which creatively hasn't been explored yet and hasn't been exploited. You must exploit it with your drawings and writing, so that the whole latter part of your life will be blooming. This will be the way, as you have already seen through analysis. By raising the love idealism up to a higher plane, where it is no longer resolved by looking for a flesh and blood person who can put you into harmony with yourself, you are assured of harmonious relationship with your inner archetype. You will find happiness within yourself, even great joy, rather than having to look to the outer world for fulfillment. This will be felt more and more precisely in the next few years. The same theme is furthered by the next card, JUSTICE, which symbolizes a balancing or harmonizing of factors. There we have the martial energies symbolized by the sword, and the balancing function symbolized by the scales. So there will be a beautiful harmony for you.

Now the next card is the ACE OF RODS, and I do associate that with intuition and the flowering of intuition, so I think that the previous cards describe a slow-moving thing. Jupiter just goes a few minutes each year in progressions, so the harmonious balancing will be felt over the next ten years.

The last card for Jupiter is JUDGEMENT, and this is a card of resurrection, so I think that Jupiter in trine with your Neptune is the key to the resolution of your problems and to the appearance of the new you. There is that same Sun rising at the top of the card that we saw in the Ace of Cups, and the floral motif that we saw in the Ace of Rods. It is a new tone in the life really, and there is a call to be answered--it's the call to let the world know what you have seen and discovered. I can't think of any better way than through that fairy tale you wrote, which was full of insights about life. We have already talked before about publishing a book of fairy tales which we have written or will write, so this is a joint venture for the future which I am sure will enable both of us to express symbolically our own insights about our archetypes and our relations to everyone else's archetypes. All right, that is Jupiter.

Now we are going to discuss the grand malefic of the Grand Experiment, Saturn. The first card is the ACE OF SWORDS. Well, Swords are associated with strife and contention in Tarot interpretations. This particular sword now appears to me in a way that I have never seen it before. The hilt has some kind of gems or embellishments that now look to me like eyes on a robot, looking left and right, every which way, and they are seeking out a victim. I am getting very paranoid reactions to this sword. Before, this sword has been described as "rather a nice sword," but I am not getting this. Those eyes are looking all around, and they are searching you out. Now the roses being split suggests to me the Twins, Castor and Pollux, or the glyph for Gemini, in which your

290

Saturn resides or lies in wait. It is kind of like a sand trap. The Twelfth House and the Saturn and Pluto conjunction is at the very end of the chart, and the fact that you have the planets in the Ninth and Tenth Houses means that in the course of the lifetime they wend their way over there to this sand trap and they catch it in the neck.

The next card for Saturn is the SEVEN OF SWORDS, and what is described there, I think, is the Twelfth House experience. Saturn moves slowly up until it reaches the position of Pluto natally, and this gives the Twelfth House experience an awful lot of power. Now let's see when this occurred in the lifetime. This is age fifteen, which we talked about before in connection with your very depressed, negative period. The progressed Moon was there also at the age of fifteen, and that is why this particular relationship of planets had a great deal of force at that time. There was not only the natal position of Saturn, but its progressed position was the same as the natal position of Pluto. So they were reinforcing one another, and then along came your pretty little Moon to step into that trap. Well, that double sword power, double strife power, is suggested by the SEVEN OF SWORDS, I think.

Now the SEVEN OF CUPS frequently suggests to me the conscious mind being overwhelmed by the unconscious. You see the head disappearing in the cup? So it is a descent into the unconscious, and it is almost like a psychedelic trip, with all the strange colors and so on. This card suggests your mind, your Mercury, being overwhelmed by Saturn, and also the Pluto in the sense of collective unconscious. This occurred at the age of twenty-eight. Was that the first time you said you went into therapy?

C: Um-hmm. It just keeps turning up.

R: O.K. That is an expression of Saturn taking over the mind. Before, we had the mind going up to where Saturn was, when we were talking about Mercury's progressions. Now this describes the same conjunction, only it is from the point of view of Saturn. Incidentally, Saturn is one of the slower-moving planets, so it is only going to move a few degrees in the lifetime; therefore, we are not doing the same type of progression that will go all the way around. What we are describing here is Saturn's relation to those planets that move up to make conjunctions with it during your lifetime.

Now the NINE OF RODS suggests confinement and imprisonment, and the figure's hat reminds me of a bandaged head. I think this is probably when the Moon became conjunct Saturn in the Twelfth House at the age of forty-three. And then for about a year or two your Moon was still in the Twelfth House, which meant confinement and hospitals. This is when you had all your operations, correct?

C: Yes, that was the time.

R: O.K. Now THE TOWER. This is really symbolic of the Saturn power that breaks things down, and I think THE TOWER is a reference to the moment at the age of fifty when the Sun moved up there to a conjunction with Saturn. So we had the Moon going up there, and the Mercury, and Saturn itself moving to a conjunction with Pluto. This would be when the Sun went into that Twelfth House conjunct with Saturn.

C: Does it get overwhelmed too? Does everything that moves into that house get overwhelmed by Saturn?

R: Do you remember my sermon in which I said one can never slip backwards and lose what has been attained? Well, the Sun can never lose its quality; it can be thwarted, but whatever Sun consciousness you have brought over from whatever experiences you have had before will never disappear. If the sum total of matter and energy in the universe can neither be created nor destroyed, your Sun consciousness can never be diminished. The Sun represents the dharma of life, and the whole zodiac is the working out of the karma of the life.

This next card, the FOUR OF SWORDS, is probably the present. We have discussed before how the Mercury and the Sun are now conjunct the position of the progressed Saturn. Remember I said that the Mercury had gone quite a way through the Twelfth House, and then it stopped and began moving backwards. And the Sun came forward and they both met during this past year. So here we have a symbolic depiction of Sun, Mercury, and Saturn, all in the same degree, three swords oppressing the knight as he lies fallen in the picture. Now having two planets at the same time under the influence of Saturn makes your temperament saturnine, which means gloomy and sluggish. The same

292

adjective also describes lead poisoning, and I think we can say that in 1970 you were suffering from a cosmic lead poisoning. Now you notice another sword beneath the knight, and this suggests to me your progressed Moon in the Sixth House in opposition to those planets in the Twelfth House. And this opposition has the same aspect as the conjunction, really, making for a gloomy, depressed personality.

As far as the future is concerned, THE HERMIT seems to describe the future experience. Your Sun and Saturn will be continuing through this Twelfth House for most of the rest of your life, and this will be the chance for the star within the lantern to shine out because this comes out in solitude again. In some ways you were kind of a misguided little girl, because if all of these experiences had worked out well for you, particularly the marriage with the political figure, I can see that maybe you would be writing columns for some left-wing newspaper, and you would be very active in political causes. But you would be cut off from your inner castles, which is the real you, actually. The creative ability and psychic ability are here, and you would never have reached the point in development where you are now, where you can open the door and reap the harvest that we talked about before, if it hadn't been for this Saturn power. It tore down all the old you, and I think THE HERMIT is the card of wisdom in the higher sense. This is what you will attain with your Sun going through Cancer in the coming years in the Twelfth House. I'm not saying you will become an actual hermit, because you will always value friends who have acted as initiatory guides for you along the path of your own spiritual development.

Now since Uranus, Neptune, and Pluto move so slowly, their progressed positions do not change appreciably during the lifetime, so I am going to delegate only one card to each of them. The first one will be Uranus, which is in your house of partners. I have associated this planet before with your animus figure. The card is the KING OF SWORDS, and it describes the inner ideal which you seek, self-reliant yet sensitive at the same time. He is a balance of masculinity and feminine sensitivity to the astral plane, symbolized by the fantastic cloud formations behind him. You have now ceased to look for him out there because you recognize that he really dwells within, and what he is doing for you now is enabling you to reflect on your own life with a little objectivity so that it has more harmony and balance. Right?

C: Um-hmm. That's a very apt description of my animus figure as we have described him.

R: THE HIGH PRIESTESS represents your feminine principle and all those elements on the shadow side of consciousness. I said earlier that Neptune was on your Ascendent, and to me this is the mark of psychic potential. The High Priestess is the one who opens the veil to the next world and initiates one into the nature of the mysteries. It is her rapport with Jupiter on the cusp between the house of mystery and the house of the higher mind that will facilitate the psychic/creative unfoldment.

At last, we are going to talk about Pluto, the god of the underworld. (Laughter). The last card is DEATH, and I had talked about Pluto in connection with transformation. I had said that it was not only the collective unconscious but the paraconscious mind. In that sense it is capable more than any other planet of conveying cosmic consciousness to the individual. Your Mercury, incidentally, will move back, continuing to go retrograde, until it hits a point that is the same position as the Pluto. This conjunction will happen in a few years and the card that summed that up before was The Hanged Man, I think. So this will be a chance for you to confront again the great mystery of the unconscious and to maybe reach a new level in the development of your own spiritual consciousness. The first card we had in the reading was the King of Cups, and the last card is DEATH. Well, that's going full circle—it's certainly the snake with his tail in his mouth. DEATH is only the birth card, the other side of the King of Cups. Seen with the enlightened vision of the seer, death is a king who bears the cup of cosmic consciousness. The last card of the life is the beginning or first card for the next life.

Well, that concludes the reading, and I believe this is the first time you have seen a horoscope or had one done for you, so it is probably difficult for you to comment on the nature of the correlation between the chart and the spread of cards, but I think there has been a very good correlation. What is your general impression of the things I said in the chart related to your own life incidents, and then related to the Tarot reading?

C: The correlation seems almost complete. The chart alone, as you got into the reading of it, even had it been not in relation to the cards, was startling to me. I felt as though you needn't ask me to comment at all but simply to corroborate what you were reading. It seemed over and over again that the cards added their corroboration to what was already in the chart. Each time we seemed to hesitate over a card or get off the track, by double checking we would see that we were wrong by a year or two, and whatever correction that was made put us right smack in connection with the chart again.

EPILOGUE BY MISS CUTLER
Easter Sunday — April 11, 1971

"This reading represents for me a climactic turning away from the destructive events and attitudes of the past toward a possible realization and fulfillment of latent potentialities that have previously been dormant, unrecognized, or frustrated.

"The horoscope alone is an astonishing record of the major events of my past life. Together with the Tarot cards, as they turned up in relation to the horoscope, the reading was nothing less than awesome. Each Tarot card substantiated the events in an accurate progression through the years, the symbols in each card corroborating and expanding the guiding precepts of the astrological chart.

"Of the sixty-four cards used in the reading, only two or three seemed somewhat obscure. Given the aptness and exactitude of the majority of the cards in conjunction with the astrological progression, one can assume that the lack of clarity lies in me rather than in any questionable aspect of the chart or in the spread of the cards. Further thought will undoubtedly bring enlightenment in these areas.

"The reading augments as well as supplements the slowly dawning insights that are taking place in analysis. It assists revelation and increases understanding, throwing light into dark corners, helping to fix the attention on significant areas of psychic disturbance, lending forewarning to portents and support to proclivities.

"For me, the immediate result of the reading was a better understanding of the powerful cosmic forces that affect an individual life. The astrological chart is a map of those cosmic forces which have their counterpart in the equally majestic energies of the archetypes of the collective unconscious. Mythology is the history of these conjunctions. Each person carries within himself his individual myth (or life journey), which will emerge as his relationship with the macrocosm unfolds. To deny this would be to deny oneself to life.

"I am deeply grateful to my beloved friend Richard Roberts for his compassionate, intuitive guidance that has led me farther along the road to spiritual evolvement."